Meditations From the Heart

African Methodist Episcopal Zion Church
Woman's Home And Overseas
Missionary Society

**MOUNTAINTOP
BOOKS, INC.**

THE HOLY BIBLE VERSIONS

The following Bible Versions were used in preparing the meditations. The version is indicated next to the Scripture reference.

KJV – King James Version
NKJV – New King James Version
NIV – New International Version
TLV – The Living Bible
NRS – New Revised Standard
RSV – Revised Standard Version
NAS – New American Standard Version
AMP – The Amplified Bible

"Scripture taken from the Holy Bible, New International Version Copyright © 1973, 1978, 1984 by International Bible Society. Used by permission of Zondervan Publishing House."

Library Of Congress Catalog Card Number 99-62306
ISBN Number: 1-880679-04-3

Please direct all correspondence and book orders to:
Woman's Home and Overseas Missionary Society
AME Zion Church
401 East 2nd Street, Suite 201
Charlotte, NC 28202

Cover by: Marilyn Gates-Davis

Published by MountainTop Books, Incorporated
Oxon Hill, Maryland

Printed in the United States of America

Woman's Home and Overseas Missionary Society
Executive Board

Meditations
From the Heart

African Methodist Episcopal Zion Church
Woman's Home And Overseas
Missionary Society

Meditations From The Heart
Table Of Content

Foreward: Janie Speaks, Missionary Supervisor Emeritus
Preface: Dr. Adlise Ivey Porter, General President
Acknowledgements: Reverend Lula G. Williams
About The Cover: Marilyn Gates-Davis

FOREWORD

Not by might, nor by power, but by my Spirt, saith the Lord. Zechariah 4:6

> Once more we come before our God
> Once more His blessings ask;
> O may not duty seem a load
> Nor worship prove a task.

The Christian Church is formed and reformed by its worship experiences. The Woman's Home and Overseas Missionary Society of the African Methodist Episcopal Zion Church has a notable history of seeking the empowering presence of God in directing its mission and purpose in Kingdom building. This has been our mandate and modus operandi.

God's Kingdom is not of this world. It is not founded on earthly power and might, John 18:36. It is the Kingdom of ministering love, where sin-forgiving is to be learned; where the frail and the weak build equally together; where the love of Christ alleviates want and misery through instructing, helping, supporting, reproving, and correcting.

In His Kingdom, the gifts we receive should gain interest, Luke 19:11-26. We are taught to serve, not rule, as Christ came to minister, and not to be ministered to. The use of this book and other devotional materials are tools necessary for the task to which we have been called, building the Kingdom of God.

We do not have strength of ourselves to help ourselves. The Word of God falls upon our ears as the sound of many waters, a mighty and great sound bringing a wonderment and acknowledgment of a force greater than human power. It is this power that we use to usher in the Kingdom of God. Therefore: *Let everything that hath breath praise the Lord, praise ye the Lord! Psalm 150:6.*

Janie Speaks, Missionary Supervisor, Emeritus

PREFACE

HALLELUJAH! PRAISE HIS NAME! THANK YOU JESUS! I express profound joy on behalf of the Executive Board for the publication of the Woman's Home and Overseas Missionary Society's book, MEDITATIONS FROM THE HEART. To God be the glory! We believe this publication will be a blessing to you in your daily walk with God as you embark upon your journey into the New Millennium.

The idea for such a volume was formed from a Presidential Initiative presented to and approved by the Executive Board in February, 1996 by the newly elected President, Dr. Adlise Ivey Porter, at the first Board meeting over which she presided. The apparent need for more spiritual food for our missionaries and others seeking to enhance their relationship with God dictated the need for such a publication. A logical source for fulfilling this need was also apparent, the Woman's Home and Overseas Missionary Society, itself, led by the Holy Spirit. Therefore, with prayer through which the vision came; the assistance of the Spiritual Life Committee, Co-chaired by Reverend Lula G. Williams and Mrs. Georgia Thompson; and, meditations written by missionaries around the world, the book was born.

MEDITATIONS FROM THE HEART is a compilation of the experiences, the triumphs, the overcoming faith, and determination of many women of the AME Zion Church. Their witness to the power of God will inspire you to a greater faith in an awesome God. The Scripture is given for each meditation. The Table of Contents lists each Missionary Supervisor and the month for which she is responsible. The author of each meditation is listed in the Table of Contents appearing before each month.

Please take time to read the explanation for the beautiful cover. You will note that it also has a spiritual basis. Let the Cover of MEDITATIONS FROM THE HEART minister to your heart.

We declare our gratitude to our Liaison and Chairman of the Board of Overseas Missions, The Right Reverend Enoch

B. Rochester; our Spiritual Life Committee; the Executive Board, especially the Missionary Supervisors who collected meditations from missionaries in their district; Mrs. Janie Speaks, former Chairperson of the Spiritual Life Committee and Missionary Supervisor, Emeritus; and all others who contributed to the fruition of this publication. Thank you for a job well done!

May your daily walk with God be blessed, strengthened, and may you prosper as you read MEDITATIONS FROM THE HEART in your home, on the job, on the plane, at school, or wherever you have quiet time with God. It is my prayer that you will also find these meditations helpful as you assemble together for corporate worship, such as prayer meetings, mass meetings, and convocations. May the fire burn in your heart that you may grow in purity and righteousness. We encourage you to share copies with friends, relatives, and to all to whom you witness as a tool to fulfill the Woman's Home and Overseas Missionary Society Motto: The WORLD FOR CHRIST!

Adlise Ivey Porter, General President

ACKNOWLEDGMENTS

It was a tremendous honor for the Spiritual Life Committee, Co-Chaired by Rev. Lula G. Williams and Mrs. Georgia Thompson, to have the opportunity to facilitate this vision of our General President, Dr. Adlise Ivey Porter.

We are grateful for the Missionary Supervisors who diligently sought meditations from women in their Episcopal Districts. To all the women of Zion who wrote meditations, we express profound gratitude. Many thanks to Mrs. June Slade-Collins for the many hours she gave to typing the first draft of this document; Mrs. Barbara Shaw, Mrs. Beulah Maxwell, Ms. Janice Guinyard, Mrs. Georgia Thompson, Rev. Lula G. Williams, and Dr. Adlise Ivey Porter for the first editing of the publication.

Certainly, we thank God for surrounding this project and those who contributed to it with His power and love, and for the courage to see it through to completion.

The Spiritual Life Committee
Rev. Lula G. Williams, Co-Chairperson
Mrs. Georgia E. Thompson, Co-Chairperson
Mrs. Estelle J. Jarrett
Mrs. Barbara S. Carr
Mrs. Faustina Ife Ekemam
Dr. Adlise Ivey Porter, Ex-officio

ABOUT THE COVER

The cover for MEDITATIONS FROM THE HEART was created with the title in mind and a number of symbolic representations of our faith. A heart was used both to show the title, but also because it is the center of life itself. While a heart and red are usually synonymous, the red on the cover represents the Blood of Jesus, which was shed for us. The leaf coming from the heart represents the fact that God's Word has fallen on good ground. Our hearts are to be open to receive God's Word and produce new life therefrom. The heart is then encased in gold, which represents His righteousness which covers us and protects us.

As we read this book we, as Christians, must allow God's Word to be planted like a seed within our hearts. That seed will grow and strengthen us and we will be able to complete the mission given to us by Jesus; to go and teach the world who He is.

Marilyn Gates-Davis

January

A new commandment I give unto you, That ye love one another; as I have loved you, that ye also love one another. By this shall all men know that ye are my disciples, if ye have love one to another.

John 13:34, 35

Mid-West Episcopal District
Table Of Contents

THE NEW YEAR:
LOOK BACK AND GO FORWARD

Scripture: Matthew 28:19 (KJV)
Go ye therefore, and teach all nations, baptizing them in the name of the Father, and of the Son, and of the Holy Ghost:

As we stand on the threshold of the New Year, it seems impossible that another year has passed. Looking back, does it seem like the year was cut short and that there are so many mission causes left undone? What is our mission in the body of Christ but to love one another and give of ourselves so that those who are outside of a right relationship with Christ will be reconciled to Him?

Will you resolve to get more involved in the mission causes this year? But first, look back and assess whether or not your last year's resolutions were kept. Many times, we talk ourselves out of keeping them. It is easier to say, "Tomorrow I'll make time or next year I'll do better."

This New Year offers a fresh beginning for me. No matter what the past, we can go forward with faith in God. As you go forward in hope, there are three points from the life of Joshua that will be helpful: take action, ask for help and do not be discouraged.

Prayer: Dear Lord, may I go forward into the New Year with vigor in the spirit of Joshua. Amen.

Adlise Ivey Porter

FACING CHANGES IN OUR LIVES

Scripture: Malachi 3:6 (KJV)
For I am the Lord, I change not; therefore ye sons of Jacob are not consumed.

So many of us seem apprehensive of change. We need to remember that everything changes, nothing ever remains the same. We should look back with fond memories on things that were and look ahead with great anticipation on things yet to come.

In all this we have the consolation of the one thing in our lives that remains constant; that is our Lord and Saviour Jesus Christ. In James 1:17 we find these words, *Every good gift and every perfect gift is from above, and cometh down from the Father of lights, with whom is no variableness, neither shadow of turning.*

Let us face the New Year with this assurance, *Jesus Christ the same yesterday, and today, and for ever.* Hebrews 13:8.

Prayer: Guide me, O great Jehovah for I am a pilgrim through a land that is sometimes barren. But I rest in the assurance that you are unchangeable, immutable, and everlasting. Amen.

Lillian E. Davis

1-2-03 Lord I am greatful that I have a saviour that never change. Lord we make a start in life, but sometime get Turned around, and change For the worst. Lord help me remain holy, and not change.

January 2

A NEW BEGINNING

Scripture: John 1:1 (KJV)
In the beginning was the Word, and the Word was with God, and the Word was God.

Genesis means beginning and the first Book the Bible tells of a number of beginnings. There are many new beginnings every single day. At the dawn of a new day God allows us to make a fresh start. Old things, thoughts, and deeds are put behind us. The mercies of God are new every morning.

When my children were young, I would put a note on the front door that they could all see when they left for school. The note stated, "This is a new day, share something good with someone." I wanted them to know at the start of a new day to do something worthwhile. In the evenings we would share the experiences of the day so they were able to see the manifestation of our daily proclamation. Usually something good had transpired for one of them, even if it was small.

Today accept the challenges and possibilities of the year that lies ahead as a new chance, a new beginning that is unfolding.

Prayer: Thank you, God, for the opportunity to begin again—a new day, a new opportunity, a new challenge, and a new sense of forgiveness. Amen.

Rosalind Washington

NEW BEGINNINGS

Scripture: Ephesians 4:23, 24 (KJV)
And be renewed in the spirit of your mind; And that ye put on the new man, which after God is created in righteousness and true holiness.

I thank God for my new arrivals on January 28, 1974 and January 2, 1977. My children's birthdays remind me that I experienced a new beginning. I knew my life would never be the same. My time was no longer my own. Now there was someone else to provide for, to nourish and nurture, to love and give spiritual guidance.

When we find Jesus, we experience a new beginning. When we touch the hem of His garment, we are made new and whole. Our lives will never be the same. We have someone who loves us and provides for all our needs.

We should want others to share this new beginning. In sharing we will truly win the world for Christ.

Prayer: I thank you, Lord, for giving me a new birth and a new beginning. Amen.

Mary F. Willis

SACRIFICE

Scripture: John 3:16 (KJV)
For God so loved the world, that He gave His only begotten Son, that whosoever believeth in Him should not perish, but have everlasting life.

When we give we usually do so out of our abundance. We do it with ease and often with self-pride and arrogance. But what if God called you to give up something that would be painful to part with? Each of us has something that would pain us deeply to give up. It is a thing that is precious to us, loved, hidden, or flaunted with pride. It soothes us to sleep at night; it defines us.

In our relationship with Jesus, He will require one day that we give, not out of our abundance or overflow, but out of our hidden treasure chest. We will know then where our devotion lies and this is His purpose.

Can you worship when giving takes your very life and it seems that in giving it that there can only be darkness, sorrow and pain? Can you raise your dagger and sacrifice the thing that is so good to you that you were sure that it was a godly thing? Will you do this without knowing whether there is a ram in the bush?

Our sacrifice to God is a seed to be sown. It will not be taken from us; we must lay it down as Jesus did.

Prayer: Prepare me for the sacrifice. I know you will not take it away from me, I must give it up. Amen.

Alisa Ginyard

January 5

RESTORATION

Scripture: Isaiah 55:10 (KJV)
For as the rain cometh down, and the snow from the heaven, and returneth not thither, but watereth the earth, and maketh it bring forth and bud, that it may give seed to the sower, and bread to the eater:

Once we have sacrificed that which is precious to us and have sown it into the ground for God's purpose, there is always a missing of the seed, and then we wait.

In the time when Jesus laid down his life, His disciples were left with an emptiness, a longing for the presence of the one who had fulfilled them and given them a sense of purpose. Their hope seemed to have perished with Jesus' last breath. So it is after we who love Jesus have sacrificed the most treasured of our defining properties, such as our ideas, thought patterns, tangible assets, physical attributes, and beloved associates. We are in pain, hurting after the cutting away and certain that we are maimed for life. But in the fullness of time, when the required season has been fulfilled, there is a promise to be received. It will surely come; no seed that has ever been sown into this good ground has remained barren. It is time for restoration, prepare your emptiness for harvest.

Prayer: Lord, thank you for teaching me to trust you with my seed. May I know that the only reason you give to me is so that I can see you as the source. Amen.

Alisa Ginyard

JESUS CALL US TO LOVE

Scripture: John 15:12 (KJV)
This is my commandment, That ye love one another, as I have loved you.

God is love. Love is the law. Love is the way. Love is the answer. Love is the magnet that attracts all that the heart is seeking. Love is the cohesive element that binds us one with another—it cements human relations—it brings people and nations together in unity. Love is not an abstract, but a real and vital expression of caring and sharing. Love forgives all and forbears all. Love sees God in all and the good in all. This is indeed a day to rejoice and be glad. God's love lifts us to new heights of accomplishment. Our religion is just a sounding brass and tinkling cymbal without love. There is no life where there is no love.

Those of us who know the Lord Jesus as our personal Saviour are acquainted with the true meaning of love. The Body of Christ must show this unconditional love of God to the lost.

Prayer: Stir me, oh stir me Lord, stir me until I can be used by you. Stir my heart in passion for the world, Stir me to give, to go, and to pray for the lost to know and accept your love. Amen.

LaFonde W. McGee

I thank you Lord for your love. I thank you Lord for your love when, at times I feel I don't deserve it. help me to love and forget. I'll always praise you.

January 7

THE GREATEST PHYSICIAN

Scripture: Matthew 9:20, 22 (KJV)
And behold, a woman, which was diseased with an issue of blood twelve years, came behind him and touched the hem of his garment . . . when he saw her, he said, Daughter be of good comfort; thy faith hath made thee whole. And the woman was made whole from that hour.

After experiencing automobile problems, an all-night journey, and arriving home from our church's annual conference around daybreak, our very brief repose was shattered by the news that our Uncle had taken seriously ill and the outlook at best was bleak. The following days were filled with anxiety. After much prayer and heart-rending contemplation, the family finally decided on surgery. Then we chose to put it all in God's hands and to trust Him.

Just as we thought that all hope was gone, God stepped in and touched our Uncle. Our Almighty Heavenly Father had done it again. Just like 2,000 years ago, when He healed the lepers, and the woman with the issue of blood, He had healed someone who was close and personal. He showed us that the Word of God that was written many years ago was relevant today and that God never changes.

Prayer: Thank you for the touch that heals, O Precious Father. Amen.

Etta Richmond

EVERYTHING OBEYS HIM!

Scripture: 1 Peter 3:13 (KJV)
And who is he that will harm you, if ye be followers of that which is good?

One of my childhood memories of God's protection still lingers as vividly as if it were only yesterday. Some especially mean wasps had positioned their nest just outside our back porch. If anyone dared venture out that door, they were soon barraged with a swarm of the buzzing and stinging insects that would send you literally running for your life. Having been chased several times, I knew that the only way to avoid their painful onslaught was to outrun them quickly. Imagine the chill of my utter fear when I saw our elderly next-door neighbor, Mother Butler, who was in her 80's, turn the corner of the house enroute to our back door. As I stood there I was frozen in fear for her, just knowing that the wasps were sure to attack her aged body. I tried to yell but nothing would come out. To my amazement, not one single wasp came out of the nest, and she proceeded to our house without incident.

Jesus has assured us of His protection, (even from the noisome pestilence, Psalm 91:3), if we believe on Him and trust in His Word.

Prayer: Father, help me to exercise my faith in the fact that you are all I need to face the trials of life. Amen.

Marilyn Fairrow

POWER IN PRAYER

Scripture: Luke 11:1 (KJV)
And it came to pass, that, as he was praying in a certain place, when he ceased, one of his disciples said unto him, Lord, teach us to pray, as John also taught his disciples.

Prayer has taught me to take one day at a time. I have stepped out on faith, leaving utter chaos to come to a calm and sweet retreat that is found at His mercy seat.

I have climbed many mountains. I have forged many streams; I am content in knowing whatever happens to me that God is able. Through prayer I have learned to I trust Him today; my understanding will come tomorrow.

God is always there in goodness, kindness and love. It took a long time for me to learn that I did not have to be anxious about how firm the grip of my hand is in God's hand. I am confident that His hand is holding mine. I begin my day in joy. I live it in love. I finish the day standing taller and stronger in Him. All because I prayed this morning.

Prayer: Dear God, thank you for the privilege of prayer. The fact that you, the Almighty, Everlasting God, takes time to talk to His children, to comfort us, and to strengthen us, awes me. Amen.

Ruby (Bethel) McCrary

GROWTH IN PRAYER

Scripture: Philippians 4:6, 7 (KJV)
Be careful for nothing; but in every thing by Prayer and supplication with thanksgiving let your requests be made known unto God. And the peace of God, which passeth all understanding, shall keep your hearts and minds through Christ Jesus.

Jesus provides us with a pattern or model for spiritual growth within and for effective service to God and our fellow human beings. *prayer should be at the top of our my agenda*

Prayer was at the top of His agenda. Jesus knew that preparation, a proper attitude, and spiritual power are needed to accomplish the task at hand. These are provided through prayer. He made prayer a habit. He believed and practiced both private and public prayer. Prayer is appropriate for all occasions. We must realize that there is nothing we should do before first consulting God in prayer. *yes remember*

Prayer: Almighty God, you draw me into a reality deeper and broader than I have known. Help me to grow, both physically and spiritually that I may not only know you, but to serve you joyfully. Thank you God that you hear and answer prayer. In Christ I pray. Amen.

Mattilyn T. Rochester

WHEN I PRAY

Scripture: Matthew 6:9 (KJV)
After this manner therefore pray ye: Our Father which art in Heaven, Hallowed be thy name.

I have so much to be thankful for. Prayer is my expression of that gratitude. I pray because I am in the Father's family. I am rooted and grounded in God's love. My prayers are my declaration of my dependence on Him. My source of refreshment is in God who dwells within me and directs me.

I have a God who is alive in my midst. My praying is the response of my mind to the overwhelming goodness and glory of God. When I pray I find some of the hidden riches of His secret place, and I find the reason to understand how very much I have to be thankful for.

I need Christ's power. I stop at His power station, because I need help in clearing my vision that the eyes of my heart may be enlightened. I need a little of the oils of joy. This is what I get when I pray.

Prayer: Thank you, God, for sending your Son. The shortest distance between two hearts is love. Your love frees me to be all that you desire me to be. Amen.

Ruby (Bethel) McCrary

OPEN OUR EYES LORD, WE WANT

Scripture: John 9:11 (KJV)
. . . and I went and washed, and I received

One morning as I was getting ready for work, I accidentally dropped one of my contact lenses while putting them in. Dropping to my knees, I began frantically searching the floor. I felt helpless because I was unable to see well enough on my own to find it. I was also afraid to move an inch fearing that I would step on it and break it. It was in that state of helplessness that I realized how helpless and blind, we really are without Christ in our lives.

At that moment, I felt a sudden and peaceful calm come over me. I realized that no matter who or what we are, God knows all about us including our physical and spiritual handicaps. He knows the areas in our lives in which we are blind. Yet, in His loving way, He looks down upon each one of us in all our weaknesses and gives sight so that we too may find our way to Him. It was while basking in that thought that I looked down only to find my lost lens. Now, I too could see!

Prayer: Father God, open my eyes to you and to your truth. May I see your will for my life. Help me to use my sight to lead others to you. Amen.

Margaret R. Anderson

TRUST GOD

Scripture: Proverbs 3:5, 6 (KJV)
Trust in the Lord, with all thine heart; and lean not unto thine own understanding. In all thy ways acknowledge him, and he shall direct thy paths.

God's will is found in His Word. To know God's will for your life is to know His Word. To follow His Word is deliverance, to forget His Word is destruction. We must seek His direction daily.

My trust is in the Lord. He is my confidence. He will unveil to me His strategies for success in every situation. Proverbs 3:26. God is in control. All His promises are true. We must simply trust, believe, and obey.

Prayer: I thank you for this day. A new day to trust you, for you are sovereign, you are great, you are Lord. Thank you for your loving kindness and tender mercies which are new every morning. I will seek you in all that I do this day that my paths are made clear and your will is done. I will give you all the praise, all the honor and all the glory. In Jesus' Name I pray. Amen.

Rosemarie Paris

help me lord to put all my trust in you, help me to trust you with all my heart help me not to lean on my understanding, my understanding is very slow. not on you in all my ways I want to acknowledge him, I no you will direct my path if only trust and acknowledge him.

I LOVE TO TELL THIS STORY

Scripture: Exodus 14:13 (KJV)
. . . Fear ye not, stand still, and see the salvation of the Lord, which he will show to you today . . .

When I came to Detroit, Michigan in 1956 with intentions of attending a large University, I found that I needed to secure a job to pay tuition. Instead of the large University I enrolled in the Lewis College of Business. When I graduated I went to a church to be interviewed for a job. I was selected and accepted the job with the thought that I would work there, enroll in the University and someday get a "better" job.

The job turned out to be a tremendous blessing in my life, I am grateful that I held onto it. The Lord gave me a job situation that I did not think could be sufficient for my needs. I found out that my sufficiency was in Him and not in the job. My position at the church helped to put my children through college. We had no outstanding loans to pay after they graduated because the Lord brought us through. One of my children is now married with two children of his own.

If you give yourself to Jesus, He will prove Himself to be your true provider. He will see you through.

Prayer: Thank you, Lord, for helping me to stand still and wait on you. Amen.

Nan E. Gaddis

Read over

CONQUERING GUILT

Scripture: Psalm 51:1 (KJV)
Have mercy upon me, O God, according to thy lovingkindness: according unto the multitude of thy tender mercies blot out my transgressions.

    In Psalm 51 we find David's moving prayer for forgiveness. It contains the message that helps us conquer the guilt of sin. We must first admit our sins. Guilt is never conquered or removed until sin is admitted. 1 John 1:9 states, *If we confess our sins, he is faithful and just to forgive us our sins, and to cleanse us from all unrighteousness.*
    We must ask God for forgiveness. David proclaims in Psalm 51:4, *Against thee, thee only, have I sinned, and done this evil in thy sight . . .*
    We must put God first in our lives. The first impulse of the forgiven sinner should be to please God, point others to Him, and praise God for His grace and mercy. You can conquer the guilt of sin by admitting your sins and asking God's forgiveness.

Prayer: Help me, O God to recognize how easily my life is possessed and twisted by unworthy motives masquerading as good. Help me to resist temptation that I may never become your enemy. Amen.

Lucille Wilkins

January 16

CONQUERING CIRCUMSTANCES

Scripture: Genesis 6:8 (KJV)
But Noah found grace in the eyes of the Lord.

Helen you need to study this [handwritten]

Many Christians are spiritually tired and life's circumstances have gotten the best of them. There are three things that will conquer circumstances:

The first is to be true to God's teachings. Noah found grace in the sight of the Lord because he was a righteous man. He did not allow the sin of his times to pull him off course.

Second, one should follow the leadership and the direction of God. Know that if you are truly serving Him, He orders your steps. After Noah found grace in the eyes of the Lord, he was given instructions on building and equipping the ark.

The third thing is to realize that looking past circumstances and seeing God can conquer them. It is not that people see too much, they see too little. Noah had the capacity to see past the wicked and corrupt world in which he lived to see God.

We too can conquer the circumstances in our lives if we will yield in faith to Him, who will make you more than a conqueror.

Prayer: God, strengthen me so that I will be able to stand in the midst of my circumstances. Amen.

Reverend Carroll Johnson

January 17

A MESSAGE IN THE THUNDER

Scripture: Isaiah 12:2 (KJV)
Behold, God is my salvation; I will trust, and not be afraid: for the Lord Jehovah is my strength and my song; he also is become my salvation.

As a child, I was petrified of thunderstorms. In the small, rural Midwest area where I lived, the storms were as certain as life itself. When they occurred, I was stuck like glue to Mom, for the comfort and consolation that she, and only she, could provide.

One day during a particularly loud and active siege of rain, lightening, and unusually loud thunder, I was at my usual place, right under Mom's arm. She said to me, in her soft and gentle, yet authoritative voice, "You know if you put your trust in the Lord and behaved when the sun was shining, you wouldn't be afraid when the storms come."

Trust in God gives us the courage, the strength, the will, the desire, and the determination to face the storms that life will surely bring. Just as He calmed the tempest of the sea, He will calm the storms of your life. You can be sure of it.

Prayer: O God, be my constant guide through the storms of life. Amen.

Evelyn Holden

FACING OUR ANTIOCH OF PISADIA

Scripture: Acts 13:51 (KJV)
But they shook off the dust of their feet against them, and came unto Iconium.

Luke gives us a very vivid example of how to handle conflict in the midst of our missionary journey. Paul's first missionary journey with Barnabas, as recorded in Acts 13, was fraught with conflict, rejection, and persecution. Jealousy, envy, and insecurity caused the Jewish leaders to turn against Paul and Barnabas. They were forced out of the district. Luke records that they left shaking the dust from their feet against them and went to Iconium.

Paul and Barnabas understood, as we must understand, that when opposition comes it is not personal. It is a response to Him whom we represent and serve. "Shaking the dust off our feet" reminds us that we cannot allow our past hurts, pains, and conflicts to negatively impact our call to share Christ. Instead of being overwhelmed by the experience, Paul and Barnabas shook it off; they dealt with it, processed it, and remained focused. He who sends us is far greater than our conflict. As they continued in Iconium, let us continue.

Prayer: Lord, as you guided Paul and Barnabas, guide me as I go forward. Amen.

Minola R. Kelly *Lord I am facing a lot of conflict in my life, guide me like you did Paul and Barnabas.*

LIFT UP YOUR HEADS

Scripture: Psalm 100:1 (KJV)
Make a joyful noise unto the Lord, all ye lands.

For those who live where there are four seasons, winter can be a desolate barren and cold venue. There is a Swahili saying: "A perfect world has been created, it is already in existence." God has granted us a limited vision of His awesomeness, in the form of this world. Can you imagine what lies ahead? Look at His creation. To behold the life cycles of the trees, as they shed their glorious foliage, saving up for the big show in spring causes us to understand God's ability to resurrect life from every dead situation. Or to watch the mother birds prepare their children for flight, as they migrate to warmer climates, is to wonder in awe how God found the time to create such a wonderful creature, oblivious to our grandiose intelligence, so adept at surviving in a world that cares little for them. To know that the world belongs to the Father in Heaven, gives any saint a reason to lift up their heads and shout with joy that they belong to a magnificent collection of wondrous creatures, existing solely to give praise and worship to our Creator.

Prayer: Thank you for showing me your Majesty through this earth created by your Hands. Amen.

Saunja Porter Townsend
(In honor of my parents: The Late Dr. Parree Porter, Sr. and Dr. Adlise Ivey Porter) *I have so much to thank God for, so while not make a Joyful noise unto the Lord, look what he has done for me.*

RELEASE! RENEW! TRANSMIT!

Scripture: Matthew 9:16 (KJV)
No man putteth a piece of new cloth unto an old garment, for that which is put in to fill it up taketh from the garment, and the rent is made worse.

As we embrace the dawning of another New Year, and release our lives of the memories of yesterday, we are blessed to be among the living. *Yes Lord*

During these Years of Jubilee, we as Christians should face the arrival of the new millenium with enthusiasm, not fear. God does not give us the spirit of fear, instead we loom anxiously for new ideas and purpose to fill our lives with joy and preparation. However, many of us are entering this chapter of our lives with heavy hearts and scarred memories.

Some of us have not released yesterday's challenges. Many lives have changed forever by love lost or love grieved. Through separation of family or friends, we find it difficult to find joy, or a simple smile, and the prospect of a new year too much for us to bear.

When we cling too tightly to yesterday, crowding our minds with fear and sadness, we do not allow God to move us into new chapters of our lives.

Prayer: Help me to let go of yesterday and embrace the new day dawning. Amen.

Shirley Norwood
(In memory of my Mother, Evelyn Norwood-Sherrill)

Lord help me to release yesterday, and help me hope for tomorrow.

January 21

PUT ON RIGHTEOUSNESS

Scripture: Ephesians 6:10, 11 (KJV)
Finally, my brethren, be strong in the Lord, and in the power of his might. Put on the whole armour of God, that ye may be able to stand against the wiles of the devil.

The Apostle Paul admonishes us to put on the breastplate of righteousness. The breastplate was used to protect the vital organs of the body such as the lungs, liver, intestines, and especially the heart. From a spiritual perspective, the heart is the most vital part of our spiritual lives. So Paul is saying that it is vital for us to protect our hearts with righteousness.

Righteousness means to conform to God's standard. It means to be in right standing with God. Once we accept Jesus Christ as our Lord and Savior, we become obligated to obey God's Word. If we fail to do so, we lose our benefits as a citizen of the Kingdom of God.

Prayer: Lord, I have no righteousness of my own so I submit those things that I consider to be my strengths to your will and to your purpose. I understand that whatever is not submitted to you will ultimately burn away and has no divine purpose. Thank you that I am now righteous through the blood of Jesus. Amen.

Wanda Merriweather *Lord place in me a spiritual heart, what ever come out of my heart you will be pleased.*

CONSIDER THE EFFECT

Scripture: Psalm 94:12 (KJV)
Blessed is the man whom thou chastenest, O Lord, and teachest him out of thy law;

Two boys sat at the table for lunch with their father. During lunch, the older brother teased the younger. When the younger brother began to complain, the father ordered him to be quiet. He raised his voice and said to his dad, "You ought to make him stop." The dad corrected the younger boy. The younger brother learned a great lesson from that incident. His brother had not hurt him but had angered him. In his anger, he showed disrespect for his father.

There are many people who disrespect our Heavenly Father by the way we live. It is easy for us to lose our souls if we do not experience something that can cause us to think properly and tune our hearts for a closer walk with God. Whatever it takes, it is the result that matters. A closer walk with God is worth suffering for.

> We would like life to be easy,
> But our needs must be met.
> So, if life brings us some hardship,
> Forbid us to regret.

Prayer: Father God, I come as an imperfect, creature, needing an experience that can change my life. Whether painful, or not, I pray that you will guide my experiences, from darkness into your marvelous light. Amen.

Olivia Christopher

REACHING OUT TO THE SICK AND BEREAVED

Scripture: Psalm 46:1 (KJV)
God is our refuge and strength, a very present help in trouble.

All of us are familiar with feelings of helplessness and despair that prevail during a serious illness or the loss of a loved one.

Reaching out is an essential part of our Christian well being. It requires that we equip ourselves with the proper working tools. Two of our most powerful working tools are prayer and God's Word. James 5:15 says, *And the prayer of faith shall save the sick, and the Lord shall raise him up . . .*

While they are powerful tools they should be done in conjunction with evangelism, missionary work and other Christian acts of love and kindness. In other words, quoting a Scripture or saying, "I'm praying for you," is simply not enough. Our reaching out requires touching God's people, going to where they are and bringing them to where they should be. Additionally, reaching out should not be limited to loved ones, friends and acquaintances. It should include hospitals, nursing homes or other areas as the need arises..

Prayer: Dear Lord, lead us and guide us as we reach out to the sick and the bereaved. Amen.

Dolores Brown *Lord give me the tools I need To do your work,*

MISSION IS OUR BUSINESS

Scripture: Isaiah 6:8 (NIV)
Then I heard the voice of the Lord saying, "Whom shall I send? And who will go for us?" And I said, "Here am I. Send me!"

"When I awoke this morning, I didn't have any doubt that Jesus Christ would bring me out," said the songwriter. Another song writer said he saw a child that was lame, and could not see because of careless parenting, a woman that could not walk, a man that could not talk, the elderly, the lonely, the hungry, and the homeless.

Then I looked around at my family. All members were whole and of sound mind. I looked at me in perfect health and rich in His Spirit and I said, "I am blessed."

I looked up to my Master, who is the Captain of my soul. I saw Jesus on the cross with outstretched arms, nails that pierced His hands, feet, and sides, suffering for our sins. I looked at me again, and I said, "Yes, Lord, mission is my business. Here I am, send me as one of your spokeswomen for Christ today.

Prayer: Lord, what can I give you today, in exchange for setting me free from my sin? I will give you a lifetime of service and thank you for suffering for me. Amen.

Janice O. Lane

[handwritten: Lord I can never thank you enough for the many blessing you gave me and I will for ever praise you.]

[handwritten: 1-24-03]

January 25

PURSUING YOUR PURPOSE

Scripture: Matthew 7:7 (KJV)

Ask and it shall be given you; seek, and ye shall find; knock, and it shall be opened unto you:

Have you ever thought about the Creator and His infinite wisdom? He is wise enough to design, develop, and set into being every living thing. He is the Architect of everything in the universe. Our lives are in His hands.

Perhaps we could save ourselves a lot of pain and time if we would just go to Him and ask Him: "Lord, what is my purpose in this life? What is it you would like for me to do?" I know that God will answer.

God has given all of us gifts and talents. These gifts and talents vary according to the purpose for which God created each of us. God wants us to use our gifts to His glory. Our talents are part of God's purpose for our lives.

Our ministry can be so much more effective and gratifying to us, if we would first seek wisdom from the Father. He knows our hearts and holds our destiny in His hands.

Prayer: O God, help me to open my heart and listen to your voice. Amen.

Shirley Norwood,
(Dedicated to my son, Quentin Orlando Norwood)

Lord just tell me what you want me to do

BEATITUDES OF CHRIST

Scripture: Matthew 5:3-11 (KJV)

Blessed are the poor in Spirit: for theirs is the kingdom of heaven. Blessed are they that mourn: for they shall be comforted. Blessed are the meek: for they shall inherit the earth. Blessed are they which do hunger and thirst after righteousness: for they shall be filled. Blessed are the merciful: for they shall obtain mercy. Blessed are the pure in heart: for they shall see God. Blessed are the peacemakers: for they shall be called the children of God. Blessed are they which are persecuted for righteousness sake: for theirs is the kingdom of heaven. Blessed are ye, when men shall revile you, and persecute you, and shall say all manner of evil against you falsely, for my sake.

In the Sermon on the Mount, Christ taught His disciples how to reach the highest level of spiritual life. Jesus said we must seek humility, penitence, meekness, a spiritual appetite for growth, mercifulness, inward purity, peacemaking skills and sacrificial suffering. What a wonderful world it would be if each of us could keep these doctrines foremost in our hearts and lives as we strive here on earth to gain our heavenly reward.

Prayer: Dear God, thank you for the many blessings you have given me. Thank you for loving me. Amen.

Kathleen R. Thompson

January 27

PRAYER AND MEDITATION

Scripture: Isaiah 26:3 (KJV)
Thou wilt keep him in perfect peace, whose mind is stayed on thee: because he trusteth in thee.

I recently experienced a deep sense of fear and helplessness when my 11 year-old grandson was not at day care when his Mom went to pick him up. As I struggled to calm my fears, I began to whisper a prayer, "Lord, we don't know where he is, but you do. Keep him in your precious loving care." As I prayed this prayer silently, my fear was released, and a calmness came over me that seemed to say, "he is in my care and he is all right."

As it turned out, he was with his teacher at an opera performance his class attended that day. He and his mother had some confusion about the time of the performance. Even in the midst of our confusion God will bring peace if we will pray and meditate on His Word.

Prayer: Lord, when my life becomes stressed and distressed and I feel I cannot hold on, help me to put my trust in you and speak your peace into my life. Amen.

Jamesena Watson *Lord when I am confusioned and stressed out, give me the peace and calmness I need.*

AFTER THE BEACH . . . WHAT?

Scripture: Matthew 4:20 (KJV)
And they straightway left their nets, and followed him.

The real work begins when we leave the seashore. Peter, Andrew, James, and John immediately left family, business, and possessions when Jesus said, "come." As we step forward into a new realm of God's glory for our lives, remember that He who called us is faithful. The Lord Jesus walks with us. When we return to familiar surroundings and begin to act on the Lord's specific instructions for using the gifts He entrusts to us, there may be some resistance perhaps from others, or maybe from our own flesh. We must allow the anointing to flow through us. Never become a swamp (stagnant pool of water) when Living Water is available to you.

Prayer: Heavenly Father, as I leave the serenity of this shore where you met me in such a special way, empower me to do what you have purposed me to do. I cast into the ocean those things that were blocking the flow of your anointing in my life. You called me, not people, and my desire is to follow only you. Use me to your glory for the upbuilding of your Church and the edification of your people with love. In the powerful name of the Lord Jesus I pray. Amen.

Vrondelia (Ronni) Chandler

January 29

TO FULFILL THE WORLD WITH CHRIST

Scripture: 2 Corinthians 5:20 (KJV)
Now then we are ambassadors for Christ, as though God did beseech you by us: we pray you in Christ's stead, be ye reconciled to God.

It is a reality that we have hundreds of churches in close proximity to each other, yet externally there appears to be little change in our world. Could it be that we are confessing one thing with our mouths and believing another with our hearts? We therefore have no power; no power to stand, witness, or live. Just as the church equipped its people to lead the battle during prohibition, the institution of slavery, segregation, and civil rights, it must now equip the Saints to be ambassadors of Christ. It is then that we will be able to be about our Father's business, fulfilling the world with Christ through reconciliation.

Prayer: Help me, Holy Father, to take seriously the privilege of my position as an ambassador for Jesus Christ, my Lord and Saviour. Amen.

Reverend Willa Estell *To be a worker for the Lord, I want to the highest, means a clean cut Christian, equipped with everything to do his work. Then we with ~~need the~~ can become an ambassador for him.*

January 30

CREATIVE SIJ

Scripture: Psalm 46:10 (KJV)
*Be still, and know that I am God: I .
among the heathen, I will be exalted in the e..*

Are we ever really silent? In church we pause
moment of silence, but what do we really do at that mome..
Silence is more than a reflective mind. We must quiet the
mental activity and the wandering of the mind as we prepare
to be receptive as we pray to God. Remember prayer is
communication with our Father. In effective communication
there is a time to speak and there is a time to listen silently.
Our listening is not effective if we are not silent. When we
allow our minds to wander or we have a multitude of
activities going on in our minds we miss parts of what the
speaker is saying. *yes*

What then, is the use of silence? In part, the stilling
of the physical aspects of life, and in part, the stilling of the
mental aspects of life. When we are both physically and
mentally silent we can be sensitive to the presence of God. *yes*

Prayer: O God, in the midst of all my turmoil, help me to be
still and listen to your voice. Grant me peace and serenity in
my life. Amen.

Gladys M. Felton *Lord help me not to crowd my mind, I need a clear mind to receive what you have for me.*

January 31

February

*Let love be without dissimulation.
Abhor that which is evil; cleave to that
which is good. Be kindly affectioned
one to another with brotherly love; in
honour preferring one another;*

Romans 12:9, 10

Mid-Atlantic I
Table Of Contents

THE MYSTERY OF LOVE

Scripture: 1 John 4:8 (KJV)
He that loveth not knoweth not God; for God is love.

It is rare to find a gift that when given away it immediately multiplies and becomes stronger, allowing both the giver and the receiver to share with others again and again. If not shared with others it can cause pain and unhappiness for the keeper. God made it the foundation of the universe. It is the meaning of life. The gift is love.

The world is hungry for love. Children, adults, animals, all things need love. But somehow, many of us have hidden our love within us. We fear hurt, rejection and misuse of our feelings. But love given freely, without pre-judgment, without blame, without criticism, cannot hurt because the things that hurt have been removed from the heart. All of us must return to that place in our hearts where God's love dwells. When we have found it, we must renew it, and then give it away; first to ourselves, then to others.

Prayer: God teach me to love whether others love me or not. Help me to love first, myself, then those who are in dire need of love, and all others that you send my way. Amen.

Dorothy E. Brunson

GOOD DOES NOT STAND ALONE

Scripture: Romans 8:28 (KJV)
And we know that all things work together for good to them that love God, to them who are the called according to his purpose

All things in and by themselves are not good, but they can work together for good. An example of this is the story of Joseph. He was loved by his father, hated by his brothers, and sold into slavery. Some of these events by themselves would be tragic occurrences in a person life. But the Lord was with Joseph, and he prospered. All of the events of Joseph's life worked together for the good; he saved his family and a nation.

Further, the Verse does not say that things work together for all people. It says they work together for the good of those who love God. For those who love God, it is an all-inclusive statement. In this month of love we need to look at our love of God and the benefits we receive because of this love. If we love Him and believe in His promises then everything that happens in our lives will work for good whether or not we can see it or understand it.

Prayer: Lord, help me to remember that all things work together for the good of those that love you. Amen.

Pamela R. Valentine *when we have the love of God in our, heart; what ever we trying to work out, put God it first, other words work togethr with God. I wont to be the one he called according to his purpose.*

February 2

AFFIRMATION

Scripture: Matthew 8:13 (KJV)
And Jesus said unto the centurion, Go thy way; and as thou hast believed, so be it done unto thee. And his servant was healed in the selfsame hour.

Despite how I may feel at the moment, affirming my strength and wholeness with God has had a powerful effect on my life. My body responds to my courageous stand for health. I know He protects me and is the source of all that is good. I acknowledge my oneness with God and let His love find expression through me.

Whenever I am at home, at work, or traveling, God is. Instead of telling myself that I feel weak or tired, I affirm: I am strong and vitally alive. I am filled with new energy. Instead of thinking of my condition as chronic or incurable, I affirm: the Holy Spirit that dwells within me renews my body. I center all my thoughts on Him.

Prayer: Father, I thank you that you have made me whole and that as I come into oneness with your purpose I am able to walk in divine health. Amen.

Esther Hendrix-Marshall *I need to change my way of feelings. When I ask God for something I need to feel that he has and will renew my body. I need to believe and say yes, God has fixed things in my life.*

February 3

GOD'S EVERLASTING LOVE

Scripture: 1 John 4:7 (KJV)
Beloved, let us love one another: for love is of God; and every one that loveth is born of God, and knoweth God.

thank you Jesus

When we sin, God does not throw us away; instead He sees us as His treasure and longs for us to return to Him. The Lord makes us His own and keeps us. Like the father welcoming home with love his prodigal son, so too does God reach out to us and always welcomes us back no matter what we have done. God hates the sin, but not the sinner. We can convince ourselves that God cannot possibly love us and that He will be angry with us for the sins we have committed. We have a difficult time doing the forgiving and accepting the love God offers. We must learn how to accept God's love and forgiveness. When others have committed sin, we must learn how to love them as God loves us, no matter what the circumstances. How much more will God love and forgive us as we forgive one another. Let us accept God's everlasting love.

Prayer: Dear God, help me to be more loving and forgiving, as you are. Let me not find fault, but always look for the good in others. Amen.

Loretta L. Sutton *Love and understanding is so important in our Christian life. Our love as Christian should flow from with in. God is always there for us because God is Love. And his love is everlasting*

WAKE UP CALL

Scripture: Philippians 4:6 (KJV)
Be careful for nothing; but in every thing by prayer and supplication with thanksgiving let your requests be made known unto God.

      Recently, upon retiring for bed, I set my alarm clock for 6:00 a.m. in order to get ready and be on time for an important meeting. The next thing I knew I was waking up to a well-lit sky and within an instant I knew I had overslept. I glanced at the clock and it had stopped at 3:00 a.m. I had to laugh at myself. I was so involved in wanting the clock to do something important for me that before I went to bed I neglected to wind it.

      As Christians, many times we go to God in prayer for something. Then, we become so anxious for Him to honor our request that we neglect to wind up our request with thanksgiving for the things He has already done for us. As a result, our prayers go unanswered. When we pray we are not only to make requests, but we are to thank God also. Philippians 4:6 states that it is with thanksgiving that our requests are to be made known unto God. Let us set our Christian clocks (lives) with prayer and thanksgiving for time is winding up.

Prayer: Lord, hear my prayer. In all things you are great, and I am thankful for those great and small things you have done in my life. Amen.

Joyce Franklin *Prayer is the answer to all our problems. I am trying to learn to take my request to God and leave it there*

February 5

A DECLARATION OF FAITH

Scripture: Psalm 27:1 (KJV)
The Lord is my light and my salvation; whom shall I fear? The Lord is the strength of my life; of whom shall I be afraid?

Like a Declaration of Independence, Psalm 27 is the Christian's declaration of independent faith. We hold these truths to be self-evident:

- The Lord is the strength of our lives.
- We need not be afraid of anyone or anything when the Lord is on our side.
- In the time of trouble Jesus will be our bridge over troubled waters.
- If we are faithful and obedient to God's will and Word no one can defeat us.
- As our praises go up unto the Lord, His blessings will flow down upon us.
- God will never forsake us, even if everyone and everything else does.

Wars have been fought and won to uphold America's Declaration of Independence. Spiritual wars must be fought and won to uphold the Christian's declaration of faith, for there are those who would have us surrender to the wicked ways of the world.

Prayer: God, may my oath of faith and my declaration of independence be pleasing unto you. Amen.

Adele M. Riley

February 6

I know the Lord is ~~the~~ my light, whith him we all will fall into darkness, the Lord helps us to look who is in controll. he gives us salvation to keep our light going I have no fear because God is my light - my salvation keeps me. The light + salvation give me stength, that god gives me, I am not afraid, because the Lord is. Stength.

BY FAITH, I BELIEVE

Scripture: Romans 1:16 (NIV)
I am not ashamed of the gospel, because it is the power of God for the salvation of everyone who believes: first for the Jew, then for the Gentile.

The message of the Holy Bible is one of great wealth. The Bible is rich, complex, and filled with relationships between God and humanity. Its content cannot be proven by science but must be accepted by faith. The Bible teaches me that God acts on my behalf through Jesus Christ and the Holy Spirit to provide eternal redemption and salvation. It is this belief upon which my faith is built.

The Bible is a book that changes lives and transforms men and women to live holy. It speaks to the rich and poor, the young and the old, the learned and unlearned. By faith, I believe the Bible gives directions from birth to death and above all, it offers forgiveness of sins and hope of eternal life in His presence.

Prayer: Dear Jesus, thank you for the Gospel of righteousness revealed by God. It is my belief that by faith the righteous will live. Amen.

Jannie R. Harris *I belive in God, I am not ashame of his word which is the Gospel, The gospel is the Power the of salvation which every on should belive.*

February 7

OUR STEPS ARE ORDERED BY GOD

Scripture: Romans 8:28 (KJV)
And we know that all things work together for good to them that love God, to them who are the called according to his purpose.

Knowing that when we love God and are called according to His purpose, that no matter what happens, it is going to work out in our best interest, is a thrill. We should not fear but always trust in God. Trust Him to do what He said He would do. He said that He would never leave me nor forsake me. We must learn to trust God and not worry. God says that we should be anxious for nothing. God is in control and will not allow any weapons formed against us to prosper. Trust God to order your steps, and He will.

Submitting to God's will is important because God knows what is best for us. Commit to the Lord in whatever you do and your plans will succeed. Furthermore, in order to know God and to trust in God, we need to grow in grace and in the knowledge of our Lord and Savior, Jesus Christ. We must study God's Word, pray unceasingly, and be in constant communication with Him.

Prayer: I pray that I will never forget that God loves me and that I will let Him order my steps according to His purpose. Amen.

Deloris White

If we love God, things will work out Fod I do belive ie I Trust God, and not worrys and let him orden my steps. and knowing This will work For the good because I Love him, I know God is in controll of my live.

Lord help me Study + understand your word, so I can grow in grace and in the knowledge of the Lord Jesus Christ

February 8

WAITING TO EXHALE

Scripture: John 4:10 (KJV)
Jesus answered and said unto her, If thou knewest the gift of God, and who it is that saith to thee, Give me to drink; thou wouldest have asked him, and he would have given thee living water.

John 4:5-42 tells of a Samaritan woman who sought to quench her spiritual thirst. Unfortunately, like so many of us today, she got lost along the journey and chose non-living water; alcohol, fornication, adultery, greed, and other behaviors outside the will of God. Such choices are insufficient to satisfy our thirst, and result in greater dissatisfaction, unhappiness, and loneliness.

We do not know her background, or how she got to such a point in her life. Was she belittled throughout her young life, causing her to lack self-esteem? Where were the sisters of her community? Did she go to the well at noon, a time when others retreated to their homes to avoid the sun, to hide from the ridicule and gossiping of her neighbors? We know that her history did not matter to Jesus. We must be more like Jesus when others are suffering because they have erred.

Prayer: I pray that I look upon those needing compassion on their journey to exhaling, with love and compassion, with a non-judgmental heart for my sisters living beneath what God has prepared for them. Amen.

Debra Dennison

February 9

[handwritten margin note:] This is what you get

[handwritten note at bottom:] We all need this living water. This water is in Jesus Christ. When we drink it we will never thirst again. Wed

THERE, BUT FOR THE GRACE OF GOD

Scripture: Leviticus 23:22 (NIV)
" '*When you reap the harvest of your land, do not reap to the very edges of your field or gather the gleanings of your harvest. Leave them for the poor and the alien. I am the Lord your God.*' "

God expects those of us who have been blessed with the necessities of life to share with the less fortunate and those in need. In the twenty-third Chapter of Leviticus, we are given an account of the various feasts the Lord appointed for the Israelites in celebration of His provision, guidance, deliverance, and protection. The Feast of Weeks was a celebration held at the end of the barley harvest and the beginning of the wheat harvest. It was in thanksgiving for the abundance of their crops. In the gathering of the harvest and in other areas of their lives, the Lord reminded them of their responsibility to the poor and needy.

As the Body of Christ, we should always be aware of God's goodness and provision for us; the intangible blessings, as well as the tangible ones. We must show gratitude and thanksgiving by having a heart and mind to care for those in need.

Prayer: Lord, may I never forget the abundance of blessings you have bestowed upon me. Keep me mindful of your amazing grace. I praise and thank you. Amen.

Nancy R. Wardlow *Lord I thank you For what you has blessed me with, help me to help someone else. help me not to heap everything For my self.* Thur

February 10

LOVE IS A REQUIREMENT

Scripture: 1 John 3:18 (KJV)
My little children, let us not love in word, neither in tongue; but in deed and in truth.

When we rise every morning by God's grace and see the blessing of a new day, do we set out to do good? Everyday is an opportunity to help someone who needs our love. As we go to work, or school, how many people do we pass and do not see? How can we show love to those we do not see?

Love is a gift from God. You always have too much of it. No matter how much you give away you will still have too much. As we support our church and missionary society with our gifts of love, we must remember love given freely is a requirement of our loving Father. God has shown us how to meet the requirement; His love for us resulted in His giving His only begotten Son, Jesus.

Prayer: Father God, thank you for loving me so much. Give me the willingness to give love to anyone I meet this day, those I know and those I do not know. In the name of the One who is love I pray. Amen.

Sheila Johnson *Show me you Love me by doing.*

Fri

February 11

THOUGHTS, WORDS, AND DEEDS

Scripture: Psalm 19:14 (KJV)
Let the words of my mouth, and the meditation of my heart, be acceptable in thy sight, O Lord, my strength, and my redeemer.

As I laid in bed early one morning, listening to a Christian radio station, the words of Psalm 19:14 were being sung. They were telling me that whatever I think, say, and do should be with God in mind. As a member of an international communications organization, a poet, and a parliamentarian, my thoughts become my words and in turn my actions. Much of what I do or say during the course of a day portrays who and what I am. People see, hear and interpret what I say through my written and oral communications. What do they see in me through my words? More importantly, is what I think, say, and do pleasing to God? Is God pleased with your thoughts, words, and deeds?

Prayer: O Lord, may I always remember to praise and thank you for your wonderful works. May I also be mindful that you created us in your image, and may I think, speak, write, and act in a way that glorifies you. Amen.

Patricia Jones Lord you are my strength
what ever I say, and what ever I
am thinking in my heart let it
be acceptable in thy shiµht
Lord help me To have The thoughts in mind
the deeds I will do with out of my
heart the words I say will be
Pleaseing to you.

February 12

GIVING

Scripture: Luke 6:38 (KJV)
Give, and it shall be given to you; good measure, pressed down and shaken together, and running over, shall men give into your bosom. For with the same measure that ye mete withal it shall be measured to you again.

Many people are trying to hide behind weak and foolish excuses pretending they have nothing to give Jesus, the same Jesus who gave all for us. God does not expect us to give what we do not have. The important question may not be what do I have to give, but rather, am I willing to give what I have?

God's blessings are promised to those who give. If we expect to have, then we must first give. Jesus told us to give to every man that asks of us. Knowing that there is a promise of blessings from God. Giving begets gifts from God. Actually, the blessing is in the giving, not in the receiving.

Remember the words of the Lord Jesus when he said, "It is more blessed to give than to receive".

Prayer: Heavenly Father, thank you for loving me so much that you gave your all. Help me to become more willing to give what I have to give. Amen.

Rose Henderson Lord teach me willing to give, Just as it is said in your word god gave us his all. I am willing to give myself.

February 13

PEACE IN TRYING TIMES

Scripture: Proverbs 3:5 (KJV)
Trust in the Lord with all thine heart; and lean not unto thine own understanding.

Oftentimes when a trouble comes into our lives it is hard for us to leave our worries in the hands of God. We want an instant solution to our troubles. God listens to our prayers and He fixes things in His time, in His way. We must trust in Him and believe that He will grant our request. If we depend on and believe that God will answer prayers, then the Lord will give true peace to those who depend on Him, because they trust Him.

Prayer: Dear Lord, I thank thee for giving me peace of mind when times are trying. You have shown me that you are there with me every step of the way. Amen.

E. Delores Nicholas *Lord when trouble come in my life. help me not to turn to my own understanding in my trying Time Lord give me The trust I need wait. I need to know, and healy belive God is the only one who can give me Peace.*

February 14

monday.

GO IN FAITH

Scripture: Matthew 28:19 (KJV)
Go ye therefore, and teach all nations, baptizing them in the name of the Father, and of the Son, and of the Holy Ghost:

Our oldest effort overseas by the church began in Brewerville, Liberia by the late Rev. and Mrs. Andrew Cartwright of Elizabeth City, North Carolina in 1876. They saw the need to reach out and touch our sisters and brothers in a foreign land. This was no easy task, but a necessary one. They went in faith, as God was truly real to them.

This religious pair understood what Christ meant in the Gospel of Matthew. We may not be able to visit other countries, but we can serve those who live in our neighborhoods and lead them to Christ. We must be obedient to God. Whenever and wherever we make contact with the unsaved we must approach them in the name of Jesus and lead them to the saving knowledge of Jesus Christ.

Prayer: Lord, let me live from day to day in such a selfless way that even when I kneel to pray, my prayer shall be for others. Amen.

Ruth Ackerman *Lord help me to use my faith, and to dought. help me here you word with my heart, as that my faith can be stronger I I want to go in faith whenever I am tempted To meet Something*

February 15

tuesday

HARVEST THE FIELDS

Scripture: Matthew 9:38 (NIV)
"Ask the Lord of the harvest, therefore, to send out workers into his harvest field."

Those of us familiar with the operation of a large agricultural concern, where migrant workers are extensively used to harvest produce, are aware of how important it is to have an adequate number of available laborers to perform the work of the harvest when a crop has properly matured. During the height of the season for that particular crop every possible laborer will be utilized to harvest the field that is now ready to be gleaned.

Today, as we carefully assess the crop of lost souls in our chaotic, troubled world that are ready to be harvested, it becomes evident that there are not enough seasoned Christian laborers, that have been properly prepared to in-gather this rich, fertile crop of souls for Christ. Let us re-assess, re-organize, re-educate, and re-tool our various ministries to meet the challenges of today's Christian field of harvest. The proper education of Christian laborers will assure ample supply of workers to send out into God's harvest fields.

Prayer: Lord of the harvest, may I always be mindful of my duty and responsibility as a Christian laborer to seek those that are lost and lead them to salvation. Amen.

Gwendolyn Dianne Ridgley *Lord prepair me To go into The harvest field. I need To be field with your spirt. give Courage, Sthength. TO face what ever I am face with.*

February 16

IN THE TIME OF TROUBLE

Scripture: 2 Corinthians 4:8, 9 (KJV)
We are <u>troubled</u> on every side, yet not <u>distressed</u>; we are <u>perplexed</u>, but not in <u>despair</u>; <u>Persecuted</u>, but not <u>forsaken</u>; cast down, but not <u>destroyed</u>;

For eyes have not seen what the Lord has in store for us. The daily struggles of this life have caused us to sometimes forget that we are just traveling through this world of woe towards a home that the Lord has prepared for us.

Here on earth, we can be sure of God's love. In heaven, we will constantly bask in that love. Here on earth, we know God accepts us. In heaven we will hold an honored place as one of God's children. Here on earth, we can strive to be Christ-like. In heaven, we will be perfect. Here on earth, we live by faith. In heaven, we will understand it all and thank God for His wisdom. Here on earth, a good work has begun in us. In heaven, our good work will be complete. Here on earth, our treasures are pitiful, shabby, and falling apart. In heaven, the treasures we stored up here on earth will abound to our account.

Prayer: I pray that in spite of all the things I endure in this life, that I will still have joy in the Lord. Remembering he has prepared the way for us. Amen.

Anna B. Crandall

In time of trouble these are the issues we are face with, we do know ~~is God God~~ ~~no~~ ge God is our refuge in all the times.

Trouble
disthessed
perplexed
despair
Persecuted
Forsaken
destroyed.

February 17

Thursday

SEEKING GOD'S FACE

Scripture: 2 Chronicles 7:14 (KJV)
If my people, which are called by my name, shall humble themselves, and pray, and seek my face, and turn from their wicked ways, then I will hear from heaven, and will forgive their sin, and heal their land.

The Bible is filled with many accounts of God's people who have been touched by a thirst to know and see Him as He is. Man yearns to feel the presence of God and to experience His goodness. Although there are varied distances we must travel in order to get closer to God, we all follow the same path to see His face.

Seeking God's face is a journey that first involves reconciling us with our Father by committing our lives to His Son, Christ Jesus. To seek God's face, we must grow in our faith and in Christ's promise for salvation. To seek God's face, we must follow Jesus' example of helping others by doing good works. Doing good for others not only exemplifies the life Christ lived among us, but reinforces our faith as we spread the good news of the Gospel and glorify the name of our Lord. To seek God's face, we must experience the fulfillment of God's peace in our lives.

Prayer: I pray that as I grow from a baby to a warrior for Christ that the face of our Father will become clearer giving me strength. Amen.

Gloria J. Simms

February 18

Friday

START LIVING FOR CHRIST NOW

Scripture: Ecclesiastics 9:10 (KJV)
Whatsoever thy hand findeth to do, do it with thy might; for there is no work, nor device, nor knowledge, nor wisdom, in the grave, whither thou goest.

How many times have we heard various individuals proclaim all that they intend to accomplish while they are on vacation, sabbatical, or once they have retired? Many have been heard pronouncing their heartiest intentions to get around to the many things they delayed doing or trying while their careers were in full bloom or their children were young.

What if Christ had delayed His ordeal of death and agony upon Calvary's cross? Would we have then been privileged to be numbered among that "royal priesthood" spoken of in 1 Peter 2:9? No we would not.

We cannot delay our living for Christ. We cannot afford to let time and eternity absorb us before we have been a faithful, committed servant of God. Daily we must strive to become more and more like our blessed Savior so that our work on earth can be done. We do not have the luxury of time.

Prayer: Lord, let what I do now uplift your name, and advance your Kingdom, and hopefully someday, I might have earned a crown of life. Amen.

Gwendolyn Dianne Ridgley

February 19

Saturday

HOLINESS

Scripture: 1 Peter 1:15, 16 (KJV)
But as he which hath called you is holy, so be ye holy in all manner of conversation; Because it is written, Be ye holy; for I am holy.

The Old Testament teaches us that atonement must be made to be set apart and made holy. The New Testament tells us that whosoever shall call upon the name of the Lord shall be saved. The Blood of Jesus has set us apart. We are the temples of God; the Holy Spirit dwells in us, and we must not defile our temples. *I need help in this error*

To keep our temples undefiled we must be obedient to the Word of God, which means we should put away corrupt speaking and speak only the things that edify. We must put away bitterness, wrath, anger, clamor, evil speaking, malice, and instead be kind tenderhearted, forgiving, and just.

When set apart for God's use every thing becomes holy. God wants all believers to be set apart when we accept Jesus into our heart. We must allow His Word to change us and set us apart for God's use.

Prayer: Father, teach me how and give me an unction to stay in your Word daily, so that I might walk in the Spirit as a holy child of God. Amen.

Essie Copeland *when I accept Jesus into my heart I try to live holy & when I am in a Conversation it should be becoming to a holy and helpful one, and pleasing to God*

February 20

Sunday

THE NAME OF JESUS

Scripture: Philippians 2:9 (KJV)
Wherefore God also hath highly exalted <u>him</u>, and given him a name which <u>is</u> above every name: Jesus

I once heard a man say that there is nothing in a name. I disagree, and Jesus is the perfect name to support my position. God gave Him a name above all other names. As Christians we are to obey that name, we are to trust that name, we are to love in that name, we are to give in that name, our very existence is in that name.

His name is not only recognized by and reacted to by Christians; the demons in hell fear His name. With all of the power associated with the name of Jesus, Christians have no reason to fail at anything we do in Jesus' name. He has given us the authority to use His name. Therefore everywhere we go we should go in His name. That man was wrong. Everything is in His name. — *Helen remember*

Like Jesus has a name that commands love, respect, mercy, justice, and peace. Our names have attributes associated with them based on how we have lived our lives. What does your name command? *Lord I need help*

Prayer: I thank you that you have given me the power of your name so that I can live a successful life. Father, as I live my life I pray that with my name would be associated those things that identify me as your servant. Amen.

Gussie Jones *I do praise God for that name Jesus, the name Jesus is very powerful, when you just say Jesus lord help me to do every thing in Jesus name, and take him everywhere I go. I dont no about anyone else but I need Jesus in my life — daily*

Monday

February 21

THE *A PRAYER OF MEDITATION*

Scripture: Psalm 121:1 (KJV)
I will lift up my eyes unto the hills, from whence cometh my help.

I lift my heart in praise for all the beauty which surrounds me day by day. As the colors of the seasons blend themselves under the direction of God as the Great Artist, I know that He has control of nature and I am comforted. As I come in touch with men, women, and children, who have about them the shining light of God's presence, I know that He is merciful and I am strengthened.

I pray He will give to the leaders of the world strength and courage to lead in Jesus' name and to the Church a renewed consciousness of her divine mission to proclaim the glad tidings of great joy to all people. I pray that we would walk in a sense of obligation to the works of the Kingdom of God. We must learn to allow Jesus to be the rock and everlasting defense for our dear ones and to protect us from the snares of the tempter, the pestilence of our thoughts, and the consequence of wicked deeds. He is able to make us fit for the tasks at home and in the vineyard by remaking our wills and our hearts, to the end that we love to do His holy will.

Prayer: Through Jesus Christ I pray for your mercy and help. Amen.

Julia M. Ingram

Lord I realize every good gift come from you, Lord help me to lift up my eyes unto the hills. I need gtty up in the moraig. I need help to deal with the cores in my family — my health, my spirtual life. I need help in every way. That why I need to look to hill.

February 22
tuesday

HE'S THERE

Scripture: Psalm 23:4 (KJV)
Yea, though I walk through the valley of the shadow of death, I will fear no evil: for thou art with me; thy rod and thy staff they comfort me.

I learned the 23rd Psalm in childhood, and many times I have stood proud to recite it. But it was in 1995 that it pulled me through when my mother became ill. I kept repeating Verse 4 over and over again. Through it all I felt a constant peace.

My mother has become ill again. Now I am experiencing another aspect of Verse 4. God has placed individuals in both our lives that have confirmed His constant presence. His presence is felt through either family or friends who have come to visit, called, sent a card, prayed a prayer, given a message, cooked a meal, baby-sat, sent e-mail messages, or given a hug.

God uses us to let His presence be known to all who are unloved, hurt, sick, lost, hungry or lonely. Share God's presence with someone today.

Prayer: Dear God Almighty, thank you for making it known to me that I am living the 23rd Psalm. Thank you for the valley times in my life that have helped me to see you face to face. Glory to your name. Amen.

Patrice Suzette Counts *Fond I am willing to walk through and valley, knowing you are with me. When fear come up on me I you to comfort me.*

February 23

Wedensday

afolonda Birthday

WHEN THE SPIRIT CALLS, ANSWER

Scripture: 1 Corinthian 2:15 (KJV)
But he that is spiritual judgeth all things, yet he himself is judged of no man.

Early one morning she was suddenly awakened. The thick clouds of billowing smoke and the strong smell of fire sent her scurrying down the stairs of her old apartment to the street below. Once outside in the pre-dawn air, she discovered it was not her building on fire, but the church next door. Had she not responded when she did the church would have been completely burned.

Many people live in that neighborhood, but it was God's plan for her to be a blessing to a congregation in need. More importantly, she answered the call for her own spiritual salvation. The following Sunday, she joined the church she had saved. A call to stop the fire at the church, became a call for her to come to Jesus.

Think how often the Spirit calls you, makes the connection, only for you to break it. Why do we cling to the emptiness of man, and run from the love of God? All we need to do is answer the call. Our lives will be transformed and we will know the love of God in ways never before imagined.

Prayer: Father, let each one of us answer when the Spirit calls. Amen.

Paula B. Davis *Lord I am willing to answer to your call please help me to recognize the Spirit. what ever The Spirit leads I will follow*

February 24

Thursday

this is to my family

FORGIVENESS

Scripture: Colossians 3:13 (NIV)
Bear with each other and forgive whatever grievances you may have against one another. Forgive as the Lord forgave you.

How many times have we encountered conflicts? We must forgive those that try to do us harm. We must forgive those persons and love them in Jesus' name. God forgave us and washed our sins away. Sometimes, our enemies will try to get us to sin by taking actions against us, but believe in the Almighty Father. He will not forsake you.

Incidents of wrongdoing will be done against you. For it is the nature of men to oppress and condemn others not considering themselves. Do not let the words of men be put in your heart or mind. If you hear with the ears of God and respond with the grace of God, you will forgive the negative things done to you.

Prayer: Dear God Almighty, I thank you for giving me a heart to forgive those who have wronged me. You are a mighty God. Thank you for giving me the strength and courage to forgive those that trespass against me. Amen.

E. Delores Nicholas *Lord thank you for giving me a willing heart to for those who wrong me. Lord I am thankful, I understand how you forgive. And remember no more.*

February 25

friday

THE REAL LIGHT

Scripture: Matthew 5:16 (KJV)
Let your light so shine before men, that they may see your good works, and glorify your Father which is in heaven.

There are many kinds of lights that are very important in our daily lives; such as, a flashlight, candle, lamp, headlights of a car, bulbs, and a match. Did you know that the glare from a match can be seen on a clear night for a mile? Did you know the light from a good flashlight can be seen on a clear night for one and half miles? Did you know that the light from a 100-watt bulb can be seen on a clear night for twelve miles? Did you know the headlights of a car can be seen for twenty miles? All these lights have something in common; they need a power source.

We are told to let our light shine. The power source for our light is Jesus. He is the light of the world. We must let others see the light of Jesus in us. We must let our light shine by what we say, how we act, what we do, and where we go. Jesus wants the world to see His light through us. Therefore we should be loving, humble, caring, peaceful, and kind.

Prayer: Jesus, I praise you for the opportunities you have given to me to let your light shine through me, and I thank you for being the source of my light. Amen.

Jimmie L. Harper *My light is the way I live - doing the things that pleas God, is the way it shine before men, helping, caring, loving, understanding, this is my way of glorifying the father in heaven.*

February 26

Saturday

THE FAITHFUL WITNESS

Scripture: Philippians 1:9, 10 (NRS)
And this is my prayer, that your love may overflow more and more with knowledge and full insight to help you to determine what is best, so that in the day of Christ you may be pure and blameless,

The purpose of your life and mine is to glorify God and praise Him forever. True fulfillment comes through obeying God. When we do, we will be showing the world who we live and die for. When we are united in His name with other believers, we will show God's enemies that their purpose will not prevail and that God still has faithful witnesses working for him.

When we live for heavenly reasons, we will contrast with those who are controlled by fleshly desires. Trying to find fulfillment while disobeying God is like starting a fire with a wet match. It will not work.

As we start to do the will of the Father, and not our own will, we discover that God has imparted His life deep within us. That life, the Holy Spirit, becomes the power that propels us to build the Kingdom of God.

Prayer: Lord, I thank you that I have the victory of your indwelling Holy Spirit. Amen.

Marlene C. Bryant

February 27

Sunday

FEAR NOT

Scripture: Jeremiah 1:8 (NIV)
"Do not be afraid of them, for I am with you and will rescue you," declares the Lord.

As a new Christian, I often struggled with decisions and new challenges. I was afraid that I would make the wrong choice or say the wrong thing. I did not want to disappoint God so I shied away from any topics or situations that would put me in opposition with non-believers. I was fearful of what my friends would think about me if I spoke out against the same activities that I use to participate in so I avoided them. Yet, in my heart I knew that I had to take a bold stand for my new life with Jesus. I was still afraid but then I came across Jeremiah 1:8. The Scripture comforted me because it was God speaking directly to my heart, which calmed me.

Prayer: Father, help me to not be afraid of what man can do to me. Strengthen me to walk boldly and proclaim your matchless name without fear. Amen.

April A. Morrow *et pays for me to take the Lord along with me every where I go, I will put my thust in God, the Lord has already said in his word I am with you. I need not be afried. Some times it is hard for me to trust God, not that I dont trust him.*

February 28

Monday

CHOSEN

Scripture: Isaiah 43:10 (KJV)
Ye are my witnesses, saith the Lord, and my servant whom I have chosen: that ye may know and believe me, and understand that I am he: before me there was no God formed, neither shall there after me.

Have you ever been the last one sitting on the bench waiting to be chosen for a team? I have. I knew I did not have the athletic skills needed to excel in sports so I honestly did not want to participate. Yet, I still felt a little disappointed because I was not selected. It did not matter how nice the team captains were, I knew that I did not have the ability to help them win; thus I was of no use to their team.

When it came to being selected to be on God's team, I was ecstatic to find that it did not matter what skills or abilities I had, but rather God chose me because of who He is and what He could do for me.

Prayer: Heavenly Father, thank you for being a great God. Thank you for choosing me and allowing me to be a part of the winning team. Amen.

April A. Morrow *Lord If you chose me as one of your ~~servents~~ servents help me to understand how to be a witness for you, and a faithful servants*

February 29

Tuesday

March

*But as touching brotherly love ye
need not that I write unto you: for
ye yourselves are taught of God to
love one another.*

                              1 Thessalonians 4:9

Western Episcopal District
Table Of Contents

UNDERSTANDING ONE'S FAITH

Scripture: Hebrews 11:1 (KJV)
Now faith is the substance of things hoped for, the evidence of things not seen.

When we walk by faith God's grace is greater than any imagined obstacle or hindrance. God has given each of us a measure of faith which must be exercised daily. This faith is the substance that allows us to rest upon His precious promises in the face of adversity. When you look at life's challenges through the eyes of faith, you recognize that all things work together for your good for you have been called according to His purpose.

Prayer: Dear God, I trust in you with my whole heart, and I lean not to my own understanding. Thank you for the grace that works on my behalf so that you will be glorified, for the faith to see things through your eyes, and for the understanding that all things will work together for the good of those called according to your purpose. Amen.

Doris M. Rogers *Lord it 'not that I don't have faith at times, it seems hard for me to let go. Knowing in my heart I have a strong belief I have exercised my faith number of times and come out victorious. I understand what the word of God mean when it say rest upon his promises. learn to hope in for the things we do not see I want to be glad to trust in him.*

March 1

Friday
wednesday

KEEP ON KEEPING ON

Scripture: Philippians 1:6 (KJV)
Being confident of this very thing, that he which hath begun a good work in you will perform it until the day of Jesus Christ:

Sometimes we may feel like giving up. We try to keep on keeping on only to find that we have fallen flat on our faces. It seems as if the two steps that we have taken forward in reality is a giant step backward. We also feel that we have failed God and that He has given up on us.

We must never forget that God knows the difficulties we face and that He promises victory in the end. Romans 8:37 reminds us that, . . . *we are more than conquerors through him that loved us.* Romans 8:38-39 states, *For I am persuaded, that neither death, nor life, nor angels, nor principalities, nor powers, nor things present, nor things to come, Nor height, nor depth, nor any other creature, shall be able to separate us from the love of God, which is in Christ Jesus our Lord.* Lord help me to press on

In the harsh light of adversity, we must go on. The work that God began in you will keep helping you to grow in His grace until the work is complete in you on that day when Jesus returns. Keep on keeping on because God is not through with you yet!

Prayer: Thank you for the good work you have begun and for that which you will perform in and through me. Your joy continues to strengthen me as I keep my mind focused on you and walk in my covenant rights and benefits. Amen.

Henrietta C. Parks Lord what ever, wont you have given me help me to have confidens to press on

March 2

JESUS HEALS

Scripture: Luke 9:11 (KJV)
And the people, when they knew it, followed him: and he received them, and spake unto them of the kingdom of God, and healed them that had need of healing.

Jesus desired to meet the needs of the people at whatever level he found them. When they needed teaching He taught them. When they needed food, He fed them. When they needed healing, He healed them. We cannot run too far or sink too low that Jesus will not reach out and reach down. He lifts us up out of our circumstances and situations in order for God to be glorified.

Jesus will meet us at the point of our need. He will not forsake us nor leave us in that hour. We simply need to let God be God and watch the healing take place.

Prayer: Thank you Lord for your awesomeness and your healing power. Thank you for saving a wretch like me. Amen.

Henrietta C. Parks

March 3

PRAYER IS POWER

Scripture: 1 Thessalonians 5:17 (KJV)
Pray without ceasing.

Be careful for nothing; but in every thing by prayer and supplication with thanksgiving let your request be made known unto God. And the peace of God, which passeth all understanding, shall keep your hearts and minds through Christ Jesus. Philippians 4:6-7. We are indeed living in evil days wherein things seem harmless, yet they are really the enemy (Satan) in disguise, waiting to deceive, devour and destroy God's children. God admonishes us to pray without ceasing. We are to remain in a state of prayer, keeping our minds and hearts sensitive to the Spirit of God so that He can direct our paths.

When we have prayed about all things and asked God for guidance, we then experience a peace that the carnal mind does not understand. Knowing that the all-powerful God is taking care of every situation we have placed before Him is the best stress medicine there is. We will not be free from trials and tribulations, but God will give us strength to deal with them, direct us around mountains, and make stumbling blocks into stepping-stones. Pray and trust God for every thing and do not forget to be thankful.

Prayer: Dear Holy Father, thank you for listening when I pray. Thank you for your grace, your omnipotent power which works on my behalf, for my benefit and for your glory. Amen.

Lord I want to give you all my troubles, and hope and belive you are going to take care of them. keep me in a spirt of prayer.

Cynthia Purnell Stuart

March 4

MY CHRISTIAN WALK

Scripture: Acts 11:26 (KJV)
. . . And the disciples were called Christians first in Antioch.

As a day care provider for an after school program, I often overhear conversations among the children. One day at snack time a group of first graders were talking among themselves. They were asking each other if they were a Christian. One after the other with excited exuberance they responded, "Yes! I am a Christian."

That conversation and their excitement stuck in my mind as I asked myself the question—could I answer with as much joy and boldness as the children?

I am reminded of the conversation that Jesus had with Peter when He told Peter that he would deny Him. Peter could not imagine himself denying Jesus. Not for all the money in the world, not under the threat of death, would he deny Jesus. Yet Jesus was barely in the grave before Peter was challenged, and he denied Jesus.

I can easily say I am a Christian when with my Christian friends, but when non-believers confront me will I become another Peter? We must ask for strength and courage as we share the love of Jesus with others.

Prayer: Lord Jesus, may I walk in boldness as a living epistle being conformed to your image so that your abundant life and love would flow from my heart to reach those who do not know you. Amen.

Shirley Davis

March 5

MY LIFE IS IN HIS HANDS!

Scripture: 1 Thessalonians 5:18 (KJV)
In every thing give thanks: for this is the will of God in Christ Jesus concerning you.

Since 1976, I have experienced three incidents wherein I knew it was nothing but the Hand of God that saved me. I was driving a van on an icy road and lost control. My family and I rolled over into the grassy ravine that divided the lanes from on-coming traffic. No one was injured. Another time I was in a ski boat that started sinking on the Colorado River. I could not swim at the time nor did I have on a life jacket. I stayed calm as I floated in the water and the Lord delivered me from drowning.

In 1988, I was on my way home from church. I was on the freeway when the car on my right crossed in front of me to get to an interchange. It was raining. I hit the brakes to avoid an accident, but skidded into the next lane. I was hit by an 18-wheeler that turned my car towards on-coming traffic. I then saw another truck coming toward me head-on. Although my car was totaled, my daughter only had a small seat belt burn on her chin.

So when I see situations in the world that seem too big for even God, I know He is able to save us from anything and everything.

Prayer: Thank you Lord for your strong Hands of protection when I face danger. Amen.

Janice Hall   *I am learning to give God thanks more and more.*

March 6

Monday

ARE YOU AVAILABLE TO GOD?

Scripture: Isaiah 6:8 (KJV)
Also I heard the voice of the Lord, saying, Whom shall I send, and who will go for us? Then said I, Here am I; send me.

I am always impressed at the resourcefulness of the Native people of Alaska and how they make use of all the resources that God provides.   Something as simple as a piece of Birch tree bark is creatively shaped into beautiful works of art. One day while browsing through the gift shop of our small Fairbanks Alaska Airport, I saw three Birch bark artifacts–a mask, a basket, and a hair barrette. I remember thinking; the raw material is not what is important but rather, how the raw material is developed.

Each one of us has been given unique talents and abilities and spiritual gifts. Our gifts (raw materials) are worthless to God unless we are willing to let Him develop and use them as a force for divine good in this world.

If you do not know what your abilities and gifts are, ask God to reveal them to you and expect an answer. Then ask Him to show you what He wants you to do with them. Your happiness and success in life will be found in fulfilling His plan for your life. Remember, God never asks about our ability or inability—just our availability.

Prayer: Dear Father, thank you for the gifts that you have entrusted to me. I am available for your glory. Amen.

Reverend Shellie M. Brown *Lord what ever you want me to do or go here am I. I'll will go where you want me To. Just Call me I am always Availabil.*

March 7

Tuesday

UNWHOLESOME COMMUNICATION

Scripture: Colossians 3:8 (KJV)
But now ye also put off all these; anger, wrath, malice, blasphemy, filthy communication out of your mouth.

I recently heard a young mother use profanity repeatedly while instructing her seven year-old daughter. The child was expected to accept the choice of words selected by the mother. The young mother was smoking a cigarette, carrying a second child in her arms, and berating her daughter.

This may seem like a pretty bleak picture of a young mother. However, use of profanity or curse words is promoted daily through their use on TV, in movies, in lyrics of popular songs and even from the mouths of Christians.

We want our children to develop habits, traits, and characteristics that are admirable and worthwhile. When children hear and see unwholesome language, habits, and behaviors, they demonstrate the same.

As we look back on our childhood we can remember certain experiences that influenced our conduct or at least our thinking. Be aware of your choices both in word and deed. Someone may carry your influence to adulthood.

Prayer: Lord, help me use wholesome communication when I speak to others. Amen.

Daisy Hogg *it is very important for us to think before we speak. our thoughts shoulds always be clean, and well thought about before we release our communication.*

March 8

wendy

MY DAILY PRAYER

Scripture: Lamentations 3:22, 23 (KJV)
It is the Lord's mercies that we are not consumed, because his compassions fail not. They are new every morning: great is thy faithfulness.

Each morning when I wake, I say I will place my hand in God's today. I know He will walk close by my side, my every wondering step to guide. He leads me with the tenderest of care, when paths are dark or I despair. No need for me to understand if I but hold fast to His hand. My hand in His knows a sure way to walk in safety through each day. By His great bounty I am fed, warmed by His love and comforted. When at days end I seek my rest, and realize how much I am blessed, my thanks go out to Him and then I place my hand in God's again.

Prayer: Thank you, Lord, for your faithfulness for you are an unchanging God. Amen.

Ethilda Robinson

A RED ROSE

Scripture: Song of Solomon 2:11, 12 (KJV)
For, lo, the winter is past, the rain is over and gone; The flowers appear on earth; the time of the singing birds is come, and the voice of the turtle is heard in our land;

My husband passed away in July of 1997. We were very close and did everything together, so I was lost, upset, and afraid.

On February 14, 1998, I was working in my rose garden, listening to the birds chirping, and children chattering, when I noticed a single red rose. It was beautiful. I could not believe my eyes because two weeks before I had pruned all the bushes.

My heart fluttered and a calm feeling came over me, as I picked the flower. The flower and the calm it caused made me know that God and my husband wanted me to be happy and do something with my life. In times of loneliness and despair, remember God is there.

Prayer: Dear Father, thank you for reminding me that I am not alone; you are there and you know my needs. You are there to help me prepare for a new beginning. Teach me to love and serve you. These are the blessings I ask in Jesus' Name. Amen.

Carol C. Winston

PUTTING GOD FIRST

Scripture: Luke 12:31 (KJV)
But rather seek ye the kingdom of God; and all these things shall be added unto you.

God gives direct instructions. He promises to provide for our needs and the desires of our heart, but we must put Him first. As we learn to put God first and apply His principles consistently in our lives, we are no longer afraid to look for miracles from God. We now expect the impossible as we encourage our children concerning their lives. We envision the invisible dreams and desires of our hearts as our faith increases with God's plan.

God has been consistent in our lives, we have been the ones that were wishy-washy. But God has waited patiently and faithfully

Prayer: Father, it is your desire to give so much to your children, but you will not violate your Word, so I must seek you first then things will be added. I thank you for keeping me in remembrance that those things to be added are not just material possessions, but, Father, it is your desire that I would also increase in my relationship with you. I thank you for my continued growth. Amen.

Kadesta Prothro-Harris What ever I desire in this world may be meaterial good, or spintial goods. Seek God First, And the boath will come to me. Lond help me seek after the things of the spirt. help me relly on your Promises.

March 11

SPEECHLESS

Scripture: John 3:3 (KJV)
Jesus answered and said unto him, Verily, verily, I say unto thee, Except a man be born again he cannot see the Kingdom of God.

The winner of the "Good Citizen's Award" made his way to the podium. Facing the cheering audience he said, "I'm speechless, absolutely speechless." This reminds me of another "speechless" man.

Matthew Chapter 22 describes a king who prepared a wedding banquet for his son. Those invited did not come, so others were recruited. The banquet was a success. However, one man who was not dressed in wedding clothes was found mingling with the guests. When the king asked him, "why," the improperly dressed man was speechless. He was cast out and punished.

I fear some of us, who believe we can "mingle" with unbelievers and somehow sneak into heaven's banquet undetected, will be speechless when asked why we are not clothed in the righteousness of Jesus. God knows His own. He even calls us by name. There is only one way to be a part of that banquet, and that is to accept Jesus Christ as your personal Lord and Savior and be properly "clothed in Him." Do it today.

Prayer: Father, help me to accept Jesus so I may be a welcome guest in heaven. Amen.

Winifred K. Sharper

March 12

Tuesday

I SUGGEST A COMMA

Scripture: 2 Peter 3:18 (KJV)
But grow in grace, and in the knowledge of our Lord and Saviour, Jesus Christ. To him be glory both now and for ever. Amen.

There is much said about being saved. Nothing we do in life is more important. Yet we handle our salvation differently. One says, "I'm saved," and puts a period at the end of the statement. I suggest a comma instead. Being saved is not the end, but the continuation of life. Salvation brings new life with new direction and there is much to learn about it.

Imagine moving to a new city. When you reach your destination, you must learn about your new home, the location of schools, and stores. Often you have to rely on others to get you from point A to point B.

The Christian journey is like that. Once we "arrive," there is much to learn.

What can I expect from God?
What does God expect from me?
What happens if I "fall"?

Again, we must rely on others to get from Point A to B. Sunday school, Bible study, and the church family are all there to help.

Prayer: Father, help me to know more about you and the gift of salvation. Amen.

Winifred K. Sharper *Lord now I am saved, I want to grow in your grace. And have the knowledge of the Lord to guide me through life.*

March 13

Monday

CALLED TO WITNESS

Scripture: Acts 1:8 (KJV)
But ye shall receive power, after that the Holy Ghost is come upon you: and ye shall be witnesses unto me both in Jerusalem, and in Judaea, and in Samaria, and unto the uttermost parts of the earth.

Even if we are not lawyers we have probably seen television programs about lawyers, so we know how important a witness can be in the courtroom. A witness is called upon to tell the truth; only those things they have seen and know to be true. No speculation or hearsay is allowed.

Our Christian witness is no different. We may think we cannot witness because we have not been to seminary or we are not able to answer someone's questions. Well, I am here to tell you that you are only asked to tell what you know to be true.

Has God delivered you from a life-style in which you felt trapped? Has He healed your body? Has He restored your family to good health? Perhaps He has simply given you a peace within that you cannot explain. If so, tell that, and only that, and you will fulfil the command to be His witness.

Prayer: Father, please give me the words, the opportunity, and the courage to be a witness for you. Amen.

Winifred K. Sharper *Lord you have done so many things For me, some I can not explain. some I have witness. it is True sometime I am lost For words to express myself, but I can be a witness For that I can put together. thank you Lord all you have done For me*

March 14

Oh some things he did

Tuesday

LET YOUR LIGHT SHINE

Scripture: Matthew 5:16 (KJV)
Let your light so shine before men, that they may see your good works, and glorify your Father which is in heaven.

When I was a young girl, I was always puzzled as to ways to let my light shine. Now that I am older, I have learned more of what is expected of us on a daily basis. A simple "Good Morning" could help lift someone's spirits. An act of kindness can cause even a very stubborn person to think differently. Receiving a greeting card, note, or phone call can let a person know that someone cares. *I need to this*

In today's world, we are constantly directed to see the "big picture." But, small person-to-person contacts can have as much impact as large ones. It is amazing how others interpret our actions, even when we are not aware that anyone is paying attention, especially younger people. Kindness and goodness can cause someone to reflect on their own life. *Lord I understand this*

Prayer: Dear Lord, help me to start each day with thanksgiving and live so that your light shines in me.

Carol Robinson *Lord let your light shin in me so every on I come in contact with, Can see your spirt in me, And I will give you phais. First I wont To be an example before my family. IF I Live by your spirt I will shine so every one can be blessed Through me. living right is a help To some who is Troubled. let Someone see the light in you when things Seam To be Takeing over your life. Lord help me Stand. And Shing bhight.*

March 15
So you can be glorifed

Wensday

remember this

CHOOSE TO LIVE A HOLY LIFESTYLE

Scripture: Romans 12:1 (KJV)
I beseech you therefore, brethren, by the mercies of God, that ye present your bodies a living sacrifice, holy, acceptable unto God, which is your reasonable service.

The end of the day is a good time to evaluate our lifestyle. We should evaluate ourselves by the standards that God has given us in the Scriptures. If we compare ourselves to our friends, co-workers, and even fellow Christians, we may measure up to their standards. However, it is when we can truthfully say we are obeying the commandments of God in every aspect of our lives that we are living a holy lifestyle.

Even when we do not quite meet all that is required of us; we must not be discouraged. We must simply tell God that we are sorry for our mistakes and make a sincere effort to do better. Being honest with God and ourselves is a giant step in our Christian walk. God is so merciful to forgive us of our misdoing, therefore we must be merciful and forgiving towards our fellowman.

Prayer: Heavenly Father, I tried to live this day in a manner that exemplified Christian character. Please forgive me wherever I fall short and strengthen me that I may become more Christ-like each day. Help me to forgive those who offended me. Lord, I leave every care and burden of this day with you. Amen.

Cynthia Purnell Stuart

Lord have mercies up on me
as I walk this christen life
Let the things I do be holy and acceptable
unto you !

March 16

Thursday

CHRISTIAN PARENTS AND THE TRAINING OF CHILDREN

Scripture: Ephesians 6:1 (KJV)
Children, obey your parents in the Lord: for this is right.

When we look at our world and see how rebellious some children are against their parents, it makes us wonder where they are getting their training and discipline. Parents need to focus more on love, understanding, and Christian training. Parents need to train children in the ways of God and to fear God.

If we are going to raise obedient children, our focus should be on:

- Spending time with our children.
- Being Christian examples for them.
- Knowing their whereabouts and their choices in friends.
- Making sure prayer is an integral part of their daily lives.

By following these instructions we can begin to raise a generation of obedient children, and our world will be a more peaceful place to live.

Prayer: Lord, help me as a parent to train my children in the ways of righteousness by living a godly life and being a Christ-like example. Amen.

Ida M. Francis Our Children, Listens to almost every word we say, and watch every thing we do, IF this send out a bad out look, Somtimes ou children will become hard to discipline. our children need To see Loving Parents, and respecteul Prants, and above all Praying Parents.

March 17

SELF SACRIFICE

Scripture: Romans 12:1 (NIV)
Therefore, I urge you, brothers, in view of God's mercy, to offer your bodies as living sacrifices, holy and pleasing to God—this is your spiritual act of worship.

There can be no real joy or happiness without sacrifice. Our greatest joy does not come from our efforts toward self-gratification, but from our loving and spontaneous service to others. This is what Jesus did. He went about helping others. Joy comes not to him who seeks it for himself, but to him who seeks it for others.

Jesus gave His best for humanity in His day, and He expects us as His followers to give our best for humanity in our day. Self-sacrifice is what He demands. Just as Jesus made daily sacrifices to tell of God's love for humanity, we too, must be willing to make sacrifices. Telling the world about God's love can alleviate the social ills of our day.

Prayer: O Lord, help me to fulfill your mission by renewing my mind daily through prayer, reading your Word, meditating and making personal sacrifices. Amen.

Ida M. Francis

March 18

"COMMAS"

Scripture: Philippians 1:6 (KJV)

. . . He which hath begun a good work in you will perform it until the day of Jesus Christ:

Many times in life we come to a point where nothing seems to be moving, everything seems to be at a standstill, whether on our jobs, or in our personal lives. We have done all we know to advance our situations and still, nothing. We are in a dry place. I believe these places are marked with inserted commas from God and are used for pauses for emphasis in our lives. We can view these pauses as negatives, and become frustrated and discouraged. Or, we can see them as periods of waiting when there is nothing we can do except be totally dependent upon God—wait it out with Him; listen, question, pray, learn, change, and learn some more.

These commas are a preparation for what is to come. Commas give us definition and character. They are an added punch to our testimonies. Whether gained through valley experiences or endless tundra, we benefit. God has not forgotten us. He is instead fighting for us trying to make us more like Him. It is to His credit that we come out of each situation with a stronger spirit, a new resolve, and a made-up mind with a more powerful story to tell. God would never deny us anything that draws us closer to Him.

Prayer: Lord, help me to view these periods of waiting as times to replenish myself in you realizing that I am not finished until your work is completed in me. Amen.

Brenda C. Harrison ˡⁱᶠ God has Saved us, and we serve him daily, Let us keep it up util he return.

March 19

Sanday

THY FAITH HATH MADE THEE WHOLE

Scripture: Mark 10:52 (KJV) (Read Mark 10:46-52)
And Jesus said unto him, Go thy way; thy faith hath made thee whole. And immediately he received his sight, and followed Jesus in the way.

In 1964, I was diagnosed with glaucoma. The doctor told me that I would be blind within one year. Thirty-four years later, after several surgeries and much growth and development in my prayer life, I still see clear enough to read God's Word by daylight.

Through the years my faith in God has grown larger than a mustard seed, which is all God requires. My daily prayer for myself is to see clearly. That prayer is continuously answered through the love and support of my family and friends. I also ask God to help me to be able to help someone else even though my sight is dim; I still want to bear fruit for Him.

God is the same yesterday, today and forever and His Word is settled in heaven. Just like blind Bartimaeus, I joyfully await the full manifestation of my healing. In the meantime and for the rest of my life, I am going to keep my hand in God's Hand knowing that He alone will lead me and guide me, from this time forth and forevermore.

Prayer: Dear Lord, help me to depend on you, to trust in, and rely on your Word. I thank you for your healing power that is real today. Teach me to wait with expectancy, as miracle after miracle unfolds in my life. Amen.

Pearl Rochon

March 20

Monday

HOW IS YOUR CONTRACT?

Scripture: Deuteronomy 5:2, 3 (KJV)
The Lord our God made a covenant with us in Horeb.
The Lord made not this covenant with our fathers, but
with us, even us, who are here alive this day.

The covenants (contracts) that God established with the children of Israel have been passed down to us. A contract is an agreement between two parties wherein each side has rights and obligations. God made promises to the children of Israel that are available to us if we abide in His Word.

As parties to the contract we must make sure we do not breach the contract—fail to perform our side of the deal. We cannot worship other gods. We cannot be a hypocrite and not live by the Scripture. Some of us just look holy to receive people's admiration and praise, but we must please God rather than man. If the contract is broken, He will bring the curse of a father's sin upon even the third generation of the children of thousands who hate Him, but He will show kindness to a thousand generations of those who keep His contract.

Prayer: Lord, help me to keep your contract in my heart, soul, and mind. Amen.

Daisy Roach

March 21

Tuesday

GIVING GOD THE BEST

Scripture: Genesis 4:4, 5 (KJV)
And Abel, he also brought of the firstlings of his flock and of the fat thereof. And the Lord had respect unto Abel and to his offering: But unto Cain and to his offering he had not respect. And Cain was very wroth, and his countenance fell.

The Bible does not say why God rejected Cain's sacrifice. Perhaps Cain's attitude was improper or his offering was not up to God's standards. God is interested in our heart condition behind the offering. When we give to God and others, we should have a joyful heart, because we are able to give.

We should not worry about how much we give because everything belongs to God. There is a story in the Bible about a woman who gave her last mite, which is equal to a penny. Jesus valued her gift more than the rich man who gave out of his wealth. The woman's gift was from her heart. God's gift of Jesus to us was from His heart. Our best should be given whether it is money, time, or talent.

Prayer: O Lord, who made the heavens and earth and everything therein, you have blessed me each day. Let my offering be acceptable in your sight. Amen.

Daisy Roach *Lord the best I can give you is my self and my service. If there is any thing better that about myself that I am not knowledgable of its yours. I am willing to give*

March 22

wednesday

GOD'S BLESSING ON MARRIAGE

Scripture: Genesis 2:18 (KJV)
And the Lord God said, It is not good that man should be alone; I will make him an help meet for him.

God's creative work was not complete until he made woman. He could have made her from the dust of the ground as He made man. He chose to make her from the man's flesh and bone. Symbolically this made man and woman one flesh. The goal in marriage should be oneness.

Each creation was made for the same purpose, to honor God. Man was used to give life to woman; woman gives life to the world.

As God created the institution of marriage it has three basic aspects:

1. The man leaves his parents, and promises in public to give himself to his wife.
2. The man and woman are joined together to be responsible for each other loving the mate above all others.
3. The two become one flesh in intimacy.

Prayer: Lord, teach me to be a wife and to follow my husband, who is head of this house, as he follows you. Amen.

Daisy Roach

My desire is to be the wife you want me to be. I do honor marriage which you gave to a man and a woman to make this marriage a Godly marriage husband and wife need to service you no matter what is going on in our lives, you are first in every marriage.

March 23

SPREAD THE GOOD NEWS

Scripture: Mark 1:28 (KJV)
And immediately his fame spread abroad through out all the region round about Galilee.

News spreads quickly. While it appears that bad news moves faster than good, it is our responsibility as Christians to spread the Goods News so that Jesus Christ will be glorified. How do we do this? The Scripture says that His fame spread abroad throughout the entire region.

Consider what caused this. There was a man possessed by demons in the synagogue. When Jesus entered the Temple the unclean spirits recognized Him immediately. The devil knows Jesus even when we do not. Jesus commanded the spirits to leave the man, and they did. The leaders of the Church were amazed. They began to talk about what they saw which caused them to want to know who Jesus was that He could heal this man.

We must begin to talk about what Jesus has done in our lives to cause people to want to know who He is that He can do such marvelous things. Then the Good News of Jesus Christ will spread throughout the world.

Prayer: Father, teach me to think about your goodness before I speak, and let me use my voice for your edification. Amen.

Daisy Roach Lord you have done so many things for me how could not spread the good news the Lord do things for us, he want us to Tell others. God is good.

March 24

Friday

KINDNESS

Scripture: Ephesians 4:32 (KJV)
And be ye kind one to another, tenderhearted, forgiving one another, even as God for Christ's sake hath forgiven you.

We receive instant gratification from each act of kindness we show others. A smile or a kind word can bring a smile to a sad face or lift the spirit of a broken heart. Small acts of kindness yield great rewards.

Prayer: Dear God, give me wisdom through your Holy Spirit that I may speak words of comfort and peace and recognize every opportunity to do good deeds. Thank you for giving me another day to do your will. I pray that when this day is over, I will have done some good deeds and cause no one harm. These things I ask in the name of Jesus. Amen.

Cynthia Purnell Stuart Lord I want so much to be Kind thoughtful, Tenderhearted, Forgiving. there are times in my life I Feel like I am being used & used - all over again. my desire is To be like Christ.

March 25

Saturday

FILLED AND OVERFLOWING

Scripture: Psalm 23:5 (KJV)
. . . thou anointest my head with oil; my cup runneth over.

As the psalmist, David was reflecting upon the mercies of God, he recognized that he was wonderfully blessed.

What a wonderful witness to the world it is to have the anointing of the Holy Ghost with our cups running over. It is a blessing to be equipped and overflowing with Holy Ghost power cascading down the halls of humility, streets of obedience, avenues of commitment, across oceans of forgiveness, valleys of despair, and vistas of life, so that Jesus may be lifted up for this dying world to see.

A cup, as referred to in the Scripture, is a form of matter that has been shaped into usefulness. As followers of Christ, we are being shaped into usefulness for the glory of God.

Prayer: Come, Holy Spirit, anoint me and make me a cup, one that is useful for your purpose. Fill me with your mercy and love anew each day. Grant that I may join David and proclaim, "my cup runneth over." Amen.

Julia Ogletree *Lord anoint my head with oil and Fill my cup with your spirT, Just let it run over and over.*

March 26

Wednesday

LOVE ONE ANOTHER

Scripture: 1 John 4:7 (KJV)
Beloved, let us love one another: for love is of God; and every one that loveth is born of God, and knoweth God.

We are living in times when it seems that real friends who care are few. It appears that our world is a cold, friendless, selfish world. We do not have to look far today to see that we condemn rather than commend, criticize rather than encourage, and refer rather than assist and show the love of God through our daily conduct.

Help the elderly, who may be alone and lonely—visit, call them, offer to drive them to church, or to go shopping. Encourage our teenagers and youth to maximize educational opportunities. Give them support and guidance in church activities. Welcome a new family into the community.

God is with us at all times, He has no hands, no feet, no tongue but ours. Let Him use us to show love.

Prayer: Dear Lord, grant me grace to meet with faith the challenge of caring for a needy world, and make me aware of the beauty in each of my brothers and sisters instead of focusing on the flaws. Amen.

Carol C. Winston

In some Cases it is hard to show Love, IF we have the Love of Christ in our heart it becomes easy to Love one another.

March 27

JESUS ADMINISTERING CPR

Scripture: Romans 5:10 (KJV)
For if, when we were enemies, we were reconciled to God by the death of his Son, much more, being reconciled, we shall be saved by his life.

We so often hear or read about doctors administering Cardiopulmonary Resuscitation (CPR) to patients in order to save their lives. I would like to let you know about Doctor Jesus' Spiritual CPR. He will never lose a patient for His CPR is life eternal.

C – is the CHANGE you will experience when you allow God to enter into your heart. You will be a new creature living in the spiritual realm.

P – is the PRODUCT that you are producing in your life, bearing the fruit of the Spirit: love, joy, peace, longsuffering, gentleness, goodness and faith.

R – is for the RECONCILIATION you received when Jesus died on the cross for our souls to be saved. He became our sacrificial Lamb, bled and died, arose on the third day, and is now sitting on the Right Hand of God, interceding for us.

Prayer: Lord, come into my heart and make the change that you alone can make. Amen.

Jeannie Williams

March 28

EQUIPPING THE CHRISTIAN

Scripture: Matthew 4:18, 19 (KJV)
And Jesus, walking by the Sea of Galilee, saw two brethren, Simon called Peter, and Andrew his brother, casting a net into the sea: for they were fishers. And he saith unto them, Follow me, and I will make you fishers of men.

Does the Church understand its mission? Are believers taught the role and definition of a disciple? Can Christians successfully disciple others without proper tools? Have you been sent out ill equipped into a world where Satan knows more about the Word than you do? God's work must begin at home.

We must study the Word of God before we can share it with others. We must have experiences with God so that we can testify of His true power. We must know the ways of God and live accordingly so that we can be an example to others. This all begins at home. Without this foundation, believers will be leading the blind into the ditch of degradation. When we get it right at home, then we can be fishers of men for Jesus.

Prayer: Father, let me get it right at home first so that my life is an example of you to attract souls to your Kingdom. Thank you, Father, for instructing me and most of all for loving me. Amen.

Anonymous

March 29

JOY IN JUST LIVING

Scripture: 2 Corinthians 1:12 (KJV)
For our rejoicing is this, the testimony of our conscience, that in simplicity and godly sincerity, not with fleshly wisdom, but by the grace of God . . .

The fear that I felt when expecting my second child is now something I can look back on with a smile. I was trying to manage a demanding job, church responsibilities, community activities, husband, home, and a very active two year-old. I could not imagine how I could fit one more thing into my chaotic life.

A burden was lifted when I remembered that I did not have to shoulder all the responsibility by myself. It is amazing how God provides what is needed at just the right time. The sense of joy that only He can give, the peace in those quiet times, and the thankfulness I have for all of the things that are right in my life are gifts from God. I am awed by His creation of the two beautiful little boys who are so full of life and curiosity, and are secure in the love that they can count on me to provide. That love is the same love that God has shown me. Now I realize my primary ministry is to my family, and it feels good knowing that I am being a good mother and a good wife.

Prayer: God, thank you for showing me how to appreciate the small things and giving me joy in just living. Amen.

Cynthia M. Harris

March 30

ABIDING IN HIM

Scripture: John 15:5, 6 (KJV)
I am the vine, ye are the branches: He that abideth in me, and I in him, the same bringeth forth much fruit: for without me ye can do nothing. If a man abide not in me, he is cast forth as a branch, and is withered; and men gather them, and cast them into the fire, and they are burned.

As Christians we are commanded to win souls for Christ through our lives, witness, and time spent in genuine relationships with the lost and sometimes members of our church. All too often we profess to be Christians, but live lives that disconnect us from the True Vine, thus preventing nutrients from establishing strong healthy roots that produce fruitful branches.

John 15:5 tells us that only fruitful Christians will remain attached to the True Vine, as they abide in Jesus. There are three keys in living a fruitful life. Christians must have a living relationship with Christ; we must be at home with Him; and we must stay in constant communion with Him. Why is this relationship with Christ so vital? It is vital because without it the Christian life is fruitless and useless. Therefore, abiding in Jesus is necessary and required if we are to live so as to win souls for Christ and produce fruit.

Prayer: Dear Jesus, help me to abide in you so that my motives will be pure; my thoughts cleansed by the Word, and my life will be in line with your will. Amen.

Fran Alexander

March 31

April

He that loveth his brother abideth in the light, and there is none occasion of stumbling in him.

1 John 2:10

Southwestern Delta Episcopal District
Table Of Contents

TRUST GOD

Scripture: Isaiah 26:4 (KJV)
Trust ye in the Lord for ever: for in the Lord Jehovah is everlasting strength:

It is not always easy to trust in God because God does not do things like we do. That is not a bad thing, but it is hard for us to understand. As human beings when we do not understand it is difficult to trust. We have to be able to rationalize and analyze actions. But God wants us to use our faith.

To get a visual picture of trust in God, picture a toddler playing with his father. The father is throwing the baby in the air and catching him. The baby is laughing and having a wonderful time. That is absolute trust. The baby is not able to even process the thought that the father would allow him to fall to the floor. No matter how close to the floor that baby gets, he knows without a doubt that his father will catch him. As a matter of fact the closer to the floor the baby gets the greater the thrill. As a little child trusts His natural father to keep him from falling, so we should as Christians trust our Heavenly Father.

Prayer: Heavenly Father, thank you for the trust, belief, faith, and your promise of your strength to sustain me in all that I may suffer. Amen.

Christine Alexander

April 1

ICY ISSUES

Scripture: Psalm 84:11 (KJV)
For the Lord God is a sun and shield: the Lord will give grace and glory: no good thing will he withhold from them that walk uprightly.

As a child, my daughter loved to play outside on hot sunny days. She would beam as she turned her face toward the sun and allowed the rays to warm her skin. One day she had a cup full of ice. She would pop a piece of ice in her mouth to suck on as she romped in the sun. When the piece of ice in her mouth disappeared she would get another piece and play some more. After a while she discovered all the ice had melted; only water was left.

The Holy Spirit used that fond memory to minister to my daughter as an adult. He showed her that the issues she faces are like the ice in her childhood memory. If she gets before the face of the Son and leaves her issues there, they will eventually melt away just like that ice.

We should seek the glorious face of Jesus, place our ice issues before Him and leave them for Him to melt away. Let us rejoice in a gracious Lord who will show Himself mightily if we allow Him.

Prayer: Father, I place my issues before you. I know they will melt away with the warmth of your love. Amen.

Shavonda Foley

THE GOOD SHEPHERD

Scripture: Psalm 23:1-3 (TLV)
Because the Lord is my shepherd, I have everything I need! He lets me rest in the meadow grass and leads me beside the quiet streams. He gives me new strength. He helps me to do what honors him the most.

Sheep are not smart. They tend to wander into the running creeks for water. Their wool grows heavy and they drown. They need a shepherd to lead them to calm water. They have no natural defense and are helpless. Sheep need a shepherd to protect them. They have no sense of direction. They need someone to lead them on paths that are right.

Like sheep, we too need someone to lead us. We tend to be swept away by waters we should have avoided. Without the Word of God, we have no defense against the evil lion (Satan) that prowls seeking whom he might devour. We too, get lost.

We need a shepherd. We need a shepherd to care for us, to correct us, and to guide us. We have one. One who knows each one of us by name. His name is Jesus.

Prayer: Father, thank you for giving me a Shepherd to guide me, to correct me, to feed me, to anoint me, to love me, and to care for me. Help me not to go astray but to follow Jesus. Amen.

Claretha H. Brooks

April 3

SAVED BY GRACE

Scripture: Ephesians 2:8 (NIV)
For by grace you have been saved, through faith—and this not from yourselves, it is the gift of God—

A world steeped in sin with no chance of returning to a state of righteousness, and no chance for reconciliation without some divine intervention; that is who we were before Jesus. In and of ourselves we had no way to redeem ourselves. Sin had become part of our nature, and a righteous and holy God does not fellowship with unrighteousness.

But our Father had an answer; He gave His only begotten Son, Jesus Christ, to reconcile the world back to Him. God did not do this because we had earned it or deserved it; God did it because He loves us. He did it because He is merciful. He did it because we had no way Home without Him.

It is only through God's grace and mercy that we are saved. God is so rich in mercy that none need to fail. I thank God for His loving kindness and forgiveness for my sins. What a wonderful opportunity we have as born-again Christians to tell others of God's precious gift of salvation through Jesus that can be theirs.

Prayer: O God, help me to reach out and touch the world in love as you did. Lead me to those who need your touch. Amen.

Jessie M. George Harris

April 4

TOO DRY FOR A COOL DRINK

Scripture: Proverbs 2:10, 11 (KJV)
When wisdom entereth into thine heart, and knowledge is pleasant unto thy soul; Discretion shall preserve thee, understanding shall keep thee:

Have you ever had a houseplant that has gone unnoticed and unwatered for a while? When you finally notice the poor plant it is wilted, and its bright yellow leaves wave at you hoping to receive a cool refreshing drink of water.

Not only is death evident by its leaves, but the soil is rock hard and dry as a bone. When watered it does not penetrate the soil, but just runs off the sides. Your next application of water just sits on top of the soil, taking a few minutes before soaking in. Finally, after several attempts to permeate the hard, dry outer-surface, the thirsty plant readily absorbs the cool drink.

As Christians we need daily cool drinks so that we may always be open to whatever the Holy Spirit wants to share for the day. There is life in God's Word—there is no life without God. Let us be mindful to stay watered. Continuous washing with the water of the Holy Ghost will leave us with a pliable and teachable heart.

Prayer: You are the Source of Living Water that I might thirst no more. Fill me with your Holy Spirit, O Precious Lord. Draw near to me as I search for you while reading your Word. Amen.

Shavonda Foley

April 5

CLEANING THE TEMPLE

Scripture: Matthew 21:12, 13 (KJV)
And Jesus went into the temple of God, and cast out all them that sold and bought in the temple, and overthrew the tables of the money changers, and the seats of them that sold doves, and said unto them, It is written, My house shall be called the house of prayer; but ye have made it a den of thieves.

There are not many times in the Bible that I would describe Jesus as angry, but in this story I picture Jesus being pushed to His limit. The temple was being defiled. Ungodly activities were taking place in the temple. People were entering the temple with an incorrect purpose of heart.

Did you know that our body is the temple of the Holy Ghost? What misuse of our temple is taking place? What impurity, mistreatment, mishandling, perversions, or corruption is taking place in the temple? This is the place where God's Spirit dwells.

It is time to clean up the temple. Someday we will have to give an account to God for the things we have done with our temple. It should be our desire that when we get to Heaven, in response to our stewardship over our temple, God would proclaim, "Well done, my good and faithful servant."

Prayer: Father, today I ask you to cleanse and purify me of all impurities that prevent me from being your house. Overthrow and cast out all that hinders me. Make me an instrument fit for your service. Amen.

Barbara Latoison

April 6

REPLACING THE WASHER

Scripture: 1 Corinthians 4:2 (KJV)
Moreover it is required in stewards, that a man be found faithful.

A faucet in your home that drips once every second could waste over seven thousand gallons of water in one year. It does not seem possible that one little drip could be so wasteful and destructive. As long as the owner of the faucet, whose mission is to be a good steward, refuses to replace the washer, the faucet will continue to drip and destroy.

It is difficult to conceive that a dripping faucet could be so destructive. Or that something as simple as a washer could be so valuable. Just like that faucet, there are simple things in our lives that when allowed to persist over time destroy our spiritual growth and eventually our witness.

It does not happen all at once, but subtly; almost without notice the gain you had made in the Lord disappears. We must replace the washer through daily prayer, study of the Word and worship.

Prayer: Lord, teach me to not be like a dripping faucet. Help me to be a builder of Christian character. Help me to daily magnify your name and fulfill the mission set before me. Amen.

Katie B. Simms

CRUCIFY HIM

Scripture: Matthew 27:22 (KJV)
Pilate saith unto them, What shall I do then with Jesus which is called Christ? They all say unto him, Let him be crucified.

What transpired between Palm Sunday and Good Friday to cause the turn of opinion? How could Jesus, who was the Son of David, the One that was to be inaugurated King on Sunday, diminish to the humiliation of the Cross? We know that it was God's will, but those who killed Him did not know it was the will of the Father. What swayed public opinion? Could it have been His desire to fulfill God's purpose here on earth?

It is easy for us to condemn those who crucified Jesus or to not understand why they did not recognize Him as the Son of God. But have you considered the fact that we are still crucifying Him. We do not call it that, but when we refuse to witness to the lost we are crying out, "crucify Him." When we refuse to obey God's Word, we are shouting out, "nail Him to the cross." When what we do does not line up with what we say, we are saying, "let Him be crucified."

In our own non-verbal ways we crucify Jesus over and over again.

Prayer: Jesus, you went to the cross for me once, it is my prayer that my lifestyle, words and/or deeds would not condemn you a second time. Amen.

Barbara Latoison

April 8

WRONG EXPECTATION

Scripture: Matthew 21:9 (KJV)
And the multitudes that went before, and that followed, cried, saying, Hosanna to the son of David: Blessed is he that cometh in the name of the Lord; Hosanna in the highest.

The triumphant entry of Jesus into Jerusalem was electrified with anticipation. The people were perched to receive their deliverer, poised to inaugurate their "Warrior King". They had faith to be delivered from the rule of the Roman Government. They knew that Jesus was the one. Jesus, however, had other plans.

How many times have we tried to impose upon God what we understood, believed, or wanted and it was inconsistent with the will of God for that season? If we are to fulfill God's purpose for our lives, we must not limit Him to our understanding. We must seek his viewpoint and align ourselves with Him.

Prayer: Father, show me areas where I have allowed my expectations to overshadow your will for the situation. Help me recognize that it only hurts me when my limited understanding and expectations are not fulfilled because I try to box you in. Help me to pray, "thy will be done" in all things. Amen.

Barbara Latoison

FALL SHORT, MISS THE MARK, LOSE THE PRIZE!

Scripture: 1 Corinthians 9:24 (KJV)
Know ye not that they which run in a race run all, but one receiveth the prize? So run, that ye may obtain.

During a football game, the chain crew is brought in to measure distances for a first down, and many times the players and fans are disappointed because their team may fall short by a few inches. Even more heartbreaking is when they miss getting that touchdown by a few inches.

In some ways, this Christian race can be compared to a football game. The prize is more than a touchdown. It is where we will spend eternity. Yes, sometimes we fall short, miss the mark, but we cannot afford to lose the prize.

In a football game only one team wins the game. In a track meet only one runner wins the race, but in the race we are running all who run the race may obtain the prize, eternal life with the Heavenly Father.

We strengthen ourselves to obtain the prize when we follow Christ and measure our progress by His Word.

Prayer: Dear God, though I fall short and many times miss the mark, please pick me up, give me an extra push so that I may win the prize. Amen.

Shirley W. Mabry

April 10

A SOLID FOUNDATION

Scripture: 1 Corinthians 3:11 (KJV)
For other foundation can no man lay than that is laid, which is Jesus Christ.

The foundation is one of the most important parts of a building. If the foundation is not strong, the rest of the building is in danger and will probably suffer damage if put to a test.

Christ established a firm foundation so that His followers would be able to stand the storms of life that we inevitably face. Death is one of those storms. Tragedy and pain are others. The foundation was completely established when He gave His life as a ransom for our sins.

As followers of Christ, we must build foundations of genuine love, so that we can teach others that Jesus Christ is the firm Foundation.

Prayer: Lord, help me to rebuild that which is leaning and torn down. Help me to humbly fulfill my mission by practicing genuine love and humility. Amen.

Katie B. Simms

STEWARDSHIP

Scripture: Matthew 25:24, 25 (KJV)
Then he which had received the one talent came and said, Lord I knew thee that thou are an hard man, reaping where thou has not sown, and gathering where thou has not strawed: And I was afraid, and went and hid thy talent in the earth: . . .

Jesus taught the parable of the talents not just to speak about money but to talk about our stewardship in general. We are to be wise stewards over all that God has given us, our possessions, our time, our bodies, our spirits. In all of these areas God will ask us to give an account of our stewardship. So we should ponder our effectiveness.

We must take our talents put them in service for the Lord so that they would reap a harvest for the Kingdom. If we have not done this we need to determine if we are like the servant who hid his talent out of fear. Do we fear that if people knew the talents we have been given they would require something of us?

The story is summed up when the master takes the talents from the slothful servant and gives them to the wise steward. Yes, to whom much is given much is required, but when you use what is given to you wisely more is given.

Prayer: Father, help me to be as Jesus, a faithful steward of that which you have given me. Show me how to overcome any thing that has hindered me. Help me to use your resources diligently and wisely. Amen.

Barbara Latoison

April 12

DO YOU WANT TO BE BLESSED?

Scripture: Micah 6:8 (NIV) Read Psalm 1
He has showed you, O man, what is good. And what does the Lord require of you? To act justly and to love mercy and to walk humbly with your God.

We have all experienced joy, compassion, love, anger, grief, stress and perhaps some depression during our lifetime. No matter what happens in our lives, we should delight ourselves in the Word of God. When we meditate on God's Word and allow the Holy Spirit to come into our heart, we are like a tree planted by the river of water whose roots run real deep, anchored in God's Word. We may feel tossed about or misused, but when we meditate on the Word, we are able to pick ourselves up, stand upright, praise God, and witness to others. God's Word challenges us to taste and see that the Lord is good. The love of Christ will help us to meet the requirement of God for our lives, to turn from evil, do good, and seek peace.

Remember: What is popular is not always right; what is right is not always popular. Do right and be blessed.

Prayer: Thank you Lord for your Word and the Holy Spirit. Help me to do justly, love mercy, and walk humbly with you today. Amen.

Classie Jones Green

April 13

TO WIN THE WORLD FOR CHRIST

Scripture: 1 Corinthians 11:1 (KJV)
Be ye followers of me, even as I also am of Christ.

The initial call of Christ to those whom He planned to utilize for the purpose of evangelizing the world continues today. We are to win the world for Christ. We must understand, recognize, and accept that this commission is for all Christian individuals, not just the church.

Jesus' first call was to fishermen, Matthew 4:18, 19. Jesus promised the fishermen that if they would follow Him, He would make them fishers of men. We are to catch souls for the Kingdom of God. When we walk upright before the Lord, the light He has placed in us attracts the unsaved. It causes them to want to know what we know. They begin to watch us, then they begin to follow us. We are to be the bait Jesus uses to catch men for the Kingdom.

It is up to us to always be that light so that the world would see Jesus and want to know Him. To win the world for Christ we must be faithful and obedient. We must be willing to deny self daily and take up our cross, sometimes denying family and possessions. We must abide in Jesus, bear good fruit, glorify God, be joyful, and love our brethren.

Prayer: Father, I thank you that I desire to follow and imitate you. I pray that you continue to give of your grace and mercy as I strive to win the world for Christ. Amen.

Wilma Littles

April 14

FISHERS OF MEN (REACHING)

Scripture: Matthew 4:19 (KJV)
And he said unto them, Follow me, and I will make you fishers of men.

      Jesus instructed us early on to be a true follower of Him, to deny ourselves, to take up the cross daily and He would make us fishers of men. The first step is to be born again. Then one has to be a dedicated and committed Christian to follow Christ. Once we are born again, dedicated, and committed, we are available to God to make us fishers of men.

      Consider the tools a fisherman uses. He uses a rod and reel to hold his catch, but he uses bait to attract his catch. We are to be the bait to attract men to the Kingdom of God. The world should see the peace, joy, love, happiness, and abundance that a life in Jesus provides, and run after us wanting to know how they to can have this kind of life.

      Once we become the bait then we should fish in all the available places. Available places are wherever we are, whenever we are there. We must witness by experience. We must teach Christ's ways by precepts and by example. We need to show that we are followers of Christ by walking the walk and talking the talk that shows Jesus in our lives.

Prayer: Heavenly Father, thank you for allowing me to be a follower of you. This is a mission that I cannot do without you. I want to be strong in you so others can see you in my life as I witness in your Name. Condition me for your will and equip me for your mission. Amen.

Imogene H. Williams

April 15

WE ARE WITNESSES

Scripture: Joshua 24:22 (KJV)
And Joshua said unto the people, Ye are witnesses against yourselves that ye have chosen you the Lord, to serve him. And they said, We are witnesses.

As we mature in the Lord and in the Church, we must come to a full understanding that everyday we are a witness. We are either a witness for God or against Him. We do not have to open our mouths. Our behavior does the talking.

Sometimes we wonder why we cannot get our family or co-workers to come to church with us. Well, what is our witness saying? We cannot praise the Lord in the morning then return late from our lunch break in the afternoon. We cannot read Scripture to the children, and then not pay our bills on time.

To witness by word, not followed by deeds is futile. We are being watched when we do not know we are being watched. The world needs hope. That light in us is their hope. When we fail in our witness it only gives the devil another opportunity to drive his nail in further. But God is merciful, forgives us, loves us, and allows us to continue to be a witness for Him.

Prayer: Father, make me a true witness. Help me live my daily life in you so that my life will reflect you and your deity. Amen.

Wilma Littles

AM I MY BROTHER'S KEEPER?

Scripture: Genesis 4:9 (KJV)
And the Lord said unto Cain, Where is Abel thy brother?
And he said. I know not: Am I my brother's keeper?

A resounding yes! God has commanded us to love one another as He loves us. God loved us so much that He gave His only begotten Son that whosoever believes in Him would not perish but have everlasting life. If we love one another like God loves us that means we are to provide for one another so that we would not perish, but have everlasting life. Our first thought is usually to provide for the natural man so we give food to the hungry, clothes to the naked, water to the thirsty, homes to the homeless, but we cannot forget about the spirit man who also needs to be fed. Consider truly keeping your brothers and giving them Jesus.

Prayer: Lord, I accept responsibility for my brothers and sisters provisions both spiritual and natural. Lord, bless me that I might be a blessing to them. Amen.

Imogene H. Williams

LETTING MY LIGHT SHINE

Scripture: Matthew 5:16 (KJV)
Let your light so shine before men, that they may see your good works, and glorify your Father which is in heaven.

Jesus instructed us to let our light shine. Some of us may not realize that we have a light within us, but when we receive Jesus we receive His light. In John 8:12, Jesus says He is the light of the world, so if we receive Him, we receive that light.

It is important to allow our light to shine, because light and darkness cannot co-exist. The light puts out darkness. Also, the brighter the light, the more darkness it dispels. So we must not only let our light shine, but also continue in the Word of God so that the brilliance of our light will continue to grow.

Prayer: Jesus, I thank you for allowing me to go forth in your name. Enable me to let my light shine. Be with me as I move from highways to hedges. You be the light for me so that I can be a light for the world. I ask this in Jesus' name. Amen.

Corlean B. Polk

BUILDING A BETTER WORLD

Scripture: Psalm 9:8 (KJV)
And he shall judge the world in righteousness, he shall minister judgment to the people in uprightness.

As we make this wonderful amazing journey through life, we should seek to make this world a better place. Too often we feel there is nothing we can do to make this world better. We cannot be led by how we feel. If we will live our lives according to the Word of God we can make great strides in improving the world.

According to Micah 6:8, God gives three principles for our lives: 1) to do justly; 2) to love mercy; and, 3) to walk humbly with our God. With these three principles, God is challenging each of us to be better which in turn builds a better world. If each of us would work daily on being the best we can be within ourselves the rest of our world would fall into place.

Prayer: Father God, I ask you to give me more spiritual strength that I may be able to face the wiles of this world and help those in the world come out of darkness to see the light. Amen.

Inez Lindsey

WALK-INS WELCOMED

Scripture: John 6:35-37 (KJV)
And Jesus said unto them, I am the bread of life: he that cometh to me shall never hunger, and he that believeth on me shall never thirst. But I said unto you, That ye also have seen me, and believe not. All that the Father giveth me shall come to me; and him that cometh to me I will in no wise cast out.

I saw a sign in a beauty shop window and it reminded me of how Jesus feels about us. The sign read, "Walk-ins Welcomed." Just as when a woman goes to the beauty shop or a man to the barber, we are welcomed just as we are, undone. We go to the beauty/barber shop to look better physically, and if the beauty shop has done its job you come out looking better.

Just like the shop Jesus is saying come as you are. He does not ask you to be right before you come. He will make you better before you leave. He welcomes you, just walk in, accept His love, and He will fix you not only on the outside but on the inside as well. When you come to Jesus, He will love you, accept you, and He will never let go of you!

Prayer: Dear Lord, I come just as I am. Thank you for meeting me where I am to do a work on the inside. Amen.

Judy Hayles

April 20

EFFECTIVE WITNESSING:
THE HOLY SPIRIT IS KEY

Scripture: Acts: 1:8 (KJV)
But ye shall receive power, after that the Holy Ghost is come upon you: and ye shall be witnesses unto me both in Jerusalem, and in all Judaea, and in Samaria, and unto the uttermost part of the earth.

Our mission is to win the world for Christ. However, winning the world begins with winning one. To win one we must be an effective witness. So we need to ask ourselves, how effective is our witness?

To be an effective witness we must have the power to walk in God's Word, to overcome our flesh, and to confront unrighteousness with the Word of God. We know that if we need it, God will provide it. This power comes from the Holy Ghost. The Scripture says we will receive power once the Holy Ghost comes upon us.

We are empowered by the Holy Spirit to be victorious in every situation and to be an effective witness.

Prayer: Father, search me. Show me those areas that defeat my witness that I might repent of them. Then, Father, empower me with the power of your Holy Spirit that I might win the world, one at a time. Amen.

Abigail D. York

CHRISTIANS LABORING FOR CHRIST

Scripture: 1 Corinthians 15:58 (KJV)
Therefore, my beloved brethren, be ye steadfast, unmovable, always abounding in the work of the Lord, forasmuch as ye know that your labour is not in vain in the Lord.

It is God's desire that every individual have knowledge of Him, and be saved. Making and multiplying disciples is the ultimate mandate of God. In order that we are able to assume this task, we must first have a personal relationship with God. We must be born again and know Him and His power for ourselves. We should be spiritual models, letting our lights shine so that others will see and come to the Lord.

Once we have established ourselves in Jesus then we must be unwavering in our beliefs and uncompromising in our convictions. We cannot be wholly sold out one minute and questioning the tenets of our belief the next. The world needs consistency, our children need to know that what you say today is going to be what you say tomorrow.

If we are not steadfast in how we think and unmovable in what we believe, those we witness to could turn our heart toward their god with some vain argument.

Prayer: Dear God, you know the great challenges and the opposition that lay ahead for your servant. Equip me. Enable me to be steadfast and unmovable as I work in your vineyard. Amen.

Linda Deamer

April 22

WITNESSING WHILE WORKING

Scripture: Acts 1:8 (KJV)
. . . and ye shall be witnesses unto me . . .

The workplace is a setting where many people spend most of their time. This environment is rich with a variety of service and witness opportunities. It is the Christian worker's responsibility to discharge his duties and meet the challenges. While at work we must be persistent in faith, so that our witnessing might bring forth fruit. Christ's message was intended for all people everywhere. Work, worship and witnessing can take place in any setting. Our witness must be an example of Christ's way of life. It must introduce a new pattern of relationships as we witness in person-to-person compassion and friendship. Tell a fellow worker about Jesus today. Complete the assignment Jesus gave to all; tell of His love for us and His great sacrifice for our sins. Christians are to be personal witnesses for our faith. Go, therefore, and make disciples of all nations. For I am with you always.

Prayer: Lord, help me to do your will and witness to others. Equip me for the work ahead. Let me draw nearer to you, so you will draw nearer to me. In your name I pray. Amen.

Imogene H. Williams

THE TIME IS AT HAND

Scripture: Ephesians 5:16 (KJV)
Redeeming the time, because the days are evil.

There is a seriousness and sense of urgency in completing the mission God has given us, bringing the world to Christ. The seriousness and sense of urgency is due to the fact that we do not know when Jesus will return. Scripture says He will come as a thief in the night. Another passage says no man knows the day or the hour. Therefore we cannot postpone our efforts to bring the world to Christ.

While we should await His return with excited anticipation, we should not wait by sitting back. Our every thought, activity, and plan should be thought of in terms of the impact it will have on building God's Kingdom. We should treat each opportunity we have to witness as though it will be the last opportunity for anyone to witness to them about Jesus. We cannot wait until next week, next month, or next year to start building the Kingdom. The time is at hand!

Prayer: O Lord, my God. This time is the only time I have. Let me use it wisely in trying to bring men to you, by lifting up your name. Please order my steps in your Word. Amen.

Linda Bush Spears

OUR CHRISTIAN MANDATE

Scripture: Matthew 28:19, 20 (KJV)
Go ye therefore, and teach all nations, baptizing them in the name of the Father, and of the Son, and of the Holy Ghost: Teaching them to observe all things whatsoever I have commanded you: and, lo, I am with you always, even unto the end of the world. Amen.

We have been given a mandate, go and teach. In order to understand the importance we assign to that work we need to understand what a mandate entails. It is an order. It is not a simple recommendation or suggestion that we go and teach. It is our Christian mandate that we do so.

While this is every Christian's responsibility, as missionaries we have expressly accepted the call. We have told the world that we have accepted the assignment. In order to carry out our accepted task we must study God's Word, attend worship service, fellowship with other Christian believers, pray daily, and allow God to continue to perfect us in all areas of our life.

Our Christian mandate requires that we work through the Christian Church as it struggles to transform the world by preaching and living the Christian Gospel.

Prayer: Lord, I praise you for keeping me ever in your care as I become what you would have me to be as a Christian missionary, keeping the mandate alive and spreading the Good News of Jesus Christ. Amen.

Wilma Littles

April 25

WORKING THE WORKS

Scripture: John 9:4 (KJV)
I must work the works of him that sent me, while it is day: the night cometh, when no man can work.

We spend a lot of time doing everyone's business except God's. What if the reverse was true? What if when we called upon God His response was, "I'll get back to you as soon as I finish what I want to do?" God will not do that. He has promised to never leave us or forsake us.

We have a finite period of time in the earth to finish the work God has planned for us. We must view each moment as precious and not waste any of them. We do not have time to harbor ill feelings toward one another. We do not have time to gossip, backbite or undermine leadership. All our efforts should be directed toward seeking the lost, the unloved, and those who are stumbling in the dark.

The earthly ministry of Jesus spanned only three years, yet there are numerous works contributed to Him during that relatively short period of time. It is because He was about His Father's business. He did not allow the traditions of men or what people thought about Him deter Him from that work. As Christians we must determine in our hearts that it is better to please God rather than man and go on about doing our Father's business.

Prayer: Dear Lord, Help me to work tirelessly, to pray without ceasing, to love unconditionally, to witness consistently, and to commit all to you. Amen.

Nancy Byers

April 26

FAITH IN GOD IS LOVE IN ACTION

Scripture: Matthew 25:40 (KJV)
And the King shall answer and say unto them, Verily I say unto you, Inasmuch as ye have done it unto one of the least of these my brethren, ye have done it unto me.

We do not always get to choose who we serve. Remember the story of the Good Samaritan, Luke 10:25-37. The story explains that thieves overtook a man, his clothes were taken, and he was beaten and left for dead. Picture it, a stranger lying in the road, half-naked, bloody, unable to move. People see him and cross to the other side of the road. Does it sound familiar?

But then comes the Good Samaritan. He does not allow what he sees to overpower his mercy. He gets down on the ground with the stranger and cleans the man's wounds. He did not stop there. The Samaritan took responsibility for his neighbor. He took him to the inn to be nursed to health and paid the bill for his care.

This is love in action. We cannot throw money at street beggars and feel we have done what Jesus asked. Jesus touched people. He put His love into action. We must be able to demonstrate our love and service to the "least of them."

Prayer: Dear Heavenly Father, please help me to exercise my faith in you by service to my neighbors through Christian love and compassion. Amen.

Henrietta Daniel

April 27

WORTHY OF THE CALLING

Scripture: Ephesians 4:1, 2 (KJV)
I therefore, the prisoner of the Lord, beseech you that ye walk worthy of the vocation wherewith ye are called, With all lowliness and meekness, with longsuffering, forbearing one another in love;

The Christian mission is to go into all nations teaching and preaching the Gospel of Jesus Christ. The Lord has called us to fulfill this Christian mission. We must come into unity with His Spirit as we attempt to respond to His call. He will give us courage to follow the right path in life so we can influence others to follow Him. He will give us the desire to follow His examples of gentleness, goodness, earnestness, compassion, humility, and patience. He equips us for His work of caring, loving, healing, helping, and teaching to make this world a better place to live is our purpose.

He will empower us to let our light shine before men that they may see our good works, and come to Him. If we walk worthy of our vocation to be effective as we witness, He will empower us to live each day in a manner worthy of the calling as followers of Christ.

Prayer: O God, help me to overcome whatever is keeping me from doing your will and commit me to a ministry that fulfills our Christian Mission. Amen.

Ora L. Finn

Lord show me my calling and I will Follow. Lord what ever the vocation you have for me open my eyes heart and mind and to follow your will, I am willing to to do your work. First let me start in my home.

April 28

PRAISE THE LORD, ANYWAY

Scripture: Ecclesiastes 3:1 (KJV)
To every thing there is a season, and a time to every purpose under the heaven:

God allows things to happen in our lives that we in our finite minds cannot begin to understand. God allows them to happen so that we may become mature Christians and that through our experiences we may strengthen others *thank you Jesus*

My husband and I, before his conversion, had been arguing for about three months over the smallest matters. I could not sleep at night for hearing his voice ring through my mind nor could I get ready for work peacefully. Reading the Bible and praying were out of the question. I was ready to pack my bags and leave, never to look back. I felt I had reached the end of my rope.

One morning I was sitting in the bathtub asking the Lord, "Why me, why must I go through this suffering and heartache?" Only then did a small still voice whisper in my ear and say, "If you never experience the persecution in your marriage, how then can you effectively witness to the next woman?" *Lord help us all to go through our troubles*

About four years later I was able to help a newly married young woman with her marital problems. So now when the persecution comes I can say, "Praise the Lord, anyway! *Lord give me that kind of peace*

Prayer: Dear God, help me to realize when persecution comes our way, God is making me stronger for the coming season. Amen.

Linda Inmor *Lord give me the knowledge to know you are with me when ever I am hearting in this way.*

April 29

WAIT ON THE LORD

Scripture: Proverbs 3:5, 6 (NIV)
Trust in the Lord with all your heart and lean not on your own understanding; in all your ways acknowledge him, and he will make your paths straight.

In 1989 I became a member of the staff of the Office of School Reform. I worked long hours, studied hard and became the person of reference on reform law. On two different occasions the position of Director became vacant and I knew the job would be mine. However, each time I was not chosen. I wanted the job and was disappointed.

In 1996, I became Missionary Supervisory of the Southwest Delta District. Neither my husband nor I had this vision in 1989, but all the skills that I had learned and developed in my secular position helped to prepare me for my new awesome responsibility. It would have been impossible to even partially fulfil the role of Missionary Supervisory and hold the position of Director in the Office of Reform, which requires a seven-day week and nearly an 18-hour day.

We do not know what tomorrow holds, but we know who holds tomorrow. God in His infinite wisdom prepared me for the job that was to come. When life does not follow our plan, know that we do not always know the plan. Trust God and let Him direct your paths.

Prayer: Father, help us to lean and depend on you, believing that all things work together for good for those who love the Lord and are called according to His purpose. Amen.

Estelle Jarrett

April 30

May

Seeing ye have purified your souls in obeying the truth through the Spirit unto unfeigned love of the brethren, see that ye love one another with a pure heart fervently:

1 Peter 1:22

Contributions From Various Episcopal Districts
Table Of Contents

BY ANY MEANS NECESSARY

Scripture: 1 Corinthians 9:22 (KJV)
To the weak became I as weak, that I might gain the weak: I am made all things to all men. That I might by all means save some.

When most people today here the words "by any means necessary", they immediately think of Malcolm X. It was Malcolm X who challenged African-Americans to seek true liberation and justice by whatever means necessary. These words also have vital meaning to disciples of Jesus Christ. The "Great Commission" Matthew 28:19, tells us that all followers of Christ have a responsibility to reach out and bring others to Christ. This should be done with a willingness to adopt a "by any means necessary" philosophy.

Paul makes it clear that he is willing to do whatever is necessary to bring someone to Christ. He recognizes that people come from different backgrounds and their level of faith is different. Paul is not suggesting that we should compromise. He is simply saying that we must be willing to minister to people in a variety of ways if we are to win the world for Christ. We cannot limit ourselves to one particular form of evangelism. We must be willing to utilize methods of reaching the unsaved that are understandable to them. Traditions can be useful, however, we must aside ineffective traditions and become all things to all men that we might save some.

Prayer: Father, give me the words to say to bring the lost, whoever and wherever they are, to you. Amen.

Reverend Kathryn G. Brown

May 1

CHRISTIAN TRAINING OF CHILDREN

Scripture: Matthew 19:14 (KJV)
But Jesus said, Suffer little children, and forbid them not, to come unto me: for of such is the kingdom of heaven.

Children are a gift from God. Therefore, as early as possible, they should be nurtured and trained in moral and spiritual living from the greatest book ever written, the Holy Bible. It is the responsibility of the parents to provide this training. Many parents have not accepted their responsibility so the local church has had to step in and do what parents are not doing. Thank God for local Christian churches.

Church School strives to get across to the children that sense of concern that God has for their personal lives and affairs, and the whole world. Church School strives to make children aware that they are vehicles through which God operates. It is through them that God's light shines.

As children are growing up they may stray from their Christian training, but the Word of God promises that if we will train a child in the way he should go, he will not depart from it. In training our children we must learn to stand on God's promises.

Prayer: Dear Father, as a parent and church leader help me to train and provide carefully for the growth of our children. Help me train our children to be strong witnesses for the Lord Jesus Christ. Amen.

Gladys G. Mack

PREPARATION TO BEAR MUCH FRUIT

Scripture: John 15:8 (KJV)
Herein is my Father glorified, that ye bear much fruit; so shall ye be my disciples.

Do I really want God to be glorified in my life? Jesus says that God is glorified when I bear much fruit. In order to arrive at the point of bearing much fruit, I must go through the process of preparation. This process includes:

1. Confessing all my sins and asking God to cleanse me of all unrighteousness, 1 John Chapter 1 and Psalms 51;
2. Allowing God to take all of the hindrances out of my life in the form of people, places, and things; and,
3. Continuously examining myself according to God's Holy Word to make sure that I am a vessel that can be used by Him.

Preparation to bear much fruit is a continuous process. Just as in the natural, seasons change and dead branches must be cut. While moving through the vineyard and working with the grapevines section by section, the Grapevine Dresser cuts away more than He leaves on the vine.

Prayer: Heavenly Father, I ask forgiveness for all of my sins of word, thought, and deed. My will is completely submitted to you. I thank you for a hunger and thirst for righteousness. In Jesus' name. Amen.

Janice L. Guinyard

BARREN YET FRUITFUL

Scripture: Isaiah 54:1 (KJV)
Sing, O barren, thou that didst not bear; break forth into singing, and cry aloud, thou that didst not travail with child: for more are the children of the desolate than the children of the married wife, saith the Lord.

I am reminded of the wonderful miracle that God performs in families. God is able to take a barren situation and make it fruitful. He is able to take a broken heart and make it whole again. After years of trying to conceive, after two years of adoption hearings and placement interviews, the judge rapped the gavel and pronounced to the world what God had ordained from the beginning, we had a son. Each year on this day we celebrate with family and friends the miracle God performed in our lives.

Prayer: Father, thank you for keeping your promises and making them real to me. Thank you for giving me an understanding of what it means to be children by adoption and joint heirs with Jesus. Amen.

Renata E. Moseley Harper

Scripture: Proverbs 1:8 (KJV)
My son, hear the instruction of thy father, and forsake not the law of thy mother:

Each year on my mother's birthday I am reminded that her mother did not raise my mother. Their father raised my mother and her three siblings during the depression because her mother died before my mother turned 3 years old. I often wonder how different my life would be had my mother's days been filled with the touch, kiss, or smile of her mother. However, Reverend Dr. Lewis Anthony taught me a valuable lesson when I heard him say, "Our parents did the best they knew how to do." Then I am reminded that there is no parent that could be more loving, more gentle, more caring than our Heavenly Father. With all of this in perspective, I marvel and thank God for my mother's ability to nurture her grandchildren and for our friendship. I praise God for the life of my precious mother whose delight is in the Lord.

Prayer: Father, thank you for loving me so much that you gave me a wonderful mother who loves me with her whole heart. Amen.

Renata E. Moseley Harper

BRIDE TO BE

Scripture: Titus 1: 15 (KJV)
Unto the pure all things are pure: but unto them that are defiled and unbelieving is nothing pure; but even their mind and conscience is defiled.

Little girls dream of the day when they will walk down the aisle escorted by their father to be given away in matrimony to their Prince Charming. We encourage their fantasies with the toys we buy them, and as they get closer to that day their dreams become our dreams of a beautiful wedding. After all of the hoping, dreaming, and planning, have we truly done all we could to prepare them for the marriage?

The first step is to teach them the importance of remaining chaste until they are married. If we do not teach them when they are young that they are to remain, chaste a wrong choice could dash those dreams forever.

As Christians we are to prepare to be the bride of Christ. Just as young boys and girls should remain chaste until they enter into a natural bond, we should remain spiritually pure to enter into our marriage with Christ. We must make the choice to live holy so that we would be acceptable upon His return.

Prayer: Father, as the unmarrieds are taught to remain chaste until they marry, keep my heart chaste in all things. Amen.

Renata E. Moseley Harper

GRADUATION DAY

Scripture: Luke 9:1 (KJV)
Then he called his twelve disciples together, and gave them power and authority over all devils, and to cure diseases.

Graduation day fills the air with joy and anticipated excitement. There are future hopes intricately connected to the receipt of a diploma. With all of this excitement the graduate must be mindful that success means sacrifice, and the sacrifice has only just begun. We oftentimes think of graduation day as the end, but it is the beginning. It is the beginning of taking all you have learned, all you have studied, and all you have been prepared for and putting it into action.

In a sense, the twelve disciples went through a graduation ceremony. There were no invitations sent out, they were robed in their ordinary clothing, and the commencement address was short. Jesus gave them power over all demons and disease. He had given them all they needed to succeed and left them with simple instructions; travel light, stay until the job is done, and leave before you are asked.

As believers and joint heirs with Jesus Christ, we have the same power and authority. We have been taught the Word of God, we have studied God's ways, we have been refreshed and revitalized over and over again, it is time to begin. It is graduation day.

Prayer: O Lord, I have been trained and I am prepared to go forth. Deposit in me the desire to declare through my actions the love of God. Amen.

Rita Colbert

May 7

this can be for anyone

GUIDANCE

Scripture: Colossians 3:16 (KJV)
Let the word of Christ dwell in you richly in all wisdom; teaching and admonishing one another in psalms and hymns and spiritual songs, singing with grace in your hearts to the Lord.

This is the time of year when we are blessed with sunny days and gentle breezes. When I sit on my back porch and observe the leafy branches moving in the direction of the wind I know that it is the work of the Lord. Although we cannot see the wind, we can hear it and see the reaction of whatever is in its path.

The tree branches are an example of how Christians should be. The branches seem to be content to move in whatever direction the wind blows them without resisting. As children of God we should listen and wait for God's voice so that we can move in the right direction, without resistance.

My inspiration comes by praying, then waiting for guidance from the Lord. Step-by-step, God shows me what to do and where to go. Wait, listen and obey.

this is my prayer

Prayer: Dear God, thank you for your divine wisdom that guides my feet and causes me to obey your Word. Amen.

Marilyn Quow

read

A HEART FOR THE POOR

Scripture: Psalm 72:4 (KJV)
He shall judge the poor of the people, he shall save the children of the needy, and shall break in pieces the oppressor.

Right in our neighborhoods where we live and worship there are needy people. We may choose not to see them, but we walk by them everyday. Consider the facts, while you worship Jesus, lift up holy hands, cry real tears for what He has done to you, there are people, maybe even sitting next to you, who are in need. How do you respond to their need? Do you ignore them, talk about them, or try to pretend you do not see their need?

Jesus cared for the poor. He instructed us to take care of the poor among us. If we are going to conform to the image of Jesus and allow His mind to be in us, then we are going to have to follow His lead with our compassion toward the needy. Let us join with our Saviour and reach out to the world in need.

Prayer: Lord, give me strength and compassion to help those in need. Amen.

Antoinette E. Joiner

May 9

JESUS WANTS YOUR HEART

Scripture: Luke 5:3 (NIV) Read Luke 5:1-11
He got into one of the boats, the one belonging to Simon, and asked him to put out a little from shore. Then he sat down and taught the people from the boat.

To love Jesus requires no great scholarship or high rank in the church—it does not take financial success or high social standing. When we come to Jesus He does not ask to see our resumes. He knows everything there is to know about us and He welcomes us in spite of who we think we are.

When Jesus came upon Peter, He found Peter distraught because of an unsuccessful night of fishing. Peter and other fishermen had been out all night fishing and had nothing to show for it. Jesus sat in his boat, suggested that he launch out a little further into the water and let down his nets. Peter told Jesus what He already knew that they had been out all night and had caught nothing. But in Peter's unbelief, he decided to give Jesus a try so he added, . . . *nevertheless at thy word I will let down the net,* Luke 5:5.

Jesus wants us to come nevertheless—regardless of what the world says, no matter what your family thinks— nevertheless, we have to give Jesus our hearts and our obedience so that He can take our failures and turn them into successes.

Prayer: Precious Lord, here is my heart. Use it according to your will and your glory. Amen.

Jacqueline Wilson

May 10

LISTEN TO HIM

Scripture: Matthew 17:5 (KJV)
While he yet spake, behold, a bright cloud overshadowed them: and behold a voice out of the cloud, which said, This is my beloved Son, in whom I am well pleased; hear ye him.

Jesus had taken Peter, James, and John into a high mountain where they had seen a changed and transfigured Jesus. During this moment, Peter was so overcome with emotion that he wanted to build an alter, but a voice stopped him and said, *This is my beloved Son, in whom I am well pleased; hear ye him.* The disciples were commanded to listen to what Jesus was trying to tell them.

Jesus warned them not to speak of the mountaintop experience when they went back down into the valley, because they did not know how to interpret what they saw. We as believers in Jesus Christ can see, hear and experience God's awesome affirmation that Jesus is the Saviour. We are reminded that God has come into our world personally. In Christ, our own nature can be transformed through commitment to Him. Therefore, there is no need to try to escape from life through selfish, mystical experience. For we are needed in the valley below for service, and Jesus is a sufficient guide and friend as we go about doing the real business of living.

Prayer: Lord Jesus, be my Master Teacher in training me to hearken to you and do your will. Amen.

Jacqueline Wilson

SHOW GOD'S BEST

Scripture: 1 Chronicles 19:13 (KJV)
*Be of good courage, and let us behave ourselves valiantly
for our people, and for the cities of our God: and let the
Lord do that which is good in his sight.*

We will never know how important our behavior is to
our Christian walk. The most important aspect is not how
our behavior affects us, but how it affects others. God
expects us to behave as conquerors and kings, being kindly
affectionate one to another. We can show God's best or the
devil's worst. It is all up to you. Before we can shout for
victory, we must realize that God must be in control. When
we allow Him to do what is good in His sight, we will truly be
conquerors.

Prayer: Lord, let the demonstration of my courage be that I
rely solely upon you. Only in yielding to you will I find what
is good. I yield not only for myself, but also for the Body of
Christ. I yield also that the world may see you clearly through
me. Amen.

Reverend Michele Owes

CALL

Scripture: Jeremiah 33:3 (KJV)
Call unto me, and I will answer thee, and show thee great and mighty things, which thou knowest not.

It is awesome to know that an Almighty God is waiting on our call. Remember the excitement and anticipation from awaiting a call from someone special. God finds you even more special and important.

He is not only awaiting your call, but He is waiting with the answers you need. He waits with the power, provisions, protection, and peace that can calm any storm. He will give more than you ask and be more than you ever thought he would be. Call Him. He will answer.

Prayer: Father, help me to first call upon you. Settle in my heart that there is no other person, place, or thing that can replace you in my life. Help me to recognize that you are willing and able to meet me at my point of need. You created me, you first loved me, and you await my call. I am someone wonderful to you. Oh, the wonders of your love. Amen.

Reverend Michele Owes

A NEW YOU

Scripture: Jeremiah 18:3-4 (KJV)
Then I went down to the potter's house, and, behold, he wrought a work on the wheels. And the vessel that he made of clay was marred in the hand of the potter: so he made it again another vessel, as seemed good to the potter to make it.

The value of a piece of pottery is directly related to the skill and craftsmanship of the potter. The slightest move of the hand or finger can completely change the shape, style, and look of his work. The potter must focus to bring it to perfection. Yet, the potter's wheel continues to move as he works.

The issues of our lives continue to move just as the potter's wheel. God ceaselessly works with precision and skill to bring peace and balance to our lives. One move from the hand of the potter can change the entire course of life. His change can only benefit you. Make that change today. Go down to the potter's house. Allow Him to work His miracles in you.

Prayer: Father, you truly are the potter. I lay myself on the wheel so that you may work a new work in me. My flaws may not appear before my eyes, but you know them. Make me again another, as it seems good to you to make me. Amen.

Reverend Michele Owes

Lord I No I need To be in the hands of the potter, I need To be on your Whell So you can Smove my life out I want to remain In the Potters hands

THE WORK CONTINUES

Scripture: Ecclesiastes 7:8, 9 (KJV)
*Better is the end of a thing than the beginning thereof:
and the patient in spirit is better than the proud in spirit.
Be not hasty in thy spirit to be angry: for anger resteth in
the bosom of fools.* yes

What a refreshing thought to know that God is not
finished with us. His desire is that we continue to grow and
develop until we are just like Him. He is the Everlasting
God. His process of perfection is a lifelong process. He
never quits. God's goal is to make us better and being the
best we can be for the Kingdom of God should be of
paramount importance to us. We will glorify the Father and
the Kingdom of God, even in our trials, as we allow this
process of perfection to take place.

Respect God's plan to make you better and look
forward to the results. Cast aside anger and agree with God.
Allow His will to manifest. Patience will have her perfect
work in you, and you will face this trial by totally relying upon
Him.

Prayer: Lord, I know that by your spirit, you will see me
through my trials from the beginning to the end. You love
me enough to make sure that at the end of this trial, I will be
better than I am today. I will lay aside anger and trust in you.
Thank you for not leaving me alone. Thank you Lord, for
investing in me. There will be a return on your investment. I
proclaim it today. Amen.

Reverend Michele Owes

May 15

CONFIDENCE

Scripture: Daniel 3:16, 17 (KJV)
Shadrach, Meshach, and Abednego, answered and said to the king, O Nebuchadnezzar, we are not careful to answer thee in this matter. If it be so, our God whom we serve is able to deliver us from the burning fiery furnace, and he will deliver us out of thine hand, O king.

There is nothing like confidence in God. The three Hebrew boys were not anxious about their problems with the king because of their confidence in God. They knew Him well enough to know that if they had to face the fiery furnace, He would be with them. You and God are always the majority. Knowing the power that works on your behalf requires a close and intimate relationship with Him.

Seek Him today. Seek His face. As the deer panteth after the water brook, so does your soul thirst for fellowship with God. Let no circumstance interrupt your fellowship with Him today. Rely upon Him. See the benefits of communication with Him through His Word. Make yourself available to Him. Watch your confidence grow as you see His miracles unfold.

Prayer: Lord, allow me to fellowship with you without distraction. Make my way clear so that my soul can be nourished with your Word. I set my heart to do your will. Thank you Lord, for being available. My confidence rests in you. Amen.

Reverend Michele Owes Lord help me To avoid distractions, when I am meditating on your word.

This is my prayer

May 16

YOU CAN'T IMAGINE

Scripture: 1 Corinthians 2:9 (KJV)
But as it is written, Eye hath not seen, nor ear heard, neither have entered into the heart of man, the things which God hath prepared for them that love him.

Your best dream or imagination cannot top what God has planned for you. Your eyes have never beheld anything more wonderful. Your ears have never heard anything more desirable. The fairy tales of this world are but mere specks of dust in comparison to what God desires for you. The timely release of your blessing is solely dependent upon you. It requires obedience. Obeying God's Word, is simply a demonstration of your love toward Him.

Just love Him. Just care for Him. Just surrender to Him. Just seek Him. Let your love and care for Him flourish into a wonderful relationship that reveals to a dying world that God is alive. Let Him demonstrate Himself clearly in you. You will be blessed beyond measure, and most importantly, you will be a blessing to others.

Prayer: Lord, I believe that you have my best interest at heart. I believe that you have a wonderful plan for my life. I surrender to it. Lead me, O Lord, lead me in your path of life. Amen.

Reverend Michele Owes

Lord all the things you have done for me and my family, I give my love to you. I will do all I know how to be obedient.

May 17

CHRIST IN YOU

Scripture: Romans 8:10 (KJV)
And if Christ be in you, the body is dead because of sin; but the Spirit is life because of righteousness.

Paul uses a very interesting conjunction in this Verse of Scripture-if. If Christ be in you, which means there is a condition to being free from the body of sin and death. We must first accept Jesus as our personal Lord and Saviour. This is our assurance that sin's control is severed through the indwelling of the Holy Spirit. His Spirit in us gives abundant life.

Once we have received Christ, the body must conform to the Word of God that says it is dead. But oftentimes the body is still much alive. Especially in those instances when the boss is on your back and you see no other way out than to "express yourself". Or when the children have hit the last nerve and you feel like mommy dearest. These are crucial times when we must depend on the Word of God for our strength. The body must not be fed opportunities to deviate from the life that is in Christ Jesus.

Because of the wonderful proclamation that we are now free from the power of sin and death, we can live the life that God has designed for us to live through the resurrection power of the Holy Spirit.

Prayer: Heavenly Father, because Christ lives in me, I am free from the power of sin and death. I thank you for making a way for me to serve you in the spirit of righteousness. Amen.

Janice McMilllian

May 18

FAVOR IN HIS SIGHT

Scripture: Esther 2:17 (KJV)
And the King loved Esther above all the women, and she obtained grace and favour in his sight more than all the virgins; so that he set the royal crown upon her head, and made her queen instead of Vashti.

As a young girl, I loved to watch beauty pageants on television. The Ms. Universe pageant was my favorite. Seeing all the beautiful women from around the world sparked a desire in me to be like them. However, there was one thing that crushed the fantasy, even if only in my mind; that was a condition called scoliosis, or curvature of the spine. This eliminated me from hope of competition.

But, when I accepted Jesus as my personal Lord and Saviour, He gave me another opportunity to receive the crown. I now am part of a royal priesthood. He has washed me in His Blood and declared my sins forgiven forevermore. Now I wear a royal crown and walk the runway to everlasting life.

Will you allow Him this day to crown your life with His unconditional love? Will you say yes, when He calls your name to receive the crown of life that is prepared especially for you?

Prayer: Father, help me this day to walk in kingdom authority. Recognizing who I am in you, a royal priesthood fit to be used in every way to the glory of your name. I stand tall, knowing that you have declared me of royal blood. Amen.

Janice McMillian

SHARING THE LORD

Scripture: Matthew 10:32 (KJV)
Whosoever therefore shall confess me before men, him will I confess also before my Father which is in Heaven.

So often throughout the course of a day, we as believers make confessions about a variety of things in our lives. A few of the more common confessions may include, deciding to be more timely, eating healthier foods, or spending more quality time with the children. Such declarations are indeed important and vital to our existence as social creatures.

However, there is a confession that garners supernatural results. Jesus, our redeemer, has given us an invitation to talk about Him and tell people who He is.

When we share the Gospel of the Lord Jesus Christ with those in need, He has declared that He will talk about us to the Father in Heaven. What an awesome thought to know that when I share Jesus, Jesus shares me.

Prayer: Dear Lord, help me to use every opportunity to share the Gospel of the Lord Jesus Christ with those I come in contact with daily. Amen.

Janice McMillian

THE TREASURE OF THE HEART

Scripture: Matthew 6:21 (KJV)
For where your treasure is, there will your heart be also.

Modern day Christians have the luxury of receiving the Word of God through a variety of formats. There are at least 20 translations of the Bible that speak of God's deity. There are churches on every street corner that welcome the sinner to repentance. And if that is not enough, the Gospel is preached throughout the world via satellite television.

With all the many different venues for receiving God's powerful and life changing Word, why is it that our hearts and minds oftentimes yearn for people, places, and especially things that are contrary to His expressed will for our lives? Is it because we are so inclined to embrace that which we can see, feel, touch, and smell, as opposed to what is really real, though invisible?

Have we replaced the God of Abraham, Isaac and Jacob, with modern day gods who come in the form of cars, homes, and fortune 500 careers? We must change focus, repent, and hold fast to that which is truly able to save our lives. Examine your allegiance today—for where your treasure is, there will your heart be also.

Prayer: Dear Lord, I am sometimes guilty of holding tight to external things that may not be profitable to my wellbeing in you. Help me to hide your Word in my heart that I would not sin against you. Amen.

Janice McMillian

PRESS TOWARD THE MARK

Scripture: Luke 17:32 (KJV)
Remember Lot's wife.

What a terrible thing to be turned into a pillar of salt. As innocent as Lot's wife may have thought looking back was, it must have held great significance with God.

After having been delivered and bought out of Sodom and Gomorrah, her looking back may have imprinted in her mind a lifestyle that God wanted her to forget. Being disobedient cost her life in exchange for a memory.

As believers in Christ Jesus, we must continuously look ahead to those things that are before us and not to the sins of the past. Any reflection of the things that kept us in bondage will only keep the ties fresh in our mind.

We must press toward the mark for the prize of the high calling in Christ Jesus. Never look back. Remember Lot's wife!

Prayer: Father, you hold my future in your hands. There is nothing that I wish to remember about my former lifestyle. Help me to look forward to the things you wish to do in my life. Amen.

Janice McMillian

MY SOUL LONGS FOR THEE

Scripture: Psalm 42:1 (KJV)
As the hart panteth after the water brooks, So panteth my soul after thee, O God.

Imagine a wonderland of trees, plants, and exotic foliage creating a landscape of symphonic beauty, typical of what one could fathom about the Garden of Eden. Everything appears, picture perfect, except the creatures of the ground roam about in search of a key necessity to their survival, water. Their search intensifies. Day and night they wander realizing that without sweet moisture, their existence is threatened.

So it is for us as believers in Christ Jesus. As the deer pants for the sweet refreshment of the water brooks, our mind, body, and soul must long for the one and only God who can guarantee, preserve, and sustain our very existence.

We must long to seek Him, pray to Him, and meditate on his divine instructions for life. Search for Him today, as one who seeks the satisfying refreshment of the water brook.

Prayer: Dear Heavenly Father, I realize that without the nourishment of your Word, I am weak and ineffective. It is you that energizes and sustains my total being. Amen.

Janice McMillian

FLOURISH IN RIGHTEOUSNESS

Scripture: Psalm 92:12 (NIV)
The righteous flourish like a palm tree, they will grow like a cedar of Lebanon.

David penned this mighty Verse of Scripture comparing the righteous to the cedar tree of Lebanon. Its root travels deep into the ground of the Middle Eastern terrain. The roots are so deep that when wind and rain attack, the cedar remains tall and firm, withstanding every assault that nature has to offer. Its branches provide widespread shade, as if it were an umbrella's protection from the elements.

God's appointed are to be like the cedar, strong in might, withstanding every attack of the enemy to the glory of God. Not allowing the situations of life to cause defeat, but rather causing them to grow even stronger, overcoming each obstacle that would seem to destroy us. Our foundation must be firmly grounded in the power and righteousness of God, through His Son, Jesus Christ. Allow the Word of God to penetrate deep in the hidden and secret places of your heart, uprooting every decayed and stale tradition of life.

Prayer: Father, my one and only desire is to be planted strong and firmly in your vineyard. Without your daily assistance, I will grow weary and fall. Uphold me with the power of your righteousness, that I might grow tall as a cedar of Lebanon. Amen.

Janice McMillian

RECOGNIZABLE FRUIT

Scripture: Matthew 7:20 (KJV)
Wherefore by their fruits ye shall know them.

If you have ever been to the orange groves of Florida, there should be no doubt in your mind as to why Florida's name has almost become synonymous with the delicious thirst quencher. Hundreds of rows of grove trees bear the fruit that gives Florida its popularity. The orange is easily recognizable in its element and even when it is transported out of its element, in particular in the grocery store.

God says that we as believers should be recognizable also by our "fruit". What type of character and likeness do we exude while in the presence of unbelievers? Does the sweet aroma of the Holy Spirit absorb them, thus likening us to the God of the Bible? Or do they relate so easily to us because they see no difference in our behavior and their behavior.

God has given us a description of the type of attributes that are typical of good fruit. Love, joy, peace, longsuffering, gentleness, goodness, faith, meekness, and temperance will produce the type of character that is recognizable in any environment or element.

What kind of fruit does your tree bear? The Holy Spirit is able to grow in His grove, sweet nectars of succulent and appealing fruit for all to recognize.

Prayer: Lord, groom me to be an appealing witness unto you. Let my lifestyle tell of the precious time that I spend daily in your grove. Amen.

Janice McMillian

May 25

THE LOVER OF MY SOUL

Scripture: Hosea 2:14 (KJV)
Therefore, behold, I will allure her, and bring her into the wilderness, and speak comfortably unto her.

God loves His people greatly. When Israel was continually unfaithful to the one and only God, He mercifully delivered them out of the wilderness and promised them a land filled with milk and honey. Even when they pursued other gods, He kept His covenant promise to them and was their Jehovah.

He delights in us so much so that He will encourage, edify, and comfort us with His most eloquent Word of life. God, like a poet, sits perched on top of the ladder of love serenading his one and only sweetheart. He speaks in ways that captivate our soul and spirit back to Him. When we want to turn the other way, He draws us nigh to Him and soothes the emptiness of our soul.

He is the only one who knows us entirely. God's love is constant and everlasting. From generation to generation, He is the God of comfort and love.

Prayer: Thank you Father, for loving me so perfectly. You have given me an example of what true love is. Your Words of love tenderly speak to my heart and mind of how much you love me. Amen.

Janice McMillian

TOGETHER AT LAST?

Scripture: Amos 3:3 (KJV)
Can two walk together, except they be agreed?

       This Verse of Scripture is often quoted to admonish us as believers to be continually mindful of being on one accord. In the Body of Christ there are many denominations that make up the earthly heavenly host. Yet, we often tend not to associate with our brothers and sisters in Christ Jesus because of the differences in the denomination. This mindset or attitude has to do with the tradition of men rather than a divine call to separate oneself from unbelievers.

       In John 12:32 Jesus said, *I, if I be lifted up from the earth, will draw all men unto me.* So if Jesus is being preached in a local church of believers, then we are all bonded together through the Blood of the Lamb. Our differences in denomination should only be minimal in comparison to the proclamation that we are all the same in Christ Jesus.

       Are we as believers walking together, on one accord or are we more concerned with what Sunday the Holy Communion sacrament will be served? Or will we be concerned with how the church down the street praises God as compared to our quiet and dignified way of hallowing His name? Jesus has given the Body of Christ all that we need to walk together without the destructiveness of division or schism.

Prayer: Father God, you have provided us an example of what togetherness is all about through the Trinity of the Father, Son, and Holy Ghost. Let us learn from you how to walk together. Amen.

Janice McMillian

May 27

A WORD IN SEASON

Scripture: Exodus 4:12 (KJV)
Now therefore go, and I will be with thy mouth, and teach thee what thou shalt say.

The thought of having to address a large audience usually causes anxiety with most people. The starched faces watching and waiting to hear what you have to say are oftentimes frightening. You rehearse in your mind with a confident flow, but as soon as the real occasion draws near, the butterflies surface.

Even when we are in situations where we feel the Holy Spirit prompting us to witness, we will choose to quench the Spirit. It is not because we do not love the Lord, but that we do not know what to say, or we think that what we have will not add to the situation. Then the desire to not draw attention to ourselves, or to not insult someone else's religious position becomes more paramount than imparting life.

God has commanded us to go and tell others that salvation is available through His Son, Jesus. No matter what situation God puts you in, you must open your mouth and allow the Holy Spirit to have His way. He knows the person and their specific needs and is clearly able to speak words of life that will edify, encourage, and comfort through us. We must obey.

Prayer: Father, often I do not know what to say, but this day, I surrender my mouth unto you. Have your way in my life that I would be an instrument used to your glory and honor. Amen.

Janice McMillian

May 28

GOD IS FAITHFUL Read Over

Scripture: Hebrews 10:23 (KJV)
Let us hold fast the profession of our faith without wavering; (for he is faithful that promised;)

Have you ever experienced such pain and suffering that you thought you would never make it through? Did you think for a moment that God had forgotten about you? The fact is, God allows us to experience His faithfulness through our life experiences. As believers in Christ, everything that we go through, whether it is a positive experience or a negative one, is for the purpose of developing our faith in the faithfulness of Christ Jesus. We are more apt to trust God when things are going well—when we are having mountaintop experiences. But, when we go through wilderness experiences, our emotions can get us so out of balance that we may even doubt whether God is on the job.

It is during these times that we must go to our secret closet, quiet our emotions, and commune with God. We can rest assured that God will never leave or forsake us. The Lord is orchestrating the events of our lives, and He has sent His precious Holy Spirit to abide with us, to comfort us when we go through trying times, to direct our steps, and to reveal Jesus in us and through us. Let us trust in God's faithfulness and allow Him to perfect us through our wilderness and mountaintop experiences.

Prayer: Lord Jesus, take me to a deeper level of understanding and experience with you. Help me see your faithfulness in all the life experiences that you lead me through. Amen.

Phyllis Cunningham

May 29

Scripture: Proverbs 25:11 (KJV)
A word fitly spoken is like apples of gold in pitchers of silver.

Imagine the serene beauty of apples of gold in pitchers of silver. The thought of such beauty lifts our spirits and refreshes our very souls. Likewise our words, our tone of voice should soothe and uplift the spirits of those we are privileged to talk to. Yet, have you ever noticed that when we get in a rush or under pressure, an unmerciful lashing of words can send a deathblow to anyone within earshot? Most often, the perpetrator is not even aware of the damage done. Indeed, the victims of our cruel retorts are often those who are closest to us—a beloved husband, a devoted wife, an inquisitive child. Can sweet and bitter water flow from the same fountain?

How do we change our delivery so that our words bless rather than curse? Only with our sincere conviction, commitment, and God's help can we tame our tongues and our tone of voice to speak life to others. We must ask the Lord to give us ears to hear not only His words, but also the tone in which the Spirit speaks. Have you noticed that when God speaks to us it is never in a harsh, vindictive, cruel or impatient tone? Hence, let us imitate our Father when speaking to others.

Prayer: Father, I pray that the words of my mouth and the meditation of my heart be acceptable in your sight. Teach me Lord to speak to others so that my words bless and uplift their thirsty souls. Amen.

Phyllis Cunningham

May 30

HUMBLE THYSELF IN THE SIGHT OF THE LORD

Scripture: 2 Chronicles 7:14 (KJV)
If my people, which are called by my name, shall humble themselves, and pray, and seek my face, and turn from their wicked ways; then I will hear from heaven, and will forgive their sin, and will heal their land.

Escalating violence, drive-by shootings, drugs, gang murders, suicide, domestic violence, teen pregnancy, and incest reign in cities across America. Throughout the world there are wars and rumors of war. In the United States, over 15 million youth are at risk—at risk of catching a stray bullet, at risk of being molested or raped, at risk of spending their lives behind bars. Neither law enforcement or government intervention can solve the world's social problems. Where does it end? How long will the Church allow the nation's moral standards to deteriorate? How many children must die prematurely before we, the Church, say no to this madness?

It may look like we are up against a hopeless situation but we can be assured that where sin abounds, grace does much more abound. Yes—there is healing in the Lord. We need a supernatural visitation from the Lord in order to defeat the devil and repossess our land. Only through our humble repentance and prayer will we receive His divine instructions to get our nation back on track.

Prayer: Father, we earnestly repent of our sins and the sins of the land and we ask for your forgiveness, healing, and restoration. Amen.

Phyllis Cunningham

May 31

June

Beloved, let us love one another: for love is of God; and every one that loveth is born of God, and knoweth God. He that loveth not knoweth not God; for God is love.

1 John 4:7, 8

Mid-Atlantic II Episcopal District
Table Of Contents

ALLOW GOD TO HELP YOU

Scripture: Psalm 46:1 (KJV)
God is my refuge and strength, a very present help in trouble.

God wants to help us, but too often our own willfulness and sense of independence causes us to become frustrated and utterly defeated.

This fact was brought home to me a few days ago as I noticed my two-year-old grandson trying to dress himself. I offered to assist him but being a typical two-year-old, he insisted on doing it himself. He started to fret and cry as he attempted to get both legs into one pant leg. He pulled and tugged as he tried to put on his jacket. Again, I offered help. He adamantly refused. Finally, when he was totally frustrated and at his wits' end, he allowed me to help.

Help was available to him all the time as God is our ever-present help. We can avoid so much frustration if we will allow Him to be our refuge, our strength, and our help.

Prayer: God, help me to recognize my weakness and accept your help. Amen.

Reverend Lula G. Williams

WHEN WE LET GOD

Scripture: Philippians 4:13 (KJV)
I can do all things through Christ which strengtheneth me.

I was asked to speak for our Missionary Breakfast. My answer without prayer or thought, was yes. I started writing my thoughts on paper, but when completed, I could not understand a thing I had written.

This is what happens when we think we are the directors of our own lives. I asked the Lord to speak to my heart, give me the words that would bring new light. Finally, I had a usable speech.

As we strive to take charge of our lives, we must realize that it is necessary to first seek the will of God. Pride says God is unnecessary and despair says God is unable. We must admit our inability to do anything in our own strength. We must then turn to God for the strength and knowledge necessary to overcome. Then and only then will we be genuine disciples anointed by the Spirit of God.

Prayer: Lord, I thank you for the knowledge to now understand what my mother was singing about when she would sing, Lord, I want to be worthy of your dying for me. Amen.

Patricia J. McGill

GOD'S PROMISES

Scripture: Genesis 18:14 (KJV)
Is any thing too hard for the Lord? At the time appointed I will return unto thee, according to the time of life, and Sarah shall have a son.

The words above were spoken to Sarah and Abraham after they questioned God about having a child in their advanced age. Sarah even laughed scornfully at God's promise that she would bare a son.

We question God's promises to us as we look at the human obstacles facing us as we work in the vineyard for Him. We allow physical health, lack of money and criticism from other people to cause us to have doubts about our ability to carry out what God has commanded.

We must learn to trust God and live one day at a time, knowing that God gives to the faithful all that is needed.

Prayer: Father, nothing is impossible for you to accomplish. Give me the ability to walk in this knowledge so that you will be glorified and others will be blessed. Amen.

Barbara L. Shaw

HE'S GOT THE WHOLE WORLD IN HIS HANDS

Scripture: Psalm 24:1 (KJV)
The earth is the Lord's, and the fulness thereof; the world, and those who dwell therein.

While riding home from church one evening with my husband and two sons, ages 4 and 5, they began singing a song that we often sing for church programs, "He's Got The Whole World In His Hands." The five year old said, "Mama, God must have great big hands." The statement surprised me because I was not aware how cognizant he was of what the words meant.

Many times as adults, we encourage children to sing, but we do not always teach the meaning with the melody. I replied, "He has you and me, the fish in the sea, the birds and the bees, the grass and trees, animals and everything that has breath in His hands."

Yes, God has great big hands. He holds us up when we are falling, and He keeps us close to Him if we desire to be kept. His hands were nailed to the cross for our sins. If we will listen to our children we can learn a great deal from the things they so innocently say.

Prayer: Dear God, help me to trust you and be assured that you hold me in your "great big" Hands. Amen.

Lessie J. Polk

BEHOLD, I STAND AT THE DOOR

Scripture: Revelation 3:20 (KJV) Read Revelation 3:14-22
Behold, I stand at the door, and knock: if any man hear my voice, and open the door, I will come in to him, and will sup with him, and he with me.

At a very early hour this morning, I watched the sunlight come through my window, quietly and uninvited. Nevertheless it came through the window. In that quietness I arose, turned to the Third Chapter of Revelation, and read the whole Chapter.

Clearly I saw the words, I stand, I knock, open. I recalled the Church to which the letter was addressed, the people were neither hot nor cold. They were comfortable in a state of neutrality, enjoying the rich and luxurious life. Yet Jesus was standing, knocking, waiting for a response.

Have our comfortable lifestyles turned us neither hot nor cold? Our hearts are the doors through which Jesus wants to enter. Our hearts are the place in which He wants to have fellowship with us. What is the condition of your heart? Is it hot or cold? Are you non-responsive to the knock of Jesus in your heart?

Prayer: Come in Lord Jesus, abide with me, you are welcome in this place. Forgive me for having kept you waiting. In Jesus' name I pray. Amen.

Gladys G. Mack

June 5

THE JOY OF THE LORD IS MY STRENGTH

Scripture: Psalm 27:1 (KJV)
. . . The Lord is the strength of my life . . .

When I think of the month of June, graduations, weddings, and children come to mind, which take my thoughts back to my teenage daughter, who did not live to graduate, have a wedding, nor have children. On February 12, 1979, my daughter died of an inoperable brain tumor. Our lives crashed and we did not know how we would pull through this tragedy. Then on February 12, 1980, the soft voice of Jesus said, "I am not a dead God, but a living God. Let my joy be your strength." I thought God was comforting me in my sorrow, but He was preparing me for what was to come.

That evening I received a call from Fort Eustis, Virginia, informing me that my son had suffered a nervous breakdown. I cried out to the Lord, "Why?" It was then that I remembered what God had spoken to me that morning. I thanked Him for His counseling, which was the only thing that pulled me through that situation.

I have learned that whatsoever state I am in to be content and to let the joy of my Lord be my strength. I have been blessed with a husband for 51 years, five living children, and seven grandchildren, one the image of my deceased daughter. My son, who had the nervous breakdown, is healed, lives a Christian life, and is married. I am now an ordained Minister. God will take care of you!

Prayer: Thank you, Lord, for your tender mercies. Amen.

Reverend Theresa M. Caldwell

JOY COMES IN THE MORNING

Scripture: Psalm 30:5 (KJV)
For his anger endureth but a moment; in his favour is life: weeping may endure for a night, but joy cometh in the morning.

In late 1989, I realized that my youngest daughter was pregnant out of wedlock. Our household and family began a period of absolute turmoil. I saw all the hopes and dreams I had for my daughter fleeing out of her grasp because of the choice she made. A close friend reminded me of what I always say to her when she is going through a struggle, "This too shall pass."

Then the child was born. The first time I held him in my arms, I realized that my night of weeping was over and my morning of joy was at hand. My grandchild and I spend a lot of time together. Just the sight of his crooked smile fills my heart to overflowing. I pray that nothing I do or say will spoil the faith and trust he has in a grandmother who he thinks knows it all, but just forgot for a moment.

We must always be mindful of our Christian duty to reach out to others. Now, whenever I see or talk to a mother in the situation I was in, I tell her, "Things may seem very dark right now, but your morning will come. Just turn it over to God. He will take care of it."

Prayer: Lord, I pray that some mother who finds herself in a tunnel of darkness will realize that there is a light at the end, and that joy really does come in the morning through you. Amen.

Patricia Griffin

GIVE THEM JESUS

Scripture: Luke 11:13 (NIV)
If you then, though you are evil, know how to give good gifts to your children . . .

    We live in a society that measures success by things. As Christians, we fall right into the trap. We work several jobs to assure that "we keep up with the Jones." Not only must we have what the Jones have, we overload our children with things to make up for the lack of time and attention they should get from us as parent.
    Our success is not found in the abundance of things we possess. Our success is in Christ Jesus. Therefore, the greatest gift we can give our children and those we witness to is Jesus. How can we give the gift of JESUS?

- Have devotional time with them;
- Take them to church and church school;
- Let them witness you praising the Lord;
- Let them see you praying and studying God's Word;
- Give them Christian tapes and videos; and,
- Give them a Bible.

    As we provide for our children's needs and wants and witness to others, let's be certain that in all of our giving, we give them JESUS.

Prayer: Lord, things pass away. Keep me mindful that the only gift I can give that will last is JESUS. Amen.

D. Diane Proctor

CHILD-LIKE FAITH

Scripture: Mark 10:15 (KJV)
Verily I say unto you, Whosoever shall not receive the kingdom of God as a little child, he shall not enter therein.

It is such a joy to watch my daughter greet her father as he walks in the door each evening from work. Her enthusiasm and energy are matchless. She dives into his arms and sends cheers throughout the house that her daddy is home.

After reading Mark 10:15, I realized that Christians must maintain a child-like spirit and enthusiasm about sharing God's Word. Unless we remain like children, eager to learn God's Word, excited about obeying His Word, and enthusiastic about loving His people, we cannot enter the Kingdom.

We must develop a child-like faith that allows us to obey our Father's Word, to go and teach all nations without question, without fear, without hesitation, and with great joy.

Prayer: Lord, restore a child-like spirit in me. Keep me excited, eager to learn, and enthusiastic about loving your people. Amen.

D. Diane Proctor

HEAVEN BELONGS TO THEM

Scripture: Matthew 19:14 (NRS)
but Jesus said, "Let the little children come to me, and do not stop them; for it is to such as these that the kingdom of Heaven belongs."

What a marvelous message of comfort for the many hurting children in the world today, so many of our children are thirsting for love, a feeling of belonging, a sense of security from the fear of abandonment and physical abuse. Thousands of children in our country and all over the world have little to smile about. Have you heard their cries?

Christian women and men must reach out to help relieve suffering and spread the joyous news that Jesus cares and loves the little children of the world. Jesus even says that the Kingdom of Heaven belongs to them. How do we communicate this Good News to families and children in our local communities? The most direct way is by our love in action—by giving of our time, talents, and substance.

Prayer: Heavenly Father, I give you thanks for the gift of children. I want to be sensitive to their cries. Use me, Lord, to meet their needs. Help me to teach them to honor your blessed name as I put my love into action. Amen.

Carmen T. Maxwell

EVERYDAY IS CHILDREN'S DAY

Scripture: Proverbs 22:6 (KJV)
Train up a child in the way he should go: and when he is old, he will not depart from it.

One Sunday in the month of June is set aside as Children's Day in our church. However, once we become parents or involved in the lives of children as guardians or teachers, everyday is Children's Day.

Those who are involved in the early development of children have the responsibility to direct, shape, and mold their thoughts toward seeking to live a good life, which is a gift from God given to those who submit to Him.

We set standards for raising or training children, but we must ask God what He wants for them. We have the responsibility to identify and develop the gifts God has given them. We cannot live their lives for them, but we can live our lives so that they see and understand that being faithful to God and trusting in God will help them live a long prosperous life.

Prayer: Lord, I thank you for the children that you have allowed to be part of my life. I now realize that they are yours and not mine. If I am in any way neglecting to train and nurture them in the way that is your plan for their lives, I ask for your forgiveness and your guidance as I prepare them for the good life. In Jesus' name. Amen.

Samantha M. Wormley

WHAT ABOUT THE CHILDREN?

Scripture: Mark 9:37 (KJV)
Whosoever shall receive one of such children in my name, receiveth me: and whosoever shall receive me, receiveth not me, but him that sent me.

Can you imagine a child entering a world of hunger, strife, and pain, and you, having abundance, sitting back and watching that child suffer? That is what we do when we do not share the Gospel of Jesus Christ with our children.

Reflect upon the parable of the Good Samaritan, Luke 10:30-37. A man attacked by thieves was suffering in the road. The priest and the Levite crossed to the other side of the road to avoid helping the man. The Samaritan stopped and ministered to the needs of the stranger. Are you crossing to the other side of the road as far as our children are concerned? We have a mandate from our Saviour to help our children, not to pass them by.

We should live our lives in such a way that a child will see the love and kindness of Jesus in the things we do. This will cause them to want to learn from us about God's love, His faithfulness, and His grace. Gather up your sons, daughters, and grandchildren, convey the message of Jesus and tell them of God's goodness.

Prayer: Help me, Dear God, to show love each and every day for all of your children, young and old. Help me, O God, to give a child hope and share the love of Jesus. Amen.

Catherine H. Whitley

June 12

TEACH A CHILD LOVE TODAY

Scripture: Matthew 19:14 (KJV)
But Jesus said, Suffer little children, and forbid them not,
to come unto me: for of such is the kingdom of heaven.

As I meditate on God's Word I am reminded of the deep concern that Jesus has for children. The tired disciples were disturbed because the parents and guardians brought their children to Jesus seeking a blessing. The disciples forbade them. They drove them away. Jesus seeing the situation said unto them, *Suffer little children, and forbid them not to come unto me. . .* The Master took them into His arms and blessed them.

Adults, fathers, mothers, shepherds of the church, sometimes like the disciples are tired and our first inclination is to send the children away. But as we strive to meet our busy schedules, we must do as Jesus did and take the young ones into our arms.

Church School, boy scouts, girl scouts, youth choirs, and other organizations that train our children need our support. These organizations teach children the way of love, peace, and joy through the example we set before them. Reach out and teach a child love today.

Prayer: Oh God, teach me so that I do not fail our children. Thank you for your love. Amen.

Gladys G. Mack

GOD'S PROTECTION

Scripture: Psalm 71:18 (TLV)
And now that I am old and gray, don't forsake me. Give me time to tell this new generation (and their children too) about your mighty miracles.

As we grow older, our conversations with our contemporaries often center on the "Good Old Days." These discussions produce a flood of memories of happy times. Sometimes we become so engrossed in the terrible conditions that exist in our world today that we forget those happy times. But it is these memories that remind us of God's constant presence in spite of the world's condition. It is His protection, which has brought us through difficult times and allows us to focus on the joy of the "Good Old Days."

People of faith must be leaders in providing for the future by planting seeds of hope through our witness of what God does for His people. When sharing our "Good Old Day" stories with the younger generation, we must continually praise God and tell about the marvelous deeds God has done, is doing, and will do for those who call upon Him. We must tell future generations about God's mighty power and His deeds of kindness.

Prayer: Dear Father, as I remember the "Good Old Days," keep me focused on the needs of the younger generations and the seeds that I plant for your Kingdom. Lord, keep me in remembrance of your mighty miracles. Amen.

Beulah F. Maxwell

STAND

Scripture: Ephesians 6:11 (KJV)
Put on the whole armor of God, that ye may be able to stand against the wiles of the devil.

As school administrators, our job is to prepare students to be successful in school. We discuss preparedness from two perspectives. First, the student must take all the right prerequisite courses to be eligible for the next level. Second, students must be willing to do the work expected by their instructors. All students must have the right stuff to succeed in life. And appropriate preparation and willingness to work are essential to school success. It is the same for the Christian. We must be prepared and willing to work to be successful in life.

Whether ready or not, students will face the pitfalls, dangers, and snares of life such as drug dealers preying on the young and innocent, boys and girls constantly dealing with peer pressure to have illicit sex, and so on. Likewise, Christians are faced with similar pitfalls thrown in life's way. As students of the Lord Jesus Christ, we must have the right stuff to be able to deal with all the curves life throws our way. The right stuff is the Word—the whole armor of God that we must put on so we can withstand the wiles of the devil.

Prayer: Dear Lord, as the fiery darts of life are hurled at me, help me to put up my shield and be ready as it comes. Amen.

Melva Polk Wright

June 15

PERFECT LOVE

Scripture: 1 John 4:18 (KJV)
There is no fear in love; but perfect love casteth out fear: because fear hath torment. He that feareth is not made perfect in love.

On our family's first white water rafting trip, my young niece stood up, the raft turned over, and everyone fell into rough water. My husband and niece disappeared from sight, while my six year-old son and I hung onto the raft for dear life. In what seemed like an instant, fear permeated my mind, soul, and body. I trembled. Suddenly I heard, "Mommy, Do you love me?"

"Yes, Aaron, I love you very much."

"Mommy, are we going to die?"

"I pray not."

"I don't hear you praying, Mommy."

I began to pray aloud, acknowledging God's love for us and our love for Him. Moments later, a man in a kayak offered a rope to me. Shaking with fear, I reached for the rope just as the current pulled me under the raft.

When I resurfaced the man and my husband were pulling the raft to safety. Before we could express our gratitude, the stranger disappeared. I realized that God's perfect love had not only conquered my fear, but had sent help to rescue me from those mighty waters.

Prayer: Thank you God for your protection, for your powerful, peaceful, perfect love that casts out all fear. Amen.

Reverend Frances M. Draper

THREE T'S OF TRAINING

Scripture: Proverbs 22:6 (KJV)
Train up a child in the way he should go: and when he is old, he will not depart from it.

What an easy Bible verse to quote. In fact, I learned it when I was a child. However, it was not until God blessed me with children that I began to meditate on this Verse. The Holy Spirit gave me three T's for training my children.

First, training takes time. We must spend quality time with our children and those we are leading to Christ. This means we may have to sacrifice something we want to do to spend time talking, listening, and participating with the children.

Second, training takes tolerance. This is where patience is helpful. We must accept the uniqueness and differences of our children and others. Training them to be God's children and productive citizens does not mean that we train them to be like us. We train them to be the best they can be.

Third, training takes teaching. Deuteronomy 6:7 says that we must teach them diligently when we sit in our home, when we walk by the way, when we lie down, and when we rise up. We are to instruct them always in God's Word.

Prayer: Lord, help me to utilize the three T's as I train my children and lead people to Jesus. Amen.

D. Diane Proctor

ABBA

Scripture: Luke 11:2 (KJV)
And he said unto them, When ye pray, say Our Father which art in heaven, Hallowed be thy name. Thy kingdom come. Thy will be done, as in heaven, so in earth.

Growing up the youngest of three girls, I was a "daddy's girl." From an early age, I sought to emulate those characteristics that seemed important to him. He read ferociously, therefore, so did I. Education was a priority for him, and so it was for me. There was a special bond between my father and me. As I think on that bond, the word that comes to mind to describe who he was to me is ABBA. Abba is the Aramaic word used by Jesus to speak of His relationship with God, the Father. Abba signifies an intimate relationship. This is the relationship that God desires to have with each one of us. Our earthly fathers are to teach us how to have that close intimate relationship with God.

In this complex world, earthly fathers are too often portrayed negatively with no mention of the many fathers who are striving to be the image that Jesus teaches them to be. It is important that our earthly fathers do their job of leading us to the Father so that in the midst of circumstances of life when only the Voice of our Father above will bring comfort, we know how to cry out, "Abba, Father."

Prayer: Abba, Father, when the uncertain little girl in me needs a Father, I know you will be there. When the confident woman in me needs a Daddy, I have your blessed assurance that I am not alone. Amen.

Rita Colbert

June 18

A FATHER'S COMPASSION

Scripture: Psalm 103:13 (NAS)
Just as a father has compassion on his children, So the Lord has compassion on those who fear Him.

As a child growing up in North Carolina, I could always depend on my father's protective hand and words of praise to God. Being a sickly child I required much attention. My mother died when I was five years old. My father was always there for me and showed me much compassion.

Then my father's high blood pressure required him to stop working. As a family we were totally dependent upon God's provision. This was not difficult for my father. Being a preacher he demonstrated abiding faith and trust in his Heavenly Father to supply the families' needs in abundance. God never failed us.

Now that I understand who God is and what He does, I understand that God responded to my father because of my father's heart toward God. My father feared and reverenced the Lord. God responded with His compassion.

Sometimes I hear people who have health problems and they sound bitter towards God. Be encouraged in knowing that our Heavenly Father loves you and knows the pain that you feel. He is waiting to show His tender mercies toward you, but that entitlement belongs to those who fear Him.

Prayer: Dear God, help me to fear you, not as one who would do me harm, but out of respect and reverence. Amen.

Ernestine Glass Burke

WE'RE ON THE SAME TEAM

Scripture: Mark 9:38 (NIV)
"Teacher," said John, "we saw a man driving out demons in your name and we told him to stop, because he was not one of us."

A team can be defined as two or more people working together toward a common goal. The goal of any Christian team is to exalt Jesus. Regardless of the type of Christian team, choir, missionary society, trustee board, the goal remains the same—to lift up the name of Jesus.

It seems that there are times when Christians forget that we are on the same team. Like the disciple John, if someone is not "one of us," we discredit God's ability to use them. There are times within the Body of Christ where we seem to be plagued with the same problem as John. We see miracles performed, we watch God use someone in a mighty way, but instead of celebrating the team's victory, we criticize.

If we are to win the world for Christ, we must remember that we are on the same team. Teammates do not all look or behave in the same manner. Some of our teammates are a different sex, culture, race, and denomination. As long as they are on the Lord's side, we should rejoice in another victory for His team.

Prayer: Father, forgive me for petty jealousies and insecurities. Help me to crucify every fleshly thing in me and celebrate your willingness to use any yielded vessel. Amen.

Reverend Kathryn G. Brown

FOLLOWING GOD'S WILL

Scripture: Luke 22:42 (KJV)
. . . nevertheless not my will, but thine, be done.

During the month of June, many sons and daughters will graduate from educational institutions with great expectations and hopes for the future. At this major crossroad, many choices and plans for life ahead must be made. Some will decide to take the road to higher education, while others may readily pursue job opportunities, or marry and start families. Many will pursue their dreams with great enthusiasm and with an attitude that nothing can hinder them from being successful.

The Holy Word says that we must lay before God all our desires and seek His help. However, before God can answer our desires and plans for the future, He must hear us saying, "nevertheless not my will, but thine, be done." God has a plan for each of our lives, and we must be willing to accept the direction He sends us.

Sometimes our plans are not God's plans. We have a choice either to obey God's will for our lives or follow our own paths. As believers, with faith and courage, we must make the ultimate decision to follow God's will.

Prayer: Dear God, as I attain new heights and make plans, help me to trust you to direct my path. Amen.

Sandra B. Crowder

A NEW BEGINNING

Scripture: Proverbs 13:19 (KJV)
The desire accomplished is sweet to the soul: but it is
abomination to fools to depart from evil.

Congratulations! Welcome to the world of the graduate. One should not think of graduation as the end, but as a new beginning which reflects growth and maturity. How well we apply what we have learned determines our future success. With that in mind, it is time to assess the value of our degree. Have we included in our curriculum courses from the Book of Life, which will reflect our Christian witness? Some of the courses that we should include are:

- Love, because Jesus told us to love Him and our neighbors as ourselves. Matthew 22:37-39;
- Conversation, for each time we open our mouths we indicate what is in our heart. I Timothy 4:12;
- Prayer, for prayer changes things, people and circumstances. Mark 11:24;
- Giving, because it is more blessed to give than to receive. Acts 20:35; and,
- Faith, because many things can be accomplished because of our faith in God. Philippians 4:13.

With hard work, perseverance, and the application of these courses, our lives can be successful.

Prayer: Dear Lord, help me to complete the curriculum on this earth that I may graduate to be with you. Amen.

Mary P. Boykin

June 22

A TIME OF CELEBRATION: GRADUATION DAY!

Scripture: 2 Corinthians 5:17 (KJV)
Therefore if any man be in Christ, he is a new creature: old things are passed away; behold, all things are become new.

Graduation is a time of rejoicing and reflecting. It is a time of new beginnings. Graduation is a time of change, moving from one stage of life to another. This process is very similar to what happens as we begin to seek Jesus and develop a personal relationship with Him. We graduate from the old man, put off the old man, and put on the new.

To begin this new phase of life, we must accept Jesus into our hearts, seek to please Him, and live Christ-like every day of our lives. We grow in His image by praying individually, as well as at Sunday school and Bible Study. We must seek the revelation of God's Word as it applies to our lives.

Ultimately, we should glorify God in everything we say and do. As new creatures in Christ, we must take on the characteristics of God, such as love, peace, joy, longsuffering and other fruits of the Spirit. See Galatians 5:22, 23.

Have you graduated? Have you changed? Are you a new creature?

Prayer: Dear God, search my heart today. Change my heart so that I may graduate to the next stage in Jesus. Amen.

Deborah J. Stanley

June 23

RUNNING THE RACE

Scripture: 1 Corinthians 9:24 (KJV)
Know ye not that they which run in a race run all, but one receiveth the prize? So run, that ye may obtain.

I watched the race between my five year-old and one year-old grandsons and was reminded of the race that we run daily. We encounter people on the highway racing to pass us. We encounter people at work racing to enter information into the computer before us. We encounter people in the supermarket racing to get in line in front of us. We encounter people complaining there is not enough time in the day to do everything so they race against time.

I wonder how many of us get up in the morning and race to have prayer and devotion before our day gets started? How many of us are racing on the highway, at work, in the supermarket or wherever our day may take us to tell others about Jesus?

Prayer: Dear God, there is only one race, one prize that counts, the prize of eternal life. Help me to run a race for your Kingdom. Father, I thank you that your prize is available to all. Amen.

Dianna R. Carver

SIMPLE WORDS

Scripture: 1 Corinthians 2:4 (KJV)
And my speech and my preaching was not with enticing words of man's wisdom, but in demonstration of the Spirit and of power:

It took me a long time to realize that God is not impressed by man's intellect. We allow ourselves to be awed by or intimidated by those who use enticing words and draw our attention with captivating, compelling orations.

It was not until I read with understanding the story of Peter following Jesus out into the water that I realized that God does not look at the depth of our words. He looks at our hearts. In Matthew 14:25-30, the disciples see Jesus walking on the water. Peter challenged Jesus to have him walk on the water also. Jesus told Peter to come on. While on the water, when Peter realized the waters were boisterous, he was afraid and began to sink. He simply cried out, "Lord, save me."

This is not to say that God does not want us educated. Paul, who God used mightily, was a highly educated man. God wants us to come to Him with our hearts pure and perfect toward Him, just as a child would. God will then put substance behind whatever words we speak.

Prayer: God, show me how to keep my heart perfect toward you that you might use my intellect for your purpose in the earth. Amen.

Angela M. Brown

ADMIT, SUBMIT, AND BE BLESSED

Scripture: 1 Thessalonians 4:7, 8 (KJV)
For God hath not called us unto uncleanness, but unto holiness.

As we grow in wisdom and understanding of God, we begin to realize the importance in checking our behavior. We no longer trust the standards we have established to measure our holiness. We begin to trust in God and His standards for holiness. We realize how quickly we react when provoked, instead of being still and acting according to God's direction. Taking a personal inventory of ourselves and confessing when we are wrong keeps us from falling into the trap of denial and ultimately exhibiting behavior that is not pleasing to God.

If we fall into the trap of denial we will view ourselves as victims. Our circumstances will be looked at only from a narrow point of view. This attitude hinders our growth and any chance to be joyous. Our deliverance lies in our willingness to be honest with ourselves.

When we examine ourselves, we are less apt to blame others and more willing to take responsibility for our actions. If we admit our wrongs and submit to God's will, God will bless us because of our obedience.

Prayer: Dear Lord, today I will admit the truth, submit to your will, and allow your Holy Spirit to bless me. Amen.

Reverend Deneen R. Jackson

WITNESSING, A WAY OF LIFE

Scripture: Mathew 28:19 (KJV)
Go ye therefore, and teach all nations, baptizing them in the name of the Father, and of the Son, and of the Holy Ghost:

We are ambassadors for Christ, and our mission is to evangelize the world. As Christians, it is our responsibility to share the Good News wherever we go—on our jobs, at school, at the grocery store, at home—anywhere we find the opportunity to tell the world of Jesus, His death on the cross, His resurrection, and His promise to return.

Witnessing must be a way of life. Our evangelistic efforts must be brought into our everyday lives. There are opportunities for witnessing all around us. Our responsibility is to develop the alertness of mind and the enthusiasm for sharing God's love to enable us to take advantage of every opportunity to be a witness on a daily basis. Paul and Silas, as they sat in a Roman jail, took advantage of an opportunity to witness to the Philippian jailer and as a result, the jailer and his whole house were saved.

Prayer: O give me, Lord, your love for souls, for lost and wandering sheep, that I may see the multitudes and weep as you did weep. Amen.

Elaine Parsons

PLANTING

Scripture: Ecclesiastes 3:1, 2 (NIV)
There is a time for everything, and a season for every activity under heaven: a time to be born and a time to die, a time to plant and a time to uproot,

Spring is a special season for me because I enjoy working in my flower garden. I plant flowers and cultivate the soil for the flowering harvest. I have found in order to reap the desired crop I must plant the right seeds, at the right time and in the right place. The same is true for our spiritual gardens. To reap the harvest of love we must sow seeds of love.

When planting seed, timing is important. Some flowers are perennials, some annuals. Some flowers do best if you plant them in the winter, others in the spring. Likewise, timing is important for our spiritual gardens. Some seeds are planted and it seems as if the harvest will never materialize. We must trust God and learn to wait on His timing, not our own. Never give up because you cannot see the harvest. Remember that we sow the seeds, but God brings the harvest. The end result will be beautiful flowers in our garden and in our lives, beautiful and loving spirits.

Prayer: Father, teach me to wait on my season to plant in your garden. I know that apart from you, I can bear no fruit. Amen.

Emily B. Simmons

GOD'S WILL vs. MY WILL

Scripture: Luke 22:42 (KJV)
. . . Father, if thou be willing remove this cup from me: nevertheless not my will, but thine, be done.

"I say yes, Lord, yes, to your will and to your way. I say yes, Lord, yes, I will trust you and obey. When your Spirit speaks to me, with my whole heart I will agree; and my answer will be yes, Lord, yes."

The melody and the words to this song are too easily erased from my memory when God gives me instructions that do not fit into what I have already planned. I must say, even as Jesus said in the garden of Gesthemane, "Nevertheless, not my will, but your will be done."

I must trust God to order my steps in His Word believing that He who began a good work in me will continue to perform it until the day of Jesus Christ, Philippians 1:6.

Prayer: Heavenly Father, I ask forgiveness for all of my sins of word, thought, and deed. Thank you for revealing your plans and purpose for my life. I thank you that I hear your voice and the voice of none other will I follow. In Jesus' name I pray. Amen.

Janice L. Guinyard

GRATITUDE

Scripture: Psalm 140:13 (KJV)
Surely the righteous shall give thanks unto thy name: the upright shall dwell in thy presence.

A young man turned to his mother one day looking at their ten year old car and said, "Mom, you take care of this car as if it were a Mercedes Benz." She turned to him and said, "It is a Mercedes Benz to me." He never forgot the way that his mother cared for each and everything that God had given her. Her stewardship over the things she had was an expression of her gratitude. When we are truly thankful for and appreciative of what we have, we take care of it.

Gratitude is not only shown in the words we speak. Our actions are the true communicator of our attitude toward our possessions. When we are grateful for our children, we spend time with them and train them according to God's Word. When we are grateful for the house we live in, we keep it clean. When we are grateful, we allow our actions to demonstrate our thankfulness. Be grateful today!

Prayer: Lord, teach me to maximize my resources and be a wise steward over that which you have blessed me with so that I might demonstrate my gratefulness. Forgive me if I have complained and been unappreciative of your blessings. Amen.

Carol Hart McCauley

July

My little children, let us not love in word, neither in tongue; but in deed and in truth.

1 John 3:18

Alabama-Florida Episcopal District
Table Of Contents

THOUGHTS OF LOVE

Scripture: 1 John 4:16, 17 (NAS)
And we have come to know and have believed the love which God has for us. God is love, and the one who abides in Love abides in God, and God abides in him. By this, Love is perfected with us, that we may have confidence in the day of judgment; because as He is so also are we in this world.

The Apostle Paul teaches in 2 Corinthians Chapter 13 that love is the great power that motivates the hearts of men. He instructs us in the development of love in our own hearts and inspires us to use it in our relationship with others.

Love is not merely a pious and gracious sentiment, but should be regarded as a way of life. It is the grandest expression of the heart of a person and should be reflected through a selfless outpouring. Love makes itself known.

God loved the world so much that He sent His Son to die for our wrongs, our mistakes, and our wicked ways. Plainly stated, our sins. He made his love known through His sacrifice. God carved the steps of the greatest love walk that has ever been taken. God is love and he who abides in love abides in God. Allow God's love to perfect you in all areas of your life and walk in His path.

Prayer: Father, help me to know your love fully and to express it to those I meet each day. Amen.

Ellen M. Richmond

July 1

GROWING FAITH

Scripture: Matthew 17:20 (KJV)
. . . If ye have faith as a grain of mustard seed, ye shall say unto this mountain, Remove hence to yonder place; and it shall remove; and nothing shall be impossible unto you.

A person with faith is rich. Faith is the activator of God's promises. For by faith we believe, and when we put that belief into action God's promises will be manifested in our lives. Faith, the size of a mustard seed, is enough for battles to be waged and won.

The great men of the Bible, Abraham, Noah, and Moses, were all counted so because of their demonstrated faith. Faith caused Noah to build an ark when it had never rained on the earth. Faith caused Abraham to prepare to sacrifice his son because he believed God's promise that out of his loins many nations would come. Faith caused Moses to lead the Israelites into the Red Sea.

Faith is the Christian's tool to operate in the principles of God. For we must believe that God is, then apply His Word in our lives. And as Hebrews 11:6 promises, He will reward those that diligently seek Him.

Prayer: Lord, give me faith to believe in your Word and move on it in my life. Amen.

Ellen M. Richmond

TAKING THE WORLD FOR CHRIST

Scripture: Acts 1:8 (KJV)
But ye shall receive power, after that the Holy Ghost is come upon you: and ye shall be witnesses unto me both in Jerusalem, and in all Judaea, and in Samaria, and unto the uttermost part of the earth.

The thought of taking the world for Christ is an awesome challenge. But God has broken it down for us. He said that we are to be witnesses in Jerusalem and Judaea—begin at home. Once we have perfected our witness at home we can then move it to the streets, our workplaces, and schools. We then have a foundation to go to the uttermost parts of the earth.

Having received the plan of attack, let us remember that we are not alone—God is always with us.

Prayer: Dear Father, help me to take one step at a time, remembering that wherever I go, you go with me as we take the world for Christ. Amen.

Reverend Brenda E. Jones

FEED US, WE ARE HUNGRY

Scripture: John 6:33 (KJV)
For the bread of God is he which cometh down from heaven, and giveth life unto the world.

We are all hungry and need to be fed. I am not referring to the hunger that is quenched by food for our natural bodies. We hunger for what will feed us spiritually. Before we accept Jesus, we hunger and do not know how to satisfy the hunger. We try to satisfy it with things or people, but the more we get, the greater the hunger. After we receive Jesus we have the answer. We must seek him diligently in His Word, in fellowship with the Saints, and through our service in His Kingdom, to have our hunger satisfied. God provides the Bread of Life that we need to never be hungry again.

Prayer: Our Father, thank you for Jesus. My cup is empty. Please fill it and let it overflow with love, mercy, and righteousness. Give me faith to remove all doubt, malice, confusion, lies, and deceit. Cleanse my heart of personal grudges, as I accept responsibility for my own mistakes and failures. I will forever praise your Holy name. Amen.

Emma L. Hibbler

RETURNING TO YOUR FIRST LOVE

Scripture: Revelation 2:4 (KJV)
Nevertheless I have somewhat against thee, because thou hast left thy first love.

"Take me back, take me back, dear Lord, to the place where I first received you. Take me back, take me back, dear Lord, where I first believed." These lyrics written by Andre Crouch help us examine where we are in our Christian walk. Sometimes we realize that we are not as close to God as we once were. We long for that place or feeling of closeness with God that we once knew.

When we feel far away from God, we have allowed something or someone to take first place in our heart. What is it that has replaced our first love? Whatever it is, we must deal with it immediately. Revelation 2:5 says that we must repent and do the things we did at first. Did you read the Bible more when you first accepted Christ? Did you pray and witness more?

We must repent, ask God for forgiveness, give Him back His first place in our lives, and do the things we did at first. Only then will we experience God's peace and joy.

Prayer: Lord, I repent for placing people and things before you. I return to you as my first love. Amen.

Reverend Brenda Shuford

July 5

FOCUS ON THE LORD

Scripture: Isaiah 53:1 (KJV)
Who hath believed our report? And to whom is the arm of the Lord revealed?

When we have done your best to obey the Lord and yet the doctor's report offers no hope, or when we are tempted to give up because life has dealt a hard blow, whose report are we going to believe?

It is imperative to know where to focus our thoughts and attention during times of adversity. If we focus on the will of the Lord, then we believe and act on His report. His report says we are healed. His report says we are more than a conqueror. His report says we have all sufficiency in Him. We must allow our thoughts to press through our tears and discouragement to focus on the Lord.

Prayer: Lord, help me to remember to keep my eyes and thoughts focused on you. You said that you would keep me in perfect peace if I keep my mind stayed on you. Lord, I choose today to focus on you and I thank you for your peace. In Jesus' Name I pray. Amen.

Reverend Barbara Rogers

July 6

TAKING CARE OF ME

Scripture: Psalm 51:10 (KJV)
Create in me a clean heart, O God; and renew a right spirit within me.

Most women will go though periods in their lives when numerous demands are placed upon them; demands from the family, the job, the spouse, the children, parents, and siblings. It is important, indeed necessary, to step back and re-evaluate our priorities from time to time, to reflect on our mission in life. It is only in nurturing our own soul that we are able to nurture and take care of others.

We should be mindful in performing our duties to give priority to developing and maintaining ourselves inwardly, as God desires. The more time we spend with God praying, studying, and meditating on His Word, the more we find our focus in life changing from self-centeredness to Christ-centeredness, which enables us to meet the needs of others.

Prayer: Father, keep me mindful of my personal needs as I meet the needs of others. I pray for understanding in this area of my development. Amen.

Ava Morrow

THE HOLY SPIRIT MAKES THE DIFFERENCE

Scripture: Acts 1:8 (KJV)
But ye shall receive power, after that the Holy Ghost is come upon you: and ye shall be witnesses unto me both in Jerusalem, and in all Judaea, and in Samaria, and unto the uttermost part of the earth.

We are called to be witnesses whose testimony will count for Jesus. The world needs to see a generation of Christians, fully empowered by the Holy Spirit and going forth as witnesses for Jesus Christ. We are witnesses of one kind or another. Unchristian behavior, such as selfishness, profane speech, jealousy, or unforgiveness, is a witness against Jesus.

We should be able to witness to the lost about the grace of God and how faith in Jesus Christ can set them free. The Holy Spirit makes the difference. He gives us the power to exercise what we believe.

Prayer: Father, thank you for the power of the Holy Spirit. Help me to walk in the power that He gives so that I can walk in what I believe. Amen.

Reverend Janice Toodle

GOD'S COMMAND

Scripture: Joshua 1:9 (KJV)
Have not I commanded thee? Be strong and of a good courage; be not afraid, neither be thou dismayed: for the Lord thy God is with thee whithersoever thou goest.

God commands us to be strong and of good courage, and to not be afraid or dismayed, because He is with us. Have you ever seen how the demeanor and attitude of a child changes when his father is with him? The same child who would not fight for himself or speak up, suddenly boldly expresses himself. What changed? The presence of the father is the difference. God wants us to have the boldness that comes from knowing your Heavenly Father is present. He is with us wherever we go, so be strong and of good courage.

Prayer: Father, let me walk in the courage and strength that comes when you know your Father is present. Amen.

Frankie Hicklin

WALKING IN TRUTH

Scripture: Psalm 119:33 (KJV)
Teach me, O Lord, the way of thy statutes; and I shall keep it unto the end.

Have you ever thought of how vital truth is? The Word says the truth makes you free. God's Word, is truth. With the knowledge of God's Word, you have His power at your access. With the knowledge of His Word, you will trust in His promises and rely on His protection. Truth will heal, sanctify, and enable you to hear God's voice. Truth guides you in the path of righteousness and comforts you when rejection, disappointment, and grief are overwhelming. You are made free from bondage, pain, and fear. Truth can be a constant companion that brings peace, joy, and love in your life and others. Let us allow truth to come alive in our hearts today.

Prayer: Father, help me to be immersed in truth today. I want to speak the truth in my heart. Let me not forget that your Word is a lamp unto my feet and a light unto my path. Lead me that I may minister by the Word of truth. Help me to be like Hezekiah as he wept before you saying, "Remember now O Lord, I beseech thee how I have walked before thee in truth." Amen.

Reverend Valerie Smith

THE WORLD FOR CHRIST

Scripture: Matthew 5:16 (KJV)
Let your light so shine before men, that they may see your good works, and glorify your Father which is in heaven.

Now and then someone tells us that they want a job in the church—that they want to become active. Indeed, the church could not run without a host of faithful workers. But in a real sense, every member has a job—to be a follower of Christ. It is defined in Matthew 5:16.

This is our commission—to be a light that shines, a candle that burns, a light that reflects the glory of God. The fact is that there are not enough titled jobs to go around in the organization of the church, but there is something for everyone to do. We can all be an active disciple of Christ. We must take our minds off of the title of the position we hold and keep our eyes on Kingdom building. Then whatever task we are assigned, we will do it as unto the Lord.

Prayer: O God, cleanse me, mold me, guide me, that I may be used by you to be a light in the darkness of today's world. Amen.

Farris Christian Williams

THE CHOICE TO OBEY GOD

Scripture: Deuteronomy 28:1 (KJV)
And it shall come to pass, if thou shalt hearken diligently unto the voice of the Lord thy God, to observe and to do all his commandments which I command thee this day, that the Lord thy God will set thee on high above all nations of the earth:

God tells us in His Word that as believers in Christ we have to be obedient to His way and will. Obedience brings success and prosperity. Obedience requires time meditating on the Word of God day and night, so that we know His will and His ways.

If we do not take time to commune with God, our spiritual life is going to be stagnant and unfruitful. When we awaken in the morning, we should have the Word on our mind. Having His Word ever present on our minds will facilitate our obedience. When His Word is on our mind, His Word is not only a resource in making decisions and choices, but our obedience to His Word becomes second nature. To obey becomes our only choice. If we want to enjoy life to the fullest, we must find ourselves being obedient to God's way and will.

Prayer: Father, teach me how to walk in your Spirit and obey your Word daily. In Jesus' Name I pray. Amen.

Evera Walton Cannon

SURROUNDED BY HIS PEACE

Scripture: Colossians 3:12-15 (NIV)
Therefore, as God's chosen people, holy and dearly loved, clothe yourselves with compassion, kindness, humility, gentleness and patience. Bear with each other and forgive whatever grievances you may have against one another. Forgive as the Lord forgave you. And over all these virtues put on love, which binds them all together in perfect unity. Let the peace of Christ rule in your hearts, since as members of one body you were called to peace. And be thankful.

Christians must always seek to imitate Christ in all we say and do. Giving thanks to God for His love and grace keeps us correctly positioned to emulate Christ.

Is our behavior compassionate? Are we kind? Do we practice humility in our attitudes and actions? Is gentleness exemplified in our interaction with others? Do we exhibit patience in responding to situations that are not as we would like them to be? Are we able to forgive?

The love of God secures all of the virtues needed to answer these questions in the affirmative. This security allows us to walk in unity and insures us that the peace of God will surround our lives.

Where there is love, there is peace. Where there is peace, there is God.

Prayer: Creator, make me an instrument of your peace in Jesus' Name. Amen.

Reverend Sondra M. Coleman

July 13

WALK IN PEACE

Scripture: Colossians 3:15 (NIV)
Let the peace of Christ rule in your hearts, since as members of one body you were called to peace. And be thankful.

As people of God, we have been called to peace—in our church, in our home, and in our relationship with others. Yes, we are different, but we are one in Christ. Christians must always seek to imitate Christ in words, deeds, and thoughts, giving thanks to God for His love and grace. This will enable us to emulate Christ in every way.

When we exhibit our faith with a spirit of compassion, kindness, gentleness, humility, patience, and forgiveness in our daily walk, we experience the peace of God that surpasses all understanding. God's love binds these virtues together and therein insures us of His peace.

Where there is faith, there is love.
Where there is love, there is peace.
Where there is peace, there is God.

By faith, walk in God's love that you might experience God's peace, thereby inviting God, Himself, to be with you.

Prayer: O Wonderful Father, may the love of Christ reign in my heart. Let me always seek to be an instrument of your peace. In Jesus' name I pray. Amen.

Reverend Sondra M. Coleman

GOD'S PROGRAM IS MISSION

Scripture: Matthew 28:18-20 (KJV)
And Jesus came and spake unto them, saying, All power is given unto me in heaven and in earth. Go ye therefore, and teach all nations, baptizing them in the name of the Father, and of the Son, and of the Holy Ghost: Teaching them to observe all things whatsoever I have commanded you: and, lo, I am with you always, even unto the end of the world. Amen.

Missionary activities encompass so much when properly executed under the direction of God. The mission of God lifts up the relevancy of Christ Jesus to a world that lacks an understanding of who He is. It teaches who He is, why He came, why He lived, why He died, and most of all, why He was raised from the dead and ascended to the right hand of God the Father. When the mission is fulfilled, people of the world are given the opportunity to accept Jesus. Fulfilling the mission means lifting up Jesus so that He may attract all mankind to Him.

Prayer: Dear God, may you use me to lift up the relevancy of Christ Jesus, that He may draw all mankind unto Himself. In the name of Jesus I pray. Amen.

Lessie B. Simpson

July 15

SERVING IN OUR MANY WORLDS

Scripture: Mark 16:15 (KJV)
And he said unto them, Go ye into all the world, and preach the gospel to every creature.

What is our mission? Our Mission can be heard in the Great Commission. We must begin to take seriously the task of fulfilling the Great Commission. If we are committed to fulfilling the great commission as Christ commanded, we have a profound responsibility. We must proclaim His redeeming love where people are suffering, starving, fighting, using drugs, and dying.

Love can be proclaimed by our service. It has been said, "love is as love does." Christ is the love of God in action and through us, that love can bless, lift, and even change the lives of others.

We must go beyond the walls of the church building. God expects us to get out of the church and go out into the many worlds of human society—business, academic, science, government—and lead people to Christ and invite them to church. Serving our many worlds is fulfilling the mission.

Prayer: Father, give me the courage to go into the many worlds and serve the needs of hurting men and women so that they can know you through me. In Jesus' name I pray. Amen.

Yvonne Q. Powell

July 16

GOD'S WITNESSES—ARE WE?

Scripture: Acts 1:8 (KJV)
But ye shall receive power, after that the Holy Ghost is come upon you: and ye shall be witnesses unto me both in Jerusalem, and in all Judaea, and in Samaria, and unto the uttermost part of the earth.

God has given us the overwhelming task of being witnesses for Him. This work should not be brushed aside through laziness or apathy, but should command our utmost attention and energy. Someday we will give an account of our service. It is possible for us to be found unfaithful and unprofitable in that day because we have looked upon our daily responsibilities as an irksome job, rather than joyously serving Him.

Our Lord Jesus Christ has given us the task of living daily for Him. Let us do all as unto Him—worshiping, witnessing, and working.

Prayer: Lord, you have given so much to me. Help me to repay a little of your gift by being a faithful witness for you. Amen.

Eula C. Goode

Lord help me to be a true witness for you... give me courage to take the

A LIVING TESTIMONY

Scripture: 2 Corinthians 5:20 (NIV)
We are therefore Christ's ambassadors, as though God were making His appeal through us. We implore you on Christ's behalf: Be reconciled to God.

As we undertake the arduous task of being God's messengers, we must be physically, mentally, and spiritually prepared and certain that we are delivering the right message.

We must take care of our bodies. Our temples should not be polluted with toxins that limit our physical capabilities. We must expand our minds and know the Word of God and the wonder of His transforming power. We must grow and mature in spirit. We must be spiritually fortified so as to avoid even the semblance of evil. Everything about us must lift the Name of Jesus.

We are messengers for Christ. He is appealing to others through us. We must seek His empowerment through the Holy Spirit. That is how we find the "right stuff" to get the job done. That is how we can effectively minister to our sisters and brothers, regardless of their need.

Prayer: Lord, magnify your light in my life so that I might be a living testimony to help win the world for Christ. Amen.

Juletha Neely French

LOVE

Scripture: 1 Corinthians 13:13 (KJV)
And now abideth faith, hope, charity, these three; but the greatest of these is charity.

Where would we be without the love of God? Love is defined as a strong affection for another rising out of kinship or personal ties, such as a mother for a child or Father God for His children. We are members of the family of God because we love God. Loving God should lead to obeying Christ.

I am a beloved person knowing that I am the daughter of God and regardless of what happens, even if I am sometimes unloved by everyone else, my Father God loves me.

They use the term love as the score of zero in a tennis game. It is also zero in life, if you do not know God. But when you know God and love as He teaches us to love, unconditionally, then you know a more excellent way. Love in its fullest meaning is true love to God and man.

Prayer: Dear Father, thanks for the joy you bring to hearts of those who love you. Please help me God, to show your love through action. Through your love I will know when to act and when to be still. Amen.

Gwendolyn Strother Smith

GOD'S WORD FOR GOD'S MISSION

Scripture: Matthew 24:34 (KJV)
Verily I say unto you, This generation shall not pass, till all these things be fulfilled.

In the Great Commission, Jesus gave His disciples the assurance of His perpetual spiritual presence with all who follow Him in preaching and teaching His precious Gospel.

Fulfilling the Mission is our way of working together to bring men and women, one by one, face to face with Jesus Christ as their Saviour and Lord.

There are those who are friendless, helpless, and homeless, whose souls have lost their way to God. Instead of wondering what will become of the present world, we must go into the world and tell the unsaved to believe and accept Jesus Christ as Lord and Saviour. If they will receive Him by faith, they too can experience all of the glorious things that are in store for the members of the true Church. We must evangelize to win the world for Christ.

Prayer: Father God, I ask for an anointing of your Holy Spirit that I might touch some soul today. In Jesus' name I pray. Amen.

Sylvia E. Parker

FULFILLING THE MISSION

Scripture: Luke 1:37 (KJV)
For with God nothing shall be impossible.

Mission Possible! God the Creator has made and sustained all that we have in our lives. He created us in His image and equips us for our daily service to Him. God would never ask His children to do anything without the instructions and equipment to do the job well.

We must not forget that with God all things are possible and He will always show us the way if we stop to ask for directions and then listen.

When we pursue guidance and understanding from the Holy Spirit by earnestly reading His Word and praying, we will fulfill the mission to His glory. This mission is possible!

Prayer: O Lord, our Heavenly Father, I, your humble servant, desire your guidance and direction. Come into my heart that I may worship you. Bless me with your Holy Spirit so I can be a blessing to others. Continue to grant me the desire to touch the lives of those who may not know you. I thank you for the opportunity to serve you. Grant me this prayer in the name of your precious Son, Jesus the Christ. Amen.

Ruby Palmer

Lord fill me with your spirit so I can understand the thing that are possible, at times Lord all we see is impassible, that why we need your spirit to guide us each day!

July 21

FULFILLING, NOT JUDGING

Scripture: Matthew 7:1 (KJV)
Judge not, that ye be not judged.

While on the mission field, we as Christians often tend to compare ourselves to others thinking that our little sin is not as big or as bad as that of our neighbors. We sometimes think that because we do not drink or smoke we are not like them. We look at the addict on the corner, the prostitute, the executive who has embezzled the company's money, the homeless who sleep in the alleyway and we feel good about ourselves. We feel especially blessed because our clean clothes fit just right, our beautiful home is air-conditioned, and our late model car is paid for. *think!*

What have we offered these people? Have we pictured ourselves in their places? Did we think about their welfare or did we judge them because of their circumstances?

When we judge, we put ourselves in God's place, and we esteem ourselves better than our brothers and sisters. This does not line up with God's Word. The Word tells us not to think more highly of ourselves than we ought. Judging is sin. Therefore let us not judge one another.

Prayer: Precious Saviour, please teach me to guard each man's dignity and to save each man's pride. May I not judge others. Help me to remember from whence all our blessings come. Amen.

Darlene M. Bennett

THE FULFILLLING PEACE OF JESUS CHRIST

Scripture: John 14:26 (KJV)
But the Comforter, which is the Holy Ghost, whom the Father will send in my name, he shall teach you all things, and bring all things to your remembrance, whatsoever I have said unto you.

Every true Christian should have a goal of fulfilling the Great Commission. This we know, but how to accomplish it can be very perplexing. Scripture assures us that we can do the same works as Jesus did and that He has fully equipped us to fulfill the mission. Jesus gave us gifts both personal and corporate. In seeking to fulfill the mission, we should be both filled and fulfilled. Jesus gave us the Comforter of the Holy Spirit that we might be filled and He gave us His peace that our joy might be full. The peace that Jesus has given us supersedes anything that the world has to offer. His peace is born out of his loving kindness toward us. Let us rest in that peace today as we move forward in reaching the world for Christ.

Prayer: Father, I pray that today I would be filled with your Holy Spirit and the loving gift of peace that was purchased by the Blood of Jesus. May I impart that peace by loving others as myself and may I see victory in my life as we seek to reach the world for Christ. Amen.

Reverend Dorothy Templeton Swafford

Scripture: Matthew 4:23 (KJV)
And Jesus went about all Galilee, teaching in their synagogues, and preaching the gospel of the kingdom, and healing all manner of sickness and all manner of disease among the people.

As we come to the close of the 20th century, we are admonished to spend our time discipling, witnessing, equipping, and teaching others in our efforts to win souls to Christ. While we are nurturing their spirits, let us not neglect their physical needs and conditions. Jesus always cared for the individual's spiritual and physical well-being.

While the power to heal as Jesus did is exercised in us at God's will, we can still provide physical gifts that will prolong and enhance the quality of the life of others. We can reach out by giving gifts of life.

The sense of well-being is exuded from the individual who is both physically healthy and spiritually sound, which in it self is a testimony to those who would be won for Christ.

Prayer: Father, instruct and guide me daily in ways that I may assist others in their spiritual, physical, and emotional needs, as they struggle on this Christian journey. Amen.

Thelma H. Cotton

EFFECTIVE WITNESSING

Scripture: Matthew 9:37, 38 (NRS)
Then he said to his disciples, "The harvest is plentiful, but the laborers are few; therefore ask the Lord of the harvest to send out laborers into his harvest."

As we seek to witness for Christ, we are reminded that we are to be God's disciples, bringing others into a saving knowledge of our Lord, Jesus Christ. However, before we can disciple others, we need to examine our hearts to make sure we are a disciple of Christ.

As we look within ourselves introspectively, there are three questions we need to ask:

1. Do I bear fruit? In John 15:8, Jesus says, *By this My Father is glorified, that you bear much fruit; so you will be my disciples.*

2. Do I study and obey God's Word? 2 Timothy 2:15 says, *Study to show thyself approved unto God, a workman that needeth not to be ashamed, rightly dividing the word of truth.*

3. Do I love others? In John 13:35, Jesus says, *By this all will know that you are my disciples, if you have love one for another.*

Prayer: Lord, I have been commanded to go into all the world and make disciples. Fill me and direct me with your love so that others watching me will want to follow you. I ask this and all other blessings in Jesus' name. Amen.

Georgia McNair Thompson

FREEDOM

Scripture: Galatians 5:1 (NIV)
It is for freedom that Christ has set us free. Stand firm, then, and do not let yourselves be burdened again by a yoke of slavery.

If we who are in Christ are to have His glorious salvation, we must unburden ourselves of those weights that enslave us and cause us to miss out on the grace, the joy, and the freedom of the Christian life. We must give up whatever endangers our relationship with God. We must learn to consciously put aside our old nature and put on the new nature that is found in Christ.

Only when we are willing to throw off those things that hinder and the sins that entangle us, are we truly free. God is in the business of freedom and newness. When we acknowledge our past and confess our sins then are we able to begin to experience His liberty.

Prayer: Father, I want to be free. I hand myself into your care and keeping. Amen.

Georgia McNair Thompson

COMPLAINT OR JOY?

Scripture: Numbers 11:4-6 (KJV)
And the mixed multitude that was among them fell a-
lusting: and the children of Israel also wept again, and
said, Who shall give us flesh to eat? We remember the
fish, which we did eat in Egypt freely; the cucumbers,
and the melons, and the leeks, and the onions, and the
garlic: But now our soul is dried away: there is nothing
at all, beside this manna, before our eyes.

Quite often we are unhappy because our focus is on what we do not have rather than on what we have. The Israelites did not look at the fact that God had set them free and that he provided for them while they wandered in the wilderness. All they could think about was the food they had left behind in Egypt. They completely forgot the cruelty they had suffered at the hands of the Egyptians. How often do we find ourselves complaining about what we do not have, rather than thinking about all of the marvelous things God has given us? If we spent less time complaining and more time being grateful, our lives would be much happier. We should be grateful that God has provided us with food, shelter, family, health, and friends. The next time you have the urge to complain, stop and find a quiet place to meditate on what God has done for you. Write down your blessings. You will soon discover that your words of complaints will turn to words of joy.

Prayer: Give me a heart of gratitude, dear God. Amen.

Georgia McNair Thompson

July 27

PRAISE YE THE LORD

Scripture: Psalm 107:21 (KJV)
Oh that men would praise the Lord for his goodness, and for his wonderful works to the children of men!

When I think about the goodness of the Lord and His kindness towards me, my soul rejoices in humble praise. How excellent are the ways of the Lord. His works are manifest from generation to generation. His love is unsearchable towards His creation. How good it is to sing praises to the God of the universe. In Him there is liberty and freedom forevermore. From the rising of the sun, to the going down of the same, His name is worthy to be praised.

He is clothed with honor and majesty. He rides upon the wings of the wind and makes the clouds His chariots. He covers Himself with light as with a garment and He stretches out the heavens like a curtain. Oh magnify the Lord, for He is greatly to be praised.

Give thanks unto the Lord; for He is good and His mercy endureth forever.

Prayer: My Lord, you are worthy of all the praise and adoration. It is in you that I live, move, and have my being. I will lift up my voice and praise your name forever. Amen.

Janice McMillian

GRACE IN THE MIDST OF THE FIRE

Scripture: Daniel 3:25 (KJV)
He answered and said, Lo, I see four men loose, walking in the midst of the fire, and they have no hurt; and the form of the fourth is like the Son of God.

Surprise was the emotion Nebuchadnezzar must have felt upon viewing the flame that was ignited to cause destruction. He had just thrown the three Hebrew boys into the pit of fire because they refused to bow and call Him Lord. But, when he looked in, he noticed a fourth figure not handled previously by human hands. It was something different about that fourth figure. It radiated above the flames causing Nebuchadnezzar to compare it to the Son of God. Astonished, he called them out of the fire and from that point on, worshipped and bowed to their God and King.

When we go through life's fiery trials and tribulations, we can be assured that the Son of God is going through the situation with us. It may not appear or even feel like He is with us, but this Scripture certainly gives credence that our advocate is a present help in the time of trouble.

If you are going through a fiery furnace situation, God is with you and will never leave or forsake you. He does His best work in the heat of the flame.

Prayer: Father, your Word proves that you are a timely God. Even when it looks and feels bad, you are there to comfort and rescue me from my enemies. Amen.

Janice McMillian

NEVER GIVE UP

Scripture: Ezra 4:4, 5 (NIV)
Then the peoples around them set out to discourage the people of Judah and make them afraid to go on building. They hired counselors to work against them and frustrate their plans during the entire reign of Cyrus king of Persia and down to the reign of Darius king of Persia.

 Have you ever felt like giving up? If you have, then you have something in common with the people of Judah. Judah was commissioned to rebuild the temple. After having received that instruction, they were submitted to the task ahead of them. But, something occurred along the way— outsiders began to interfere and frustrate their resolve to finish. Does this sound familiar?

 Many times our hearts are committed to carrying out what God has called us to do. We take on the assignment with enthusiasm and proceed fervently. But after awhile, we run into strong and consistent opposition. It slowly pinches at our resolve, not totally overtaking us, but enough to frustrate our purpose. It is almost synonymous to a helium balloon. Over time the balloon slowly looses air, causing it to be ineffective in its original purpose.

 If this is where you are today, know that God has a plan and purpose for your life. Nothing, absolutely nothing, can interfere with your appointment with destiny.

Prayer: Lord, I sometimes get frustrated with the everyday nuisances of life. Help me to hold on to the divine promises in your Word. Amen.

Janice McMillian

July 30

FIERY TRIAL OF FAITH

Scripture: 1 Peter 1:7 (KJV)
*That the trial of your faith, being much more precious
than of gold that perisheth, though it be tried with fire,
might be found unto praise and honour and glory at the
appearing of Jesus Christ:*

The word "faith" is recorded in the Bible 246 times.
In the book of Hebrews alone, it is recorded 30 times. Faith
is the belief or trust in someone or something greater than
ourselves. God has commanded that we have faith in Him.
He even goes further to say that without faith, it is impossible
to please Him. This suggests that in order to get His
attention, our faith must be alive and active.

If faith is important to God, then it is understandable
that it is also important to our adversary the devil. He
realizes that once we step out into the atmosphere where
faith dwells, then he can no longer attack and assault our
minds with doubt and discouragement. God has warned his
children to expect such assaults. Even though our faith may
wane, the Word of God promises victorious results, if we
believe.

Prayer: Heavenly Father, you declare in your Word that you
are the author and finisher of my faith. Help me to walk in
the knowledge that whatever happens in my life, you will
sustain me to a glorious end so that I might walk by faith and
not by sight. Amen.

Janice McMillian

July 31

August

*Beloved, if God so loved us, we
ought also to love one another.*
1 John 4:11

Eastern West Africa Episcopal District
Table Of Contents

BLESSINGS UNREALIZED

Scripture: Luke 15:31 (AMP)
And the father said to him, Son, you are always with me, and all that is mine is yours.

Many Christians do not realize the blessings they have from God. When they do not understand their correct position, they can neither see the glorious handiwork of God nor hear His Word.

Once there lived a little child who fell ill at birth. As a result of the illness, the child lost her sight and sense of hearing. The mother had to do everything for the child. Because of this situation, the child did not receive the mother's acts of kindness as her mother's love—they were taken as necessities of life. The child did not recognize the blessings she received as such.

Similarly, the elder son in the parable of the prodigal son did not realize his earthly father's blessings and love for him. He could not understand why the father would bless his unfaithful brother in a manner that the father had never blessed him. The father had to declare, "Son, all that is mine is yours," in order for the elder son to grasp the reality that his father's blessings were there for the taking.

God's abundant blessings belong to His children, yet the spiritually blind and deaf Christian is not in position to realize this. God's spiritually disabled children will always take their Father's blessings for granted.

Prayer: God, help me to remember each day the price Christ paid to give me many blessings. Amen.

Mary Hope

August 1

STEWARDSHIP

Scripture: Matthew 25:21 (KJV)
His Lord said unto him, Well done, thou good and faithful servant: thou hast been faithful over a few things, I will make thee ruler over many things: enter thou into the joy of thy Lord.

Most people do not like to take responsibility—they want to avoid giving account of their stewardship. Some take responsibility but dodge accountability. The Bible tells us the story of a master who went on a journey and gave his servants some talents to use. The story helps us to know how the wise servants used their talents. The master blessed and rewarded those who used their talents judiciously. On the other hand, he cursed the foolish servant, took his talent and gave it to one of the other servants.

As Christians, we must try to make use of our talents. We must use them to God's glory rather than bury them in our own irresponsibility. When we use our talents, God's commendation will be our reward.

Prayer: Our most gracious Father, help me to identify my talents and to make good use of them to your glory. Amen.

Patience N. Udechuku

EXCHANGE FOR LIFE

Scripture: Exodus 30:16 (KJV)
And thou shalt take the atonement money of the children of Israel, and shalt appoint it for the service of the tabernacle of the congregation, that it may be a memorial unto the children of Israel before the Lord, to make an atonement for your souls.

God asked Moses to take the census of the children of Israel. Everyone counted, both rich and poor, was to give an offering not less than half a shekle (ten Gerahs) for atonement for their souls.

Jesus is the atonement for our souls, but God still expects us to participate in His offering. It is through our giving that God is able to provide for our lives. This is the principle of sowing and reaping. If we sow in good ground, we will reap a good harvest. Galatians 6:8 says, . . . *he that soweth to the Spirit shall of the Spirit reap life everlasting.* We will be beneficiaries of the fruit of the Spirit, Galatians 5:22-23. Our lives and our properties will be well protected, even from devourers, Malachi 3:10-11. So, . . . *let us not be weary in well doing: for in due season we shall reap, if we faint not.* Galatians 6:9.

Prayer: Lord, help me to give liberally to you that I might be eligible for your higher calling now and always. Amen.

Inemesit Ebito

GOD'S LOVE

Scripture: Ephesians 2:4 (KJV)
But God, who is rich in mercy, for his great love wherewith he loved us,

When I imagine what God looks like, He appears incomprehensible. When I see my reflection in a mirror, I see one created by God in His own image and I come to appreciate God's love and care for man. Man provokes God, but God still loves and cares for us.

God allowed His Son to come to earth in human form that we might have everlasting life. Jesus passed through the odds of life and finally died a humiliating death on the cross of Calvary for man's sake. This practical demonstration of love shows how God loves man, John 3:16.

Man is God's vessel and for God to fulfill His mission, we must allow God's love and care to be shown through us as we serve others. It takes God's love to win the world.

Prayer: Father God, I know that I do not deserve your loving kindness for the precious blood shed on Calvary. Help me to share your love with others thereby drawing nearer to you. Amen.

Patience N. Udechuku

SELFLESS SERVICES

Scripture: Matthew 16:25 (NIV)
For whoever wants to save his life will lose it, but whoever loses his life for me will find it.

There was a woman named Sister Ruth who once said that in her daily service to God, she felt she was not doing enough to satisfy God. She felt this way because it appeared to her that she was only achieving her own self-satisfaction. These acts included fasting and praying for her health and salvation, singing, and seeking the blessings of God. She therefore decided to reach out to others by sharing the Word of God, caring for the aged, feeding the poor, and clothing the naked. According to her, serving others made her feel more like she was satisfying God.

We must remember that it is more blessed to give than to receive. We ought to form the habit of looking out for others. Serving others does not always mean giving material possessions. We render service to others when we remember them in prayers, visit the lonely, comfort the depressed, and teach the less privileged. When we do this, we are equally rendering service to God. He who sees the sincerity of the heart will reward us abundantly.

Prayer: Lord, help me to understand those things I ought to do to serve you and humanity in Jesus' name. Amen.

Dorathy Eze

August 5

GOD'S SIGNET

Scripture: Haggai 2:23 (KJV)
In that day, saith the Lord of hosts, will I take thee, O Zerubbabel, my servant, the son of Shealtiel, saith the Lord, and will make thee as a signet: for I have chosen thee, saith the Lord of hosts.

The children of Israel had abandoned the completion of the temple in favor of building their own homes and God was not pleased. God spoke through the prophet, Haggai, to Zerubabel, saying that he had been chosen to act on God's behalf to get the people to complete the building of the temple. God chose Zerubabel to be His signet bearer and entrusted him with kingdom authority. A signet was a royal seal used to authenticate any document. The bearers of a signet had to be carefully selected because they were entrusted with royal authority. Zerubabel successfully completed his assignment and found favor with God.

In this dispensation, all Christians have been chosen to be signet bearers. The Christian's assignment is to complete the ministry of reconciliation. We have been given God's authority as ambassadors of Christ, to witness and cause the world to take up their cross, deny themselves, and follow Christ

Prayer: Seal me, O God, with your Holy Spirit that I may witness for you. Amen.

Ethel Igbagiri

DOING GOOD ALL THE TIME

Scripture: Mark 3:4 (KJV)
And he saith unto them, Is it lawful to do good on the sabbath days, or to do evil? to save life, or to kill? But they held their peace.

I used to think that the good you do on Sunday carried more weight than other days because it was done on the Lord's day. Jesus showed us that doing good is a twenty-four hour thing, seven days a week. It has no special time or special day. Every opportunity you have to do good, do good. We must project Jesus and His redemptive power in and out of season.

Our zeal to be like Jesus must not be poisoned by those who do not understand all Jesus endured because he was good. His life admonishes us to do good whether people praise or criticize us. Let us not relent in our effort to do good even on a Sabbath day.

Prayer: Surely, goodness and mercy shall follow me all the days of my life and I will dwell in the house of the Lord for ever. Amen.

Reverend Umoh L. Udofa *I will remember, every opportunity I get I will try with all my hart to do good*

LOOKING BEYOND WHAT YOU SEE

Scripture: Psalm 119:66 (KJV)
Teach me a good judgement and knowledge: for I have believed thy commandments.

Sometimes when faced with a dilemma, what you see in the natural seems like the answer. Yet, you hear the voice of the Lord telling you that this is not the answer. If at this point, you fail to ask God to help you look beyond the natural and yield to His voice, you will assuredly make a mess.

Samuel was faced with this dilemma when he set out to anoint the next king of Israel. Samuel was sure that Jesse's oldest son, Eliab, was the next king, but God had rejected him. Samuel was looking at Eliab's outward appearance.

We must include God in our daily decision making. When looking for people to head offices in the church, we should look beyond their fine suits and persuasive speech to examine the fruit in their life. Yielding to God will always lead to the right choice.

Prayer: Order my steps, Oh Lord, so that I may not stumble and be a disgrace to you. Open my spiritual eyes that I might see your answer to every situation. Amen.

Esther Ebinyasi lord help me not to look out of my natural eye when I am face with that seam impossible.

August 8

BE THANKFUL

Scripture: 1 Chronicles 29:13 (KJV)
Now therefore, our God, we thank thee, and praise thy glorious name.

David wanted to build a house for the Lord. During the planning and brainstorming period, he stopped to give thanks to God for having the opportunity to build the Lord's house.

No matter what project you have been assigned to undertake, you must first be grateful to God, who gave you the opportunity. As Christians, we must reflect a spirit of gratefulness. This gratefulness will come from being used as an instrument to do God's Work. It is reinforced through our commitment to the assignment.

As you prepare to work on your next project or assignment, stop and thank God for instilling in you all that you will need to complete the assignment. Thank Him for the opportunity to bring glory and honor to His Kingdom by using you as His chosen vessel.

Prayer: Oh Lord, our heavenly Father, deliver me from the spirit of ingratitude and help me to witness through thanksgiving to the people around me in Jesus' name. Amen.

Dorathy Anderson

August 9

Scripture: John 9:5 (KJV)
As long as I am in the world, I am the light of the world.

God called the church to be a body of true believers and to be the light of the world. Where a true church exists works of darkness such as immoral acts or works of the flesh are eradicated.

Our Lord teaches us that the mission of the church is to be a light and has equipped the church with everything it needs to be that light. When the church ceases to shine for the Lord, it automatically losses its power to end the works of darkness.

Prayer: Father, let my light so shine before men so that they may see my good work and glorify you in Heaven. Amen.

Arit Jimmy Essien

BELIEVER'S LIFE

Scripture: John 15:1, 2 (KJV)
I am the true vine, and my Father is the husbandman. Every branch in me that beareth not fruit he taketh away: and every branch that beareth fruit, he purgeth it, that it may bring forth more fruit.

It is one thing to believe that Jesus Christ is the Son of God, but it is equally important to admit and confess our sins and heed His plea to follow. The Lord knows those who follow Him by their fruit. Joining the church or becoming a member of any church society does not equate to abiding in Him.

The branch cannot bear fruit of itself except it abides in the vine, and every branch in Him that does not bear fruit He takes away. Every branch that bears fruit, He purges it so that it may bring forth more fruit.

To those that abide in Him and are bearing fruit, we are now to go and teach all nations, baptizing them in the name of the Father, and of the Son, and of the Holy Ghost. Teaching them to observe all things whatsoever God has commanded.

Prayer: Father God, help me to abide in you and may I be purged to bear fruit that will bring more souls to your Kingdom. Amen.

Arit Jimmy Essien

HOW OLD SHALL YOU BE?

Scripture: Jeremiah 1:7 (NIV)
But the Lord said to me, "Do not say, 'I am only a child.'
You must go to everyone I send you to and say whatever
I command you."

There is an important role for the youth in the task of taking the world for Christ. Jeremiah, like Samuel, was called as a child to go and say to Jerusalem, "Thus says the Lord... "

The Lord continues searching for young hearts to plant His message and young mouths to fill with His Word for the world and the church.

According to Jeremiah 1:17, young people must be ready to gird up their loins, arise and say everything that the Lord commands. The Lord spoke the following to Jeremiah in his youth: *See, today I appoint you over nations and over kingdoms, to uproot and tear down, to destroy and overthrow, to build and to plant.* See Jeremiah 1:10. God further says in Jeremiah 1:19, . . . *they shall fight against thee; but they shall not prevail against thee; for I am with thee, saith the Lord, to deliver thee.*

If anyone asks how old shall you be respond, "I am the right age."

Prayer: O Lord, let not my youth make me deaf to your call or timid to proclaim your message. Amen.

Obot Francis Williams

August 12

VERIFY YOUR COMMISSION

Scripture: Exodus 3:13 (KJV)
And Moses said unto God, Behold, when I come unto the children of Israel, and shall say unto them, The God of your fathers hath sent me unto you; and they shall say to me, What is his name? What shall I say unto them?

Before Moses received his commission he thoroughly ascertained who commissioned him to deliver Israel from the land of bondage. Throughout his mission, Moses acted with confidence, certainty, and authority because he had sufficient knowledge and full proof of his God.

In Judges Chapter six, we read also about Gideon's call to deliver Israel from the hand of the Midians. Gideon displayed authority and courage only after conclusive verification of his call and proof of the God who called him.

The Lord will not get angry if we earnestly seek confirmation from Him of our call and clear assurance of His presence in our endeavors to spread the gospel. God would not have His children ignorant. In the Old Testament God's people looked for signs of God's presence; Moses had the burning bush, Gideon used the wet grass/dry ground fleece. Today, we have God's Spirit dwelling on the inside to lead and guide us to all truths. We must use God's Word to confirm His directions to us.

After receiving confirmation, we must then walk in full assurance of that call and trust that God will lead us every step of the way, as He led Moses and Gideon.

Prayer: Father, clarify my assignment and let me know I am equipped to accomplish the task. Amen.

Grace Eyewan

August 13

IDENTIFY YOUR GIFT

Scripture: 1 Corinthians 12:7 (KJV)
But the manifestation of the Spirit is given to every man to profit withal.

A young man by the name of Prosper was discovered by his Pastor at a tender age as being hardworking and submissive. Prosper was always willing to do anything without being asked. He would come to the Pastor's house every Saturday to see whether the lawn needed to be mowed or if the pews in the church needed to be polished. He volunteered to drive the guests around during conferences or conventions. He did all this with a broad smile on his face humming the song "Take My Life and Let It Be."

God never gives a person a task without providing the tools for it. According to W. W. Dawley, "God gave Moses a rod, David a sling, Samson the jawbone of a donkey, Shamgar an Oxgoad, Esther the beauty of person, Deborah the talent for poetry, Dorcas a needle, Apollos an eloquent tongue, and to each the ability to use the gift. In so doing, everyone of them did most effective works for the Lord."

The Lord has provided us with all kinds of spiritual gifts. It is left to us to use these gifts to bless the church amd to be a channel of blessing to others around us so that we would be blessed.

Prayer: Take my life and let it be consecrated, Lord to you. Amen.

Ifeoma Onyeyiri

THE CANDID CAMERA

Scripture: John 1:47 (KJV)
Jesus saw Nathanael coming to him, and saith of him, Behold an Israelite indeed, in whom is no guile!

As a school guidance counselor, I have observed students with different personalities. There is the personality where a student presents himself as a good child in front of his parents; then in another way to please his peer group; and finally, there is the real person. If this student cannot manage the three personalities, it will boomerang in the adolescent stage into what we call the stormy stage.

This Christian journey does not need multiple personalities. Too many talk about folks in the morning and shout "Praise the Lord," in the evening. Let your life be a living testimony all of the time. Let us be a mirror where others will look and see Jesus. Let your light shine, let it shine, let it shine, let it shine.

Prayer: Lord, let me be a living witness for others to see and glorify your name always. Amen.

Faustina Ife Ekemam

PLAY YOUR PART

Scripture: Acts 9:15 (KJV)
But the Lord said unto him, Go thy way: for he is a chosen vessel unto me, to bear my name before the Gentiles, and kings, and the children of Israel:

"Saul, the Lord Jesus . . . has sent me that you may regain your sight," said Ananias, who was sent by the Lord to aid Saul. Saul had just completed a mission to destroy the Christians. God chooses the vessels to use. He assigns the parts we will play. Who would have ever thought Saul, later named Paul, would have served God the way he did. Saul was a persecutor of Christians. Then God touched him, which changed everything.

When God has chosen you, you must accept the part assigned. The society or department where you belong has a mission that needs you. You have a part to play in the fulfilling of the Mission. You may not be the head of the society or department, but you are commissioned to make the body a whole.

Fulfilling the Mission requires all working together in the direction of the goal. When we do not get involved it only delays Kingdom building.

Prayer: Lord, help me to identify, accept and appreciate the part you assigned to me. If I cannot be the instrument, make me a suitable support to the one chosen. Amen.

Eunice E. Isong

BELIEVER'S EXERCISE

Scripture: John 15:5 (KJV)
I am the vine, ye are the branches: He that abideth in me, and I in him, the same bringeth forth much fruit: for without me ye can do nothing.

The work of preaching and teaching the Gospel and adding new souls to the faith is a continuous exercise for the believer. In order to succeed in this duty, Christ must be magnified in our lives. *According to my earnest expectation and my hope, that in nothing I shall be ashamed, but that with all boldness, as always, so now also Christ shall be magnified in my body, whether it be by life, or by death.* Philippians 1:20.

The meaningful part of the exercise is the believer setting the Lord before him. Psalm 16:8 says, *I have set the Lord always before me: because he is at my right hand, I shall not be moved.* This exercise requires us to get right and stay right with God, for without God we can do nothing."

Prayer: Father God, help me to serve you in Spirit and truth so that my life, teaching, and preaching may add new souls daily to the fold, in Jesus' Name I pray. Amen.

Arit Jimmy Essien

WORSHIP HIM

Scripture: James 4:8 (KJV)
*Draw nigh to God, and he will draw nigh to you.
Cleanse your hands, ye sinners; and purify your hearts,
you double minded.*

There are questions as to how we should worship God. Some prefer to sing just hymns and not choruses, while others like to hear the Scriptures and sermons and to pray only. Others do not want to be bothered at all. They come and worship the Lord their own way and leave quietly. One thing we dare not overlook in our disagreements about worship is that God demands praise always. There is no bargaining about it. *Let everything that hath breath praise the Lord. Praise ye the Lord.* Psalm 150:6.

In the Old Testament the privilege of worshipping God was reserved for the priesthood. The principle still remains that only those who are pure in heart can move into the holy place of worship and fellowship together in spirit and truth. However, God has provided Jesus that we might be cleansed. God sees us through the Blood of Jesus, so now all those covered with the Blood of Jesus are entitled to the privilege of worshipping the Almighty, Everlasting God.

Prayer: Lord, please give me a clean heart that I may worship you in my lifetime. Amen.

Faustina I. Ekemam

THE EVALUATION

Scripture: John 21:17 (KJV)
He saith unto him the third time, Simon, son of Jonas, lovest thou me? Peter was grieved because he said unto him the third time, lovest thou me? And he said unto him, Lord, thou knowest all things; thou knowest that I love thee. Jesus saith unto him, Feed my sheep.

Peter was asked three times if he loved Jesus. It had gotten to the point that Peter was offended. There was a reason for asking the question over and over. Sometimes we need to be tested. We need to evaluate what we say against what we do. God wanted to know how committed Simon Peter was in Kingdom building. God decided to give Peter an evaluation on patience, long-suffering and dedication. Even though, Simon Peter almost lost his cool, he passed the evaluation before God gave him the assignment of feeding His sheep.

Jesus wanted to make sure that Peter would not say one thing with his mouth and act differently. All our works must be tried before we can withstand an evaluation.

Before we enter the mission field we should take an evaluation to ensure that we can carry out the great commission. If the mission field is your place, you will love missions, talk missions, and act missions.

Prayer: Father Almighty, I humbly beseech you to help me recognize the importance of individuals in world missions. Help me to reach the masses by lifting Jesus up in my life. Amen.

Iquo Otu Bassey

August 19

A THORN IN MY SIDE

Scripture: 2 Corinthian 12:7 (KJV)
And lest I should be exalted above measure through the abundance of the revelations, there was given to me a thorn in the flesh . . .

My next door neighbor was cutting a mango tree close to his house. He cut it so far down to the stump that its growing back again was written off. I felt real bad because this tree produces the most delicious, big mango fruits. I asked him why he cut the tree. He answered, "Believe it or not, it is too close to my bedroom window and it disturbs my sleep." But to my great surprise, by next rainy season, it was all covered with green leaves again. So my neighbor got frustrated and let it alone.

Like my neighbor who viewed that tree as an irritant, there are things in our lives that we see as irritants. But God has put them in our lives for a purpose. We may not see or understand the purpose, but until it is fulfilled, we should not try to remove them—God only allows them to come back.

Prayer: Lord, help me to lean on you when the going gets tough. Amen.

Affiong I. J. Akpan

WATCH YOUR STEP

Scripture: Leviticus 10:3 (KJV)
Then Moses said unto Aaron, This is that the Lord spake, saying, I will be sanctified in them that come nigh me, and before all the people I will be glorified. And Aaron held his peace.

Leviticus Chapter 10 speaks against both moral and spiritual laxity. We read about Priests who were threatened with death if they were not well groomed or stayed away from the tabernacle. People dropped dead for not worshipping correctly. Yet today, people come to church dressed any way. They smoke and do other things on the church premises. This new laxity may bring a measure of happiness and joy for a moment, but before God, those things are sinful or as filthy rags. We are to have holy conduct before God, for He is Holy. Without God's holiness, our worship is mere trash.

A British Theologian, P. T. Forsyth once wrote, "Sin is but the defiance of God's holiness, grace is but its action upon sin, the cross is but its victory, and faith is but its worship." As believers in Jesus, we must remain reverent before Him.

Prayer: Lord, help me to refrain from sin so that I can join the angels to sing holy, holy, holy. Amen.

Reverend Umoh L. Udofa

POWER OF PRAYER

Scripture: James 5:16 (KJV)
Confess your faults one to another, and pray one for another, that ye may be healed. The effectual fervent prayer of a righteous man availeth much.

Two children were friends. One was a powerful prayer warrior while the other was weak in prayer. One day the mother of the girl weak in prayer was sick. The sick mother called her daughter near to her bed and asked her daughter to pray for her. The girl prayed citing her inadequacy, "Lord, you know that I don't take prayer seriously. But now, Lord, kindly hear my request and heal my mother because she is my only hope." God, being very merciful, heard her prayer and healed her mother. After that experience the girl saw the need for cultivating a strong prayer life.

Prayer requires reverence, commitment, and dedication. If you have these three prerequisites, you can ask anything and it will be granted unto you. That is why the children of God are encouraged to pray because prayer changes things. Pray when things are good and pray when things are bad.

Prayer: Father, prayer is my way of communicating with you. Keep my heart always in a position to pray and give me the desire to pray. Amen.

Patricia Yellow

GIVING IS LOVE

Scripture: John 3:16 (KJV)
For God so loved the world that He gave His only begotten Son, that whosoever believeth in him should not perish, but have everlasting life.

An old widow, whose only son declared his obedience to God's call to the mission field, became upset reasoning that the boy would be her helper as she grew older. Later, John 3:16 changed her outlook, catching her attention in a way it never had. The thought came to her to reciprocate God's gift of salvation. She would release her son to heed his calling. The highest expression of love is found in giving. We could not experience His love towards us without His wonderful gift to mankind. This should prompt us to reciprocate by giving the gift of Jesus to all we meet.

Prayer: Lord, help me to follow your footsteps of love. Amen.

Dorathy Eze

GREAT PROVIDER

Scripture: Matthew 6:31, 32 (NIV)
So do not worry, saying, 'What shall we eat?' or 'What shall we drink?' or 'What shall we wear?' For the pagans run after all these things, and your heavenly Father knows that you need them.

Human nature being what it is, we tend to worry. We worry about the necessary and the unnecessary to no avail. Our worrying does not provide us a solution to what we are worrying about. In Isaiah the Lord reminds Israel that He had been carrying them from their birth. See Isaiah 46:3, 4.

Children of God need to understand that God, who created us, knows our needs and cares for us. God has never made a promise that He did not keep. His Word is faithful. Trust Him and it shall be well with you. Let God do the thinking and worrying for you.

Prayer: Lord God, you are my provider. I have no need that you have not provided for. You are my Bread of Heaven and you feed me until I want no more. Amen.

Justina Ekpeowo

FACE THE CHALLENGE

Scripture: Luke 18:29, 30 (NIV)
"I tell you the truth," Jesus said to them, "no one who has left home or wife or brothers or parents or children for the sake of the kingdom of God will fail to receive many times as much in this age and, in the age to come, eternal life."

Former President Nixon once said, "He who is on the mountain does not know what the person in the valley is going through until you come down to the valley." Some self-sufficient individuals are so comfortable where they are that they are not willing to leave their comfort zone for the sake of the Gospel. They are apathetic to the suffering of others. They are neither willing or ready to sacrifice their time and financial resources for their brothers and sisters.

Each new day should be a day of challenge and opportunity. It is a day to challenge our faith by trusting God in new areas and for new provisions. It is a day which provides new opportunity to grow in our relationship with God by reaching out to those less fortunate both naturally and spiritually. To take advantage of this new day we must learn to deny self. Give up some of those comforts that we have become so used to and take a stand against forces that would quench the Gospel.

Prayer: Lord, help me to be mindful of the cross and to do what is right in your sight all the days of my life. Amen.

Uduak Isong Williams

August 25

THE REAL THING

Scripture: Hebrews 4:12 (NIV)
For the word of God is living and active. Sharper than any double-edge sword, it penetrates even to dividing soul and spirit, joints and marrow; it judges the thoughts and attitudes of the heart.

I have a friend who will not take heed to the Word of God. Instead of listening to the preacher he prefers to follow his own life's experiences rather than follow God's instructions. My friend feels tired of God yet God is not tired of my friend. God even pays attention to the very air my friend breathes.

God knows our hearts, He has provided His Word to correct our hearts. We must allow the Word of God to penetrate to the dividing of the soul and spirit so that our attitudes will be corrected. We cannot allow ourselves to tire of that which gives us life. We think that we have heard this before so we have no need to listen to the preacher. God's Word is real; it is alive; and it is inexhaustible. God is able to do exceedingly, abundantly more than we could ever imagine if we will allow Him.

Prayer: Lord, renew me, help me to take advantage of your Word and feed on it for my daily nourishment. Amen.

Grace Eyeanwan

FORGIVENESS

Scripture: Matthew 6:14 (KJV)
For if ye forgive men their trespasses, your heavenly Father will also forgive you: But if ye forgive not men their trespasses, neither will your Father forgive your trespasses.

When I was a child growing up, I was taught by my Sunday School teacher that if I have a grudge against my brother or friend and refuse to forgive and make up with him, God will not forgive my sin. I have since then lived with that concept and have found it very beneficial. It is healthy to forgive. It purges the mind and gives peace to the soul. You feel free physically and spiritually.

Whenever you find yourself offended by someone, be quick to forgive, and take it one step further—forget the offense, for God is quick to forgive us of our transgressions against Him, and He remembers them no more.

Prayer: Lord, keep me in remembrance that no greater offense was suffered than that suffered by Jesus on the cross for me. He who was without sin took on my sin that I might be reconciled back to you. Father, I ask for a clean heart toward my brothers and sisters, so that as I follow you, I will serve them. Amen.

Grace Ufot

SAY IT LOUD

Scripture: Proverbs 19:5 (NIV)
A false witness will not go unpunished, and he who pours out lies will not go free.

It is often said that you can fool most people most of the time, but we cannot allow that to make us believe that we can ever fool God. He is omniscient, omnipresent, and omnipotent. He hears all we say and sees all we do, therefore we should be honest with Him. After all He knows everything. We begin being honest with God by being honest with ourselves.

If honesty begins at home that means we must learn to see our own faults rather than the faults of others. When we think our actions are not so bad as compared to our neighbors or that God is pleased with us when we know that we are not following God's Word, we are being deceived. It is a self-perpetuating deception—we fool ourselves. Truth is bittersweet but it is precious. It is through truth that we gain our freedom. Allow truth to reign loudly in your life and in your witness to gain freedom.

Prayer: Father, I give you control of my lips and my mind. Help me to make an accurate assessment of who I am, my attitudes and actions that I might serve you in truth and honesty. Amen.

Boyne Fyncountry

LAUNCH OUT INTO THE DEEP

Scripture: Luke 5:4 (KJV)
Now when he had left speaking, he said unto Simon, Launch out into the deep, and let down your nets for a draught.

What disappointment the disciples must have felt after spending all night long toiling on the sea, to no avail, still unable to hook a fish. This was their craft, and the substance of their livelihood—no fish, no income. They were no doubt at their human wall of limitation—probably ready to give in and quit. Much like most of us. But, at the point when it seemed hopeless, Jesus stepped in.

That is the kind of God we serve. He always steps in on time. When we are at a point where we can no longer see what is ahead of us and disappointment is about to encompass our mind and soul, Jesus provides a way. He told the disciples to launch out into the deep and let down their nets. He used that circumstance to bless them. Jesus' message to us in this Scripture is when all seems dismal and unattainable, I can still work a miracle.

When they let down their nets, they were abundantly blessed. The net was overflowing with fish. They relinquished all human effort and depended on the sovereignty of God. Jesus was teaching the disciples the principles of faith. Believe the impossible. What are you believing God for? Launch out into the deep and let your net down.

Prayer: Father, continue to build my faith up even in the midst of the most difficult circumstances. Amen.

Janice McMillian

August 29

LAYING A SOLID FOUNDATION

Scripture: Proverbs 22:6 (KJV)
Train up a child in the way he should go: and when he is old, he will not depart from it.

The nation's headlines today speak of shocking deeds being carried out by our teenagers. Killings and other forms of destruction have escalated to an all time high. What do these children know about violence and its affect? How is such a callous mind formed? Seemingly, we think we have the solutions, but never do we actually deal with the real reasons behind such atrocities. We demand more metal detectors in the schools, armed guards, and gun control. But is that really what we need?

The Bible has given us clear instructions as to the development of a sane and moral society. We look for the answers, but never really consider the source. God tells us in His Word to train, mold, develop, instruct, and teach our children about Him in the formative years. When we instill the Word of God in their hearts and minds and walk uprightly before them, they are able to choose life. No matter what situations come their way, they will have the foundation that will never fail.

Prayer: Lord, I submit my children unto you. Before they were formed you knew who they were and what they would become in the earth. Help me to become a more positive influence in their life. Amen.

Janice McMillian

August 30

THE GOOD FRUIT OF WORK

Scripture: 2 Chronicles 15:7 (KJV)
Be ye strong therefore, and let not your hands be weak: for your work shall be rewarded.

Many times the saints of God get weary and laden down in the everyday demands of life. Where once there was an appreciation for the nine to five job, we now find ourselves tired, overworked, and unfulfilled. The industrious attitude of early years has now been replaced with a rat race mentality. The only incentive to work is the bi-weekly paycheck.

God ordained in the very beginning that work was good. Since we are made in His likeness, this should also be our attitude toward work. We tend to associate what we do with whom we are doing it for. In seeing it from that perspective, it is understandable why we would be weary. But God, who is rich in mercy, has proclaimed that if we would only be strong in whatever we put our hands to, our work would be rewarded.

God wants us to take comfort in knowing that as we work to His glory and honor, we work to build the Kingdom of God here on earth. The physical movement of paper is inconsequential as compared to the bold statement we make as we joyfully work unto the Lord.

Prayer: Lord Jesus, help me to be mindful of who I work for. You are my Alpha and Omega, the Beginning and the End. Everything that I do starts and ends with you. Amen.

Janice McMillian

August 31

September

Put on therefore, as the elect of God, holy and beloved, bowels of mercies, kindness, humbleness of mind, meekness, longsuffering; Forbearing one another, and forgiving one another, if any man have a quarrel against any: even as Christ forgave you, so also do ye.

Colossians 3:12, 13

Western West Africa Episcopal District
Table Of Contents

PARENTS' PARENTS

Scripture: 2 Timothy 1:5 (NRS)
I am reminded of your sincere faith, a faith that lived first in your grandmother Lois and your mother Eunice and now, I am sure, lives in you.

They are back-up caretakers, vessels of wisdom, and transmitters of faith, history and heritage. They have been there with open arms for extra hugs, and undivided attention. "Nana," "Paw-Paw," "Big-Ma," "Grand Dad," and many other names identify the parents of parents. Revered are the sainted people we call grandparents.

Our grandparents have been the connecting link to our spiritual growth and development. They rest in the wisdom and faith of Almighty God—our ultimate Parent. God in His infinite wisdom would so have it that these treasures would be available to care for His little ones and enhance His earthly kingdom through their patience, insight, unconditional love, and support.

We pay special tribute to these unsung heroes and heroines whose mid-years and retirement years—the fun years, are freely given to help nurture, teach, and raise so many of their grandchildren to walk with and put their faith in a never failing God.

Prayer: Thank you, God, for the comfort and strength found in our grandparents that so often makes the difference in who we are and who we can become. Amen.

Aurelia S. Brown

September 1

THE WORD

Scripture: 2 Timothy 3:16, 17 (KJV)
All scripture is given by inspiration of God, and is profitable for doctrine, for reproof, for correction, for instruction in righteousness: That the man of God may be perfect, thoroughly furnished unto all good works.

Children, youth, and adults are in continuous stages of natural and spiritual growth. Our willingness to avail ourselves to countless opportunities to learn determines our success in life.

As Christians, we can rely on the Word of God to guide us through the daily trials and triumphs of life. This instructional guide for Christian living and spiritual growth informs and inspires every age.

If we heed God's Word, we are challenged to be open to His wisdom, knowledge, and understanding. Our paths are charted and we are guided into spirit-filled, productive living. Our lives then become examples for others. Our homes, our communities, and our world become better places for all. As Christians, our lives should be living examples of Kingdom living right here on Earth.

Prayer: Dear Lord, open my mind and my heart to your Word. Instill in me a boundless desire for knowledge and understanding. Discipline me in ways of study and learning that I may be an example of your wisdom. With a humble heart, I pray. Amen.

Aurelia S. Brown

TEACHING

Scripture: Acts 8:31 (KJV)
And he said, How can I, except some man should guide me? . . .

Teaching is vital to the spiritual and intellectual growth and development of all human-kind. It is a gift to be shared precisely and creatively with boldness and commitment. Those who receive and respond to this gift answer the mandate of our Lord. As teachers we must become students, diligent in study, so as to be wise and clear in our imparting of the same.

Once we identify the fact that we have this gift, it is our responsibility to keep it stirred up so that Jesus would be glorified. Our ministry gift must be used for building and nurturing families, congregations, and citizens of the world at-large.

Prayer: Heavenly Father, Master Teacher, sharpen my mind, open my heart to wisdom. Bless anew those whom you have chosen to teach. May I remain humble before you and learn of you. For Christ's sake, I pray. Amen.

Elizabeth Hatchfu

September 3

REACHING OUT

Scripture: Acts 3:4-5 (KJV)
And Peter fastening his eyes upon him with John, said, look on us. And he gave heed unto them, expecting to receive something of them.

In response to the Lord's commission in Matthew 28:19, the need for the Church to reach out to get the message of God to the lost is paramount.

In Africa, illiteracy and lack of education often impedes missionary efforts. Communication is problematic. As we approach a new millennium, with the help of sophisticated communication systems and state-of-the-art equipment, rural people must be given easy access to education to equip and prepare them adequately to receive the message of Christ with understanding.

As it was when the lame man caught the attention of Peter and John, thus it is when we introduce Christianity to people; their appetites are whetted and they too expect to receive great things from us. The church, its missionaries, and evangelists can be of great service as they minister to the whole person.

Prayer: Dear Lord, as I fulfill the mission to win the world for Christ, tear down any language, education, or cultural barriers so that I may lift the Savior up for all who need Him. Amen.

Reverend Dorothy E. Dennis

September 4

MISSIONS—THE CHURCH IN ACTION

Scripture: Matthew 28:19 (KJV)
Go ye therefore, and teach all nations, baptizing them in the name of the Father, and the Son, and of the Holy Ghost:

The fulfillment of the great commission is a challenge that is met when the Church is in action. Our spiritual strength and fervor attracts those outside the Body of Christ to seek that which we have found—worshipping and praising God for the joy felt when we remember His sufferings and sacrifice for us.

The Word of God gives insight into the character and person of Jesus Christ. We are given opportunity to learn of the Master and from the Master. This realization compels us to act, to work, and to serve. Our sisters and brothers at home and overseas, the church, and community become our parish. We begin to see needs and opportunities that we had not seen before. We respond to hunger, nakedness, illiteracy, and poverty so that souls to be saved can witness a caring Father through His Body, the Church. The cycle is continuous: evangelism, education, and service intertwining and overlapping so that the great commission may be fulfilled.

Prayer: O Lord, give me strength and vision to act with boldness and power as I evangelize, educate, and serve the world for Christ. Amen.

Reverend Felicia Amoah

September 5

THE MINISTRY OF RECONCILIATION

Scripture: 2 Corinthians 5:18 (KJV)
And all things are of God, who hath reconciled us to himself by Jesus Christ, and hath given to us the ministry of reconciliation;

RECONCILIATION! To be reconciled is miraculous. Yet the miraculous will never become reality unless someone makes the first move. With whom do you need to reconcile? God—He has made the first move. That is why He sent Jesus to repair the breach between God and His creation.

The work Jesus was sent to do is finished. With reconciliation now available, we can live the life God planned for us in Him. Jesus left us responsible for sharing His ministry with others. He wants people to drink from the water of life and appoints us to be His fountain of living waters. Jesus wants His harvest to be bountiful and appoints us to be reapers. Do not let anymore time go by without committing yourself to the ministry of reconciliation.

Prayer: Father, I have been touched by the comfort of your love so let my heart agree that it is toward my brothers and sisters that I should move to tell them about Jesus and to bring them to you. Amen.

Elizabeth Djokotoe Dumashie

DO YOU HAVE A NEW NAME?

Scripture: Revelation 2:17 (NIV)
. . . To him who overcomes, I will give some of the hidden manna. I will also give him a white stone with a new name written on it, known only to him who receives it.

A few days ago, I met a lady on public transportation declaring to others that she had accepted Christ as her personal Savior. She was boasting to her two friends whom she was going out with that the "Man" she has now met is greater than the idols they are still worshipping. When I asked her name, she said she was baptized after 35 years of idol worshipping, and she decided that her new name should be Mary. She is now called Mary.

Why the name change? I am sure for that woman her name change signifies her new belief in Jesus Christ and the rejection of her past life and beliefs. A name is important. Will you let this gift of a new name change your life?

Prayer: Jesus, my God, you have given me a new name and erased all those sins that were under the old name. Now it is only your name that I trust. Amen.

Elizabeth Djkotoe Dumashie

THE ARMOUR OF GOD

Scripture: Ephesians 6:13 (KJV)
Wherefore take unto you the whole armour of God, that ye may be able to withstand in the evil day, and having done all, to stand.

Equipping oneself before undertaking an assignment is necessary. As followers of Christ, we need to equip ourselves with the spiritual armor of Christ on our Christian journey. Before a teacher goes out, the teacher must have a good knowledge of the subject matter. They must prepare a lesson plan and get the necessary materials in order to deliver the lesson in a satisfactory manner. It is the same for Christians. Before we take on any assignment for God, we must prepare ourselves. We must put on the whole armor of God.

The Apostle Paul tells us to avoid living as endorsed by the world and be transformed by the renewing of our mind to do God's perfect will. Therefore, let us stand firm with the breastplate of righteousness, with the helmet of salvation, and the sword of the Spirit which is the Word of God. We put on the armor of God through our rich devotional time with God and delving into His Word. Then we are prepared to be soldiers of Christ.

Prayer: As a soldier of Christ, I arise and put my armor on, strong in the strength which God supplies through His eternal Son, strong in the Lord of Hosts and in His Mighty Power. Amen.

Elizabeth Djokotoe Dumashie

TURN TO THE LORD: HE IS LOVE

Scripture: 1 John 4:8 (KJV)
He that loveth not knoweth not God; for God is love.

God is a God of Love. His love will never end. He has redeemed us and has given us victory over the enemy. But man has turned from God to follow his own wicked ways causing God's anger to burn against us. The Psalmist in Psalm 103:9 says that our God will not harbour His anger forever. Therefore, forsake your sins and return to the Lord today. He is our righteousness, Jehovah-Tsidkenu. Come to Jesus now. He has paid the price for our righteousness. The promise to Abraham's seed is yours now, if you repent.

Prayer: It is with my whole heart that I turn to you my God, for you are love. You have redeemed my soul and I thank you. Amen.

Love-Grace Amenuvor

September 9

RETURN TO YOUR FIRST LOVE

Scripture: Revelation 2:4-5 (NIV)
Yet I hold this against you: You have forsaken your first love. Remember the height from which you have fallen! Repent and do the things you did at first. If you do not repent, I will come to you and remove your lampstand from its place.

Do you remember your first days of salvation? Do you remember your thirst and hunger for the Word when the fire of God's Spirit overshadowed everything in your life? There is fresh fire with our first love. We need to stay on fire for Jesus by continually maintaining our first love for Him through the study of His Word and prayer.

Thessalonians 5:17 urges us to pray continually. If we pray continually, fresh fire from God will keep us close to our first love, God, and it will be manifested in our outward expression of love and compassion toward mankind.

Prayer: God of love, let your Holy Spirit recreate in me that hunger and thirst I felt in my first days of salvation. Amen.

Love-Grace Amenuvor

YOUR JOY IN THE LORD IS A SOUL WINNER

Scripture: Ephesians 5:18, 19 (KJV)
And be not drunk with wine, wherein is excess; but be filled with the spirit; Speaking to yourselves in psalms, hymns and spiritual songs making melody in your hearts to the Lord;

A happy and joyful spirit of praise is the result of being filled with the Holy Spirit. A joyful spirit of praise and worship renews the believer. It also attracts the unbeliever and makes him desire a similar experience. Does your behavior attract people to the Lord? Or do people shy away because of your fits of rage? I once read a story about a professed Christian woman who was anxious for her husband to find Christ. One day her minister spoke to her husband about his soul. The minister was shocked when the man answered that he was not particularly an irreligious man, but if Christianity should make him full of wrath like his wife, then he would have no part in it.

Brethren, you see, uncontrolled anger can mar our efforts for evangelism. Likewise, our joy, our songs of praise and worship, and our happy dispositions can win souls for God's Kingdom.

Prayer: Lord, let my life exhibit your joy and peace and draw perishing souls to you. Amen.

Love-Grace Amenuvor

September 11

MAKE USE OF YOUR TALENTS

Scripture: Matthew 25:24-25 (NIV)
Then the man who had received the one talent came. 'Master,' he said, 'I knew that you are a hard man, harvesting where you have not sown and gathering where you have not scattered seed. So I was afraid and went out and hid your talent in the ground . . .'

      Christ's servants receive gifts and talents from Him. Thus His church can identify with the parable about the servants whose master left them with talents. Upon his return, two of the servants had made good use of their talents, giving their master a return. The third servant hid his talent and his master was not pleased.

      Jesus has left gifts and talents that are necessary for His church to carry out its purpose. Some of us have taken those talents and buried them like the slothful servant. The church suffers when we bury our talents because all gifts are necessary to bring us to the unity of faith. Christ's gifts are rich and valuable. Let us not hide them away.

Prayer: Father, as you take account of my service to you and your people, it is my prayer that you would say to me, "Well done my, good and faithful servant." Amen.

Love-Grace Amenuvor

CONTROL YOUR TONGUE

Scripture: Proverbs 16:23, 24 (KJV)
The heart of the wise teacheth his mouth, and addeth learning to his lips. Pleasant words are as an honeycomb, sweet to the soul, and health to the bones.

How easy it is to hurt others with our tongue by the things we say or the way we say them. The Book of James says that a tongue is like a tiny spark, which can start a huge fire.

Think of some of the words we use that are hurtful. For example, how often do we respond sharply, mockingly, rudely, crossly, or bitterly? Sometimes when we regret making a crude remark we say, "I just said it without thinking." But if we are going to control our tongue, we must always think before we speak.

Let us be sure that we always use our tongue for good—that our words are always kind, loving, and helpful. May words of praise, never curses come from our lips. The wise man's mind guides his speech. Kind words are like dripping honey—sweetness on the tongue and health for the body.

Prayer: Father, out of the abundance of my heart my mouth speaks. Fill my heart with your precious Holy Spirit so that only love and kindness would come from my mouth. Amen.

Theresa Acolatse

BE GOOD STEWARDS OF GOD'S GRACE

Scripture: 1 Peter 4:10 (KJV)
As every man hath received the gift, even so minister the same one to another, as good stewards of the manifold grace of God.

One of the great truths of the Christian faith is that everybody has something to offer. Each person is unique; uniquely loved, and uniquely gifted.

Peter says whatever gift, not if you have a gift. He gives a lovely picture of Christians dispensing the grace of God. On a long car journey, petrol stations are very important. In the same way Christian's gifts are very important in the journey of life.

Of ourselves we have nothing to offer. However just as petrol flows through the petrol pump, so the life and power of the Holy Spirit flow through us to others.

As stewards of God Almighty, there is no limit to our resources and gifts.

Prayer: Dear God, while there is no limit to my resources as your child, let me be ever so mindful to be a wise steward over that which you have given me. Amen.

Theresa Acolatse

TRUST IN WHAT GOD CAN DO

Scripture: 1 Kings 18:21 (KJV)
And Elijah came unto all the people, and said, How long halt ye between two opinions? if the Lord be God, follow him: but if Baal, then follow him. And the people answered him not a word.

Three years after Elijah told Ahab there would be no rain, Elijah met Ahab again. In their meeting Ahab, a false prophet, blamed Elijah for the trouble Israel was having. Elijah promptly advised Ahab that it was not Elijah who was the problem but the fact that Ahab and his whole house were following Baal. Elijah presented Ahab with a challenge to see who was the True God. Ahab accepted.

All the people gathered on Mount Carmel to see whose God had real power. The test was to see which God could provide fire for the sacrifice.

While it appeared that Elijah was outnumbered by the prophets of Baal, Elijah had God's mighty power behind him. He trusted completely in what God could do.

Prayer: Lord, I confess that my faith does not measure up to that of Elijah, but I pray that my little faith grows as I trust you more and more each day. Amen.

Theresa Acolatse

September 15

BE ADAPTABLE AND SELF-DISCIPLINED

Scripture: 1 Corinthians 9:22, 23 (KJV)
To the weak became I as weak, that I might gain the weak: I am made all things to all men, that I might by all means save some. And this I do for the gospel's sake, that I might be partaker thereof with you.

Some of us adapt ourselves to others' ways of behavior and belief because we want to get along with them. We take the easy road. Others of us make no attempt to understand lifestyles different from our own. Maybe we consider them to be inferior. Paul's reason for adjusting to those who differed from him is made clear. He said he was made all things to all men so that he could save some. He adapted for the Gospel's sake.

He learned this from Jesus. When Jesus was in the earth, He became like us so that He could save us. He became like us, but He did not sin. Paul made it clear that this behavior was not to give him an excuse to sin. This approach demands self-discipline. There is no greater privilege than that of leading people to Jesus. But there is also the great responsibility of keeping our standards in order to complete successfully our task of witnessing to all.

Prayer: Father, show me how to become as those to whom I witness so that I might win some for the Gospel's sake. Amen.

Theresa Acolatse

September 16

BE HOLY IN ALL YOU DO

Scripture: 1 Peter 1:15 (KJV)
. . . as he which hath called you is holy, so be ye holy in all manner of conversation;

God wants us to be holy and to consecrate our lives to belong to Him. Left on our own, we could never become holy. But Christ, through His death on the cross, has redeemed us. He has paid the price for our sin and freed us from its power. Now, when we repent, He cleanses us from our sin and makes us holy.

A person who gets a job in a new business has to learn the office procedures of that company. Someone who marries and joins a new family has to learn the way things are done in that family. When we become Christians, we belong to God in a new way and have to learn God's way of living. Walking with God affects every area of our lives.

Prayer: Father, I am a member of a new family now. Teach me your ways that I might be pleasing in your sight. Amen.

Theresa Acolatse

KNOW THE TRUTH ABOUT JESUS

Scripture: 1 John 2:23 (KJV)
Whosoever denieth the Son, the same hath not the Father: [but] he that acknowledgeth the Son hath the Father also.

In the early church, preachers arose from time to time to teach new ideas. Some of them denied that Jesus was Christ, the Son of God. Christians were confused by these new teachings so John wrote to them about how they could distinguish true ideas from false.

Our faith is based on Jesus, who He was, and what He said and did. When a new teaching goes against Jesus, it is clearly false. We have the New Testament to help us know and understand Jesus better. We also have the Holy Spirit, who lives in our hearts guiding us into the truth.

Prayer: Lord God, I hear many different things about Jesus. Teach me by your Spirit to know the truth, so that I can remain faithful. Amen.

Theresa Acolatse

WE NEVER WORSHIP ALONE

Scripture: Revelation 7: 9, 10 (KJV)
After this I beheld, and, lo, a great multitude, which no man could number, of all nations, and kindreds, and people, and tongues, stood before the throne, and before the Lamb, clothed with white robes, and palms in their hands; And cried with a loud voice, saying, Salvation to our God which sitteth upon the throne, and unto the Lamb.

John was in exile on the island of Patmos. In a vision, he saw God sitting on a throne and Jesus at His side like a lamb killed in a sacrifice and raised to life again.

This vision helped John know that he was not really alone. He was part of a great multitude praising God and one day he would join them in praising God face to face. Whenever we pray or worship, we join millions of others, past and present, who are lifting up their voices to God. What a tremendous thought this is, especially for those who are not able to share in public worship.

Prayer: O God, as I worship you, help me realize that I am part of a great multitude on earth and in heaven who are worshipping you. Amen.

Theresa Acolatse

LET GOD PURIFY YOU

Scripture: Psalm 24:3, 4 (KJV)

Who shall ascend into the hill of the Lord? or who shall stand in his holy place? He that hath clean hands and a pure heart; who hath not lifted up his soul unto vanity, nor sworn deceitfully.

If we take a pair of shoes to the shoe repair or clothes to the dressmaker to be mended, we often ask whether they are worth repairing. The craftsman will look at them and picture what they will be like when he has finished working on them. He then decides whether or not it will be worth his time and our money to do the repairs.

God believes that we are worth forgiving, repairing, and purifying. He longs to pardon and rid us of everything that spoils us. God purifies and corrects because he loves us. It is His desire that we would be new and clean.

Prayer: Father, you have said that I am worthy of repair and you sent your Son to accomplish it. Thank you that you have purified me. Amen.

Theresa Acolatse

SPIRITUAL FITNESS IS IMPORTANT

Scripture: 1 Timothy 4:7 (KJV)
But refuse profane and old wives' fables, and exercise thyself rather unto godliness.

Those who wish to succeed in sports spend a lot of time and trouble to be physically fit. Paul said spiritual fitness was even more important.

Today some people seek to draw attention to themselves by destructive behavior. On the other hand, spiritual fitness produces pleasant behavior, honesty and reliability. These attributes will draw people's admiring attention.

We keep ourselves spiritually fit by doing spiritual exercises. We must take the time and trouble to get to know God better through reading the Bible, praying, and worshipping with other Christians. We need to obey Christ, our spiritual trainer. He knows what is best for us, far better then we do. When we are obedient to do these things, we shall experience life in all its fullness.

Prayer: Lord, help me to be spiritually fit for your service. Amen.

Theresa Acolatse

September 21

THE ESSENCE OF MAN

Scripture: Galations 5:17 (KJV)
For the flesh lusteth against the Spirit, and the Spirit against the flesh: and these are contrary the one to the other: so that ye cannot do the things that ye would.

Man is both flesh and spirit. This makes man complete as a tool for God to use to proclaim His Word to the unsaved. However, in order for man to be used as that tool he must crucify his flesh. The flesh wars against the Spirit. We must die to self to fulfill God's purpose for our lives.

Paul, in Romans 7:15-25, explains that there is a war going on between his mind and his flesh. When he would choose to do God's will, his flesh would choose to sin. If we remain carnally minded we will succumb to the desires of the flesh, but when we are spiritually led, we are valuable tools for God.

Prayer: Holy Spirit, lead me, teach me, encourage me, and strengthen me to be spiritually led. Amen.

Reverend Paulina Kumadey

CHILD-LIKE HEARING

Scripture: Nehemiah 8:2, 3 (KJV)
And Ezra the priest brought the law before the congregation both of men and women, and all that could hear with understanding, upon the first day of the seventh month. And he read therein before the street that was before the water gate from the morning until midday, before the men and the women, and those that could understand; and the ears of all the people were attentive unto the book of the law.

Sometimes children have selective hearing when it comes to parental instructions. They hear only what they want to hear. For example, children seem to block out instructions such as, 'do your homework,' or 'clean your room.' But they always seem to hear statements such as, 'you can watch TV now,' or 'you can go out to play.' It is frustrating for a parent.

As I was thinking of a parent's frustration, I began to ponder how God feels when we, His children, exercise selective hearing. We hear, 'And these things shall be added,' but we do not hear, 'seek ye first the Kingdom.' Matthew 6:33. We must exercise the same patience with our children that God exercises with us. He gently and lovingly corrects us until we get it right.

Prayer: Gracious Lord, you have been so patient with me. Let me show the same patience toward others. Amen.

Reverend Dr. Myrtle Bowen

September 23

TO KNOW HIM

Scripture: Philippians 3:10 (KJV)
That I may know him, and the power of his resurrection, and the fellowship of his sufferings, being made conformable unto his death;

Jesus gave the disciples opportunities to understand who He was and He taught them the importance of exercising faith and belief in Him. As Christians, we too must look to the Lord revealing Himself to us at all times and in all manners of creation.

The Lord Jesus is with us in the midst of our problems. He demonstrates to us that He is Lord over our lives at every turn. Jesus promised He would not leave us nor fail us. He will be with us even unto the end of the world. Therefore we must always be ready to do the Lord's work because His presence is with us.

Prayer: Lord, give me grace to know you and to trust you when life's burden seems too much to bear. Dispel the darkness with new hope and help me rise above despair. Amen.

Vinolia Vanderpuye

YOU ARE A CHOSEN VESSEL UNTO THE LORD

Scripture: Acts 9:15 (KJV)
But the Lord said unto him, Go thy way: for he is a chosen vessel unto me, to bear my name before the Gentiles, and kings, and the children of Israel:

It appears that we have chosen God because we must make a conscious decision to ask Jesus into our hearts. We determine to live a holy and righteous life, and we decide to work for the Lord. But in reality, God chooses us first. He choreographs the events in our lives to lead us to Him. He moves every obstacle out of the way so that we will see His glory and then He puts people in our path to nurture us into Him. Think back on your own salvation experience and how God led you to Himself. Oh, it requires a volitional act of our wills, but we are chosen vessels.

Prayer: Dear Lord, thank you for choosing me. I make myself available for your work and to be used for your glory. Amen.

Love-Grace Amenuvor

CALLED TO THE MINISTRY RECONCILIATION

Scripture: 2 Corinthians 5:18 (KJV)
And all things are of God, who hath reconciled us to himself by Jesus Christ, and hath given to us the ministry of reconciliation;

Ministry to build up the church is not just for the ordained ministry. It also involves general spiritual service. Every believer is to be fruitful in every good work and to project the Word of Life. Though we may not be called to the pastorate, we are called to the ministry of reconciliation.

When we accept Jesus as our Lord and Savior, we become a new creature, old things have passed away and all things become brand new. God through Christ changed us from enemies into His friends and gave us the task of making others His friends. What a friend we have in Jesus all our sins and griefs to bear. *Yes Lord*

Prayer: Lord Jesus, I thank you that I have a friend in you and that you have opened the way for me to approach the Father as a friend. Amen.

Alberta O. Nyaku

Lord I am glade I accepted You in my life, I have put the old life behind me, and now living a brand new life in Jesus Christ. Lord keep my heart and mind on you!

September 26

FULFILLING THE MISSION THROUGH SACRIFICE

Scripture: John 12:3 (NIV)
Then Mary took about a pint of pure nard, an expensive perfume; she poured it on Jesus' feet and wiped his feet with her hair. And the house was filled with the fragrance of the perfume.

In the Scripture, Mary used a valuable ointment to anoint Jesus' feet. Additionally, she allowed her hair to flow in public as she wiped them. Without fear or shame, Mary did not hold back. She made a costly and valuable sacrifice. Mary gave her best to the Master. This is a valuable lesson for each of us to learn. We too must be willing to give up that which is considered valuable to us in order to serve the Master. *Thank you Jesus, I will*

Yes, the Gospel is free to all who believe, but we must daily pay the price of self sacrifice, presenting our bodies as living sacrifices, holy, and acceptable to God. We must be willing to sacrifice anything which would cause others not to see Jesus in us. Sometimes that means sacrificing an attitude, having things done your way, or winning an argument. Let us follow Mary's example and be willing to give up that which is valuable to us to fulfill our mission.

Prayer: Father, we are so thankful that you gave your Son, Jesus, for our salvation. Grant us the strength to share the joy and your love with others. Be ever merciful to us for Christ's sake. Amen. *thank you Jesus for opening*

Louise D. Brooks-Koffa *in heart and mind to under the importance of Sacrifices.*

September 27

FULFILLING THE MISSION THROUGH WORSHIP

Scripture: John 4:24 (KJV)
God is a Spirit: and they that worship him must worship him in spirit and in truth.

We are very busy visiting the sick, giving to the poor, caring for the bereaved, serving in soup kitchens, manning homeless shelters, and lending a listening ear. But has God sent us to perform these works? Have we stopped long enough to receive direction from Him? Have we spent time acknowledging His holiness?

It is essential for our spiritual growth and witness that we worship God in all that we do. Our mission projects and deeds carry little substance when the Church carries out our mission work no differently than national and local government agencies. Our duty is to rely on Him for all that we are able to do, not with a spirit of pride, but one of humility to thank Him, to praise Him, and to worship Him in spirit and truth, using our talents and resources. To God be the glory!

Prayer: Father, help us remember that our worship is vital to our growth and productivity. Let all that we do bear witness to your mighty acts of mercy and grace. Thank you, Lord. Amen.

Gladys Donkor

September 28

WHERE ARE YOU?

Scripture: Genesis 3:9 (NIV)
But the Lord God called to the man, "Where are you?"

Adam had just done the one thing that God told him not to do. Instead of coming to God and confessing what he had done, he covered himself and hid. When God called to him, God was not interested in his physical location. He wanted Adam to realize what he had done.

Has God ever called to you, "Where are you?" And if He did, what was your response? Did you try to cover up and hide? How did you get there? Were you drawn away by your lusts? Did you forget to cast down those imaginations? Have your thoughts developed a life of their own?

Before God calls to you, examine your walk. But if He has already called, do not try to cover up your sins. Answer the call with the words found in the 51st Psalm.

Prayer: Father, forgive me for the times I have allowed sin to reign in my life. Cleanse me from my hidden faults. In Jesus' name. Amen.

April A. Morrow

A LESSON LEARNED

Scripture: Philippians 4:6, 7 (KJV)
. . . let your requests be made known unto God. And the peace of God, which passeth all understanding, shall keep your hearts and minds through Christ Jesus . . .

During a particularly trying season in my life, I had taken the day off from work to re-focus and spend quiet time before the Lord. Before shutting myself in, I made a trip to my favorite local Christian bookstore. While there, I overheard a conversation between a mother and her child. The conversation was one sided because the child had not yet spoken. But I could tell the child was very much a part of what was going on.

As time passed, the mother's questions became more direct. I began to wonder why the mother would make the child struggle if she knew what he wanted. Then the light bulb went off. The mother was teaching the child how to ask for what he wanted. Finally after a few more questions, I heard the child speak these words; "Will you help me?"

My joy over the mother's success was short lived because I then realized that this was the cause of the season I was now enduring. I did not ask for what I wanted. That day I learned that God knows my desires, but He wants me to bring them to Him.

Prayer: Father, thank you for being a loving Parent and teaching me how to surrender my life to you. Amen.

April A. Morrow

October

Now our Lord Jesus Christ himself, and God, even our Father, which hath loved us, and hath given us everlasting consolation and good hope through grace, Comfort your hearts, and stablish you in every good word and work.

2 Thessalonians 2: 16, 17

North Eastern Episcopal District
Table Of Contents

FILLED WITH A SENSE OF DUTY

Scripture: Romans 8:4 (KJV)
That the righteousness of the law might be fulfilled in us, who walk not after the flesh, but after the Spirit.

Have you ever started something, but never quite finished it? We often begin a project or assignment with great zeal. We plan our strategy, solicit ideas and support, gather materials, and set out to do the work. However, somewhere along the way we get distracted or let obstacles get in our way. The task is never completed. We intend to get back to it but we never do.

So it is with our mission mandate—*Go ye therefore, and teach all nations, . . .* Matthew 28:19. We are to be dutiful and complete the assignment that was given to us by Christ, just as He completed His assignment and ascended back into heaven.

Be filled with a sense of duty to reach the world for Christ, because you love God and want everyone to experience His saving grace. Nothing can stop you as long as you are prayerful and dutiful.

The hymn writer admonishes, "O Zion, Haste, Thy Mission High Fulfilling . . . Behold how many thousands still are lying bound in the dismal prison house of sin . . ." We must tell the world about Jesus.

Prayer: Father, give me the boldness and confidence to never quit when you place something in my heart. Amen.

Vanessa Clayton

October 1

STOP, THIEF

Scripture: Isaiah 51:11 (KJV)
Therefore the redeemed of the Lord shall return, and come with singing unto Zion; and everlasting joy shall be upon their head: they shall obtain gladness and joy; and sorrow and mourning shall flee away.

It had been a glorious day. During church school, the children shared their love for Jesus through song and my Pastor preached on the wonders and joy of knowing Jesus. I was on a spiritual high. Then it happened. Someone blocked my car in because I inadvertently parked in a space reserved for people seeking tax help. A man emerged from the tax office stating that he put his car there deliberately. Words of condemnation and profanity spilled out of his mouth. Somehow I was as cool as a cucumber. When the tirade was finished, I introduced myself, apologized, and offered suggestions to help prevent this from happening again. The man softened and moved his car. I thanked him and left.

Driving home I realized how easy it is to succumb to the evil that is so pervasive, thus allowing the devil to steal your joy. Even in the difficulties of daily living, God requires our faithfulness. Our joy must be strong and deep enough to withstand every attack. It must be rooted in our knowledge that we are God's people and that He is in control.

Prayer: Dear God, help me to have faith in difficult times, so that your joy would flow through me and be displayed in all situations. Amen.

Reverend Carolyn H. Dixon

October 2

RIGHT WHERE YOU ARE

Scripture: Matthew 28:19, 20 (KJV)
Go ye therefore, and teach all nations, baptizing them in the name of the Father, and of the Son, and the Holy Ghost: Teaching them to observe all things whatsoever I have commanded you: and, lo, I am with you always, even unto the end of the world. Amen.

Being called into ministry as a middle-aged woman, I often sought God concerning the purpose and direction of my ministry. I knew my calling was sure and clear. As a middle school counselor, I found myself ministering to students and colleagues alike. It became clear that along with my duties at church, I was called to serve right where I was.

Christians too often seek a "captive" congregation to proclaim the Good News. If we submit to God's will, He will use us wherever we are—in the grocery store line, in our civic group, or even in our office uplifting words of hope that salvation is found in Jesus Christ. Church folk need a word from the Lord, but we must not only "preach to the choir," but also to the lost. Jesus came to set all the captives free, wherever they may be.

Every day brings wonderful opportunities to be used by God in the reconciliation of His people. We must worship Him, serve Him, and witness for Him right where we are.

Prayer: Dear God, use me where I am. Amen.

Reverend Carolyn H. Dixon

October 3

A LIVING TESTIMONY

Scripture: Acts 1:8 (KJV)
But ye shall receive power, after that the Holy Ghost is come upon you: and ye shall be witnesses unto me . . .

In the world's great cities, magnificent sculptures and buildings bear the names of those who once lived and did great things. Yet, these monuments are often cold and dead—they are only mute representations of former life and glory.

I, however, am a living witness. I stand for Him who has given me life. I testify to the goodness of God. I exist because of His love. Although I have been burdened with troubles, I know He is with me, otherwise, I would have given up long ago. My testimony is based on what the Almighty, Omnipotent, Omnipresent, Omniscient God has done for me, in spite of my unrighteousness. It is a testimony of His grace and His love.

My God is not a lifeless monument. His greatness is not limited. His magnificence surpasses anything we can imagine. Simply . . . God is God!

When was the last time you gave God praise? Have you taken His goodness for granted? Your testimony may bring someone hope or lighten someone's burden. Your testimony could encourage others to seek Christ. Do not let a day go by without giving your testimony.

Prayer: Father, thank you for your omnipotent grace and mercy working on my behalf. Help me to be a living testimony so others may see you through me. Amen.

Reverend Carolyn H. Dixon

October 4

A LIGHT IN DARKNESS

Scripture: 2 Samuel 22:29 (KJV)
For thou art my lamp, O Lord: and the Lord will lighten my darkness.

So often we sing about letting our light shine for Jesus. One night while attending a conference in the Bahamas, I was awakened by a storm that rolled in from the sea. As I looked out of the hotel window, the nearby shoreline, beach, and treacherous rocks were concealed by thick, gray fog.

From where I stood, the only thing visible was the light flashing from the historic lighthouse on the nearby rock ledge at the entrance of the harbor. Certainly, without that strong beam of light, large cruise ships would be thrown off course by the strong winds into the rocks and the hotels that extended out toward the beach.

Many of us do not really know the importance of light. We have not been in darkness with our very life depending upon our ability to see that which surrounds us. When I sing "Send a gleam across the wave," I will think about that lighthouse in the Bahamas and how the Lord allows His light to shine through us.

Prayer: Dear Lord, I thank you for being such a caring Father who watches over me in the light and darkness. Amen.

Shirley V. Jackson

October 5

TAKE MY LIFE

Scripture: Galatians 2:20 (KJV)
I am crucified with Christ: nevertheless I live; yet not I, but Christ liveth in me: and the life which I now live in the flesh I live by the faith of the Son of God, who loved me and gave himself for me.

The songwriter said, "Take my life . . ." It sounds like a lot to ask. But just think, Christ gave His life for us that we could live life here on earth more abundantly. The hymn "Take My Life, and Let It Be" speaks of being consecrated to the Lord. We must set ourselves apart for God. Can we give to Christ the life that He so freely gave to us on the cross? Take my feet . . . to walk the path of righteousness. Take my lips . . . witnessing to God's goodness. Take my will . . . willing to live by faith knowing that God never leaves us alone. Take my love . . . loving one another as our Father loves us. Christ lives in each of us and in Christ we should live. Give your life to Christ through faith. Take my life and let it ever be only for Thee.

Prayer: O God, teach me to act according to your will. Amen.

Vicki L. Lewis

A CALL TO PRAYER

Scripture: Luke 18:1 (KJV)
And he spake a parable unto them to this end, that men ought always to pray, and not to faint;

We constantly hear and read about the dangers and problems of stress. Our own experiences indicate how easy it is to feel rushed, worried, and frightened as we cope with everyday problems.

In some Christian traditions, believers are called to pray several times during the day to renew their strength and composure. Through out the day, we can certainly find reminders to turn our thoughts to God. The chimes of a clock in our home or the bells of a nearby church can be such a signal. Perhaps we could be aware of the passing of each hour when a TV or radio program changes.

However the hours are marked, it is rewarding to have a brief period of prayer and meditation several times each day. During those moments, we can take time to lift our thoughts to God and give thanks for the day. We can pray for a member of our family, a friend, or a stranger near us. We can ask for guidance in our work. Being quiet in mind and body for a short time can bring great renewal to our lives.

Prayer: Father, your great strength and wisdom are ours for the taking. May we reach out and receive them through divine prayer. Amen.

Helen Jones

MERCY IS TWICE BLEST

Scripture: Micah 6:8 (KJV)
He hath shown thee, O man, what is good: what doth the Lord require of thee, but to do justly, and to love mercy, and to walk humbly with thy God?

One day I was rushing around to complete some tasks during my lunch hour. I was off to the post office, the dry cleaners, and the bank. There was only one car at the bank's drive-thru window. In the interest of time, I used the drive-thru window. All I had to do was to cash a check. I went to my employer's bank because my bank was out of the way and I had my employee identification card.

Oh no, a new teller. Now, I knew I was going to return late to work. Conscious of time, I did not bother to count my money. Once back at work, I counted my money and realized I had fifty dollars too much. I called the bank and asked for the drive-thru teller. The new young teller was so grateful, and it made me feel good to know I had done the right thing.

Prayer: God, help me to do what is just and to love mercy as much when it is directed to others as when I receive it. Amen.

Sharon Hagerman

MANDATED TO FULFILL OUR MISSION

Scripture: Matthew 9:37 (KJV)
Then saith he unto his disciples, The harvest truly is plenteous, but the labourers are few;

If we are Christians, and we are; if we have embraced the Christian faith, and we have; then we are mandated to fulfill God's mission by going out into the vineyard. We must realize as a body of believers that we are commissioned to spread the Gospel of Jesus Christ throughout the world.

In recent years, we have had several Bishops who have either re-established work or brought new work into the African Methodist Episcopal Zion Church both in the U.S. and abroad. Many of us have accompanied our Episcopal leaders to the ripe fields. Others have given financial support, and still others have prayed. If we will accept the Christian mandate, we can fulfill the Great Commission and be used to gather a great harvest for the Lord.

Prayer: Dear Lord, prepare me for the mission fields. Help me to become a radical Christian and to be used to create and maintain worldwide churches. Prepare me to boldly proclaim, "Here am I, send me." Amen.

Betty V. Stith

October 9

SOMETHING TO THINK ABOUT

Scripture: Lamentations 3:22, 23 (KJV)
It is of the Lord's mercies that we are not consumed, because his compassions fail not. They are new every morning: great is thy faithfulness.

      Each day that the Lord awakens you to a new day, He provides new mercies. Throughout your new day, keep your eyes and mind focused on Jesus. The only true witness and testimony you have on any given day is not what you say, but how you live.

      God spared your life to be a light to a dark and fallen world in this new day. Let your light so shine that all people will see your good works and glorify your Heavenly Father.

      The new day should be used to be good, kind, thankful, peaceable, trustworthy, and dependent on God, because every good and perfect gift is from above. What will you choose to do with the new day that has been given to you?

Prayer: Father, help me to take advantage of the opportunity to tell someone about you in this new day. Amen.

Michele Augustine

October 10

FULFILLING THE MISSION:
BRINGING CHRIST TO MY WORLD

Scripture: John 14:17 (KJV)
Even the Spirit of truth; whom the world cannot receive, because it seeth him not, neither knoweth him: but ye know him; for he dewelleth with you, and shall be in you.

Am I fulfilling the mission by bringing Christ to my world? Am I living by the Bible's standard so that the people in my world (job, home, all the places I frequent) can see Jesus Christ in me? Am I in love with Christ enough to say yes to His will and really mean it? In other words, am I walking the walk as well as talking the talk? These are questions we must ask ourselves if we truly desire to live a life that is pleasing to our Heavenly Father. By doing our part, we can help expose the world to Christ, fulfill the mission, and bring Christ to a lost and dying world. However, we deceive ourselves if we think we can fulfill anything without the indwelling of the Holy Spirit.

Prayer: I invite you, Holy Spirit, to live big in me so that I might live a life that is pleasing in your sight. Strengthen me to do my part to help bring Jesus Christ to the world by walking the walk as well as talking the talk. In Jesus' name I pray. Amen.

Oturia W. Lambert

October 11

ON MY MISSION TO SELFLESSLY SERVE

Scripture: Ephesians 3:8 (KJV)
Unto me, who am less than the least of all saints, is this grace given, that I should preach among the Gentiles the unsearchable riches of Christ;

      Time and time again the human element leads us to shift our focus inwardly, thinking only of ourselves, brooding in self-pity, and dwelling on how hopeless life appears. A sure way for one to lift herself up is by helping to lift up someone else. Turning our focus to someone else's situation or dilemma can be our best means of self-help.

      Therefore, I will fix my mind and efforts on fulfilling the mission set before me, by spending some portion of my day helping someone else. I will volunteer to provide someone with a basic need, but more importantly, I will give them Jesus. No matter how bleak my dawn, my sunset will be radiant, as I daily minister to those in need of truth. *For God so loved the world, that he gave his only begotten Son, that whosoever believeth in him should not perish, but have everlasting life.* John 3:16.

Prayer: Father God, I am truly grateful for your goodness, and I am answering your call to serve. Amen.

Willie Mae Davidson

October 12

THE BEAUTY OF HIS HOLINESS

Scripture: Psalm 29:2 (KJV)
Give unto the Lord the glory due unto his name; worship the Lord in the beauty of holiness.

The month of October in New England is a time of beauty as the leaves turn from green to an array of autumn colors. People come from far and wide to view the foliage and to see the beauty of God's handiwork. Yet there are some who live in the midst of this extraordinary sight and miss it each season.

The prophet Isaiah said of the Messiah, . . . *he hath no form nor comeliness; and when we shall see him, there is no beauty that we should desire him.* Isaiah 53:2. When Jesus came, He did not come in elegance although He was a King. He came wrapped in the beauty of simplicity and humility. He was a servant to all who gave testimony of His Father.

We are called to be humble servants whose lives should give testimony of Jesus. Beauty is all around us if we only take the time to admire what God is doing and has done in our lives. We can see that beauty when we put God first and self last.

Prayer: Heavenly Father, I am grateful for your love for me and for the beauty of the earth. Help me to be mindful of your love. I pray in Jesus' name. Amen.

Irene Romney

October 13

WORK WHILE IT IS DAY

Scripture: Ecclesiastes 3:1 (KJV)
To every thing there is a season, and a time to every purpose under the heaven:

October represents the fall season when nature prepares for winter. There are changes in the weather patterns. Fall can also be seen as a time of maturity in our lives. Hopefully, we are embracing wisdom and passing it on to those in the spring and summer months of their lives.

Jesus was on earth for only a short period of time, yet He accomplished everything He was sent to do. Like Jesus, we are here for only a short time. Our purpose for being here is to proclaim the Word of God.

The season is short and limited. The work must be done and we do not have forever to accomplish it.

The task that God has given to you for today must be done while there is still daylight. When the season for opportunity leaves, it is gone forever. We cannot afford to put off for tomorrow what we can do today.

Prayer: Father, your wisdom is infinite. Please help us to understand the meaning of our lives. Grant us courage to accomplish the work, which you have given to us. In Jesus' name we pray. Amen.

Irene Romney

PATIENTLY WAITING FOR GOD

Scripture: Isaiah 40:31 (KJV)
But they that wait upon the Lord shall renew their strength; they shall mount up with wings as eagles; they shall run, and not be weary; and they shall walk and not faint.

When we give our lives to Jesus Christ, we are constantly reminded that our lives are not our own. For that reason, we must surrender our will so that God's will can be done. Yes, at first glance this sounds simple, but there are times when impatience has its way with us. We find ourselves tied up in knots, burning nervous energy, and looking for our change to come. In times like these, we must remember to wait for God's direction. Resting in His peace will allow us to rise above all challenging circumstances and to soar freely on the clouds like an eagle. It is good to know that God loves us and is only a prayer away. Are you seeking a response from God? *But let patience have her perfect work, that ye may be perfect and entire, wanting nothing,* James 1:4.

Prayer: Dear God, give me the patience and grace to wait for an answer from you. Amen.

Reverend Shelley D. Best

October 15

DO THE RIGHT THING

Scripture: Esther 4:14 (KJV)
For if thou altogether holdest thy peace at this time, then shall there enlargement and deliverance arise to the Jews from another place; but thou and thy father's house shall be destroyed: and who knoweth whether thou art come to the kingdom for such a time as this?

One of the most challenging ministries Christians have today is taking faith into the workplace. When I worked as a public relations executive in a child welfare agency, a case came to my attention in which a baby was fatally injured and the system was at fault. When the media came knocking, it was my job to put a spin on the story to make my organization look good. The Holy Spirit was with me, and He urged me to help an investigative reporter get the information he needed to uncover the systemic flaw, so more children would not be hurt. I obeyed His leading knowing that sometimes God places us in positions, where we are called like Esther, to stand up for what is right, even if it may cost us our lives. Why are you in your current position? Perhaps it is for "such a time as this."

Prayer: Dear God, give me the courage to trust in you when you call me to speak up. Amen.

Reverend Shelley D. Best

DON'T TRY TO BLEND IN

Scripture: Matthew 5:14-16 (NIV)
You are the light of the world. A city on a hill cannot be hidden. Neither do people light a lamp and put it under a bowl. Instead they put it on its stand, and it gives light to everyone in the house. In the same way, let your light shine before men, that they may see your good deeds and praise your Father in heaven.

Have you ever tried to just blend in? It may be a meeting, where prior to arriving you told yourself to be silent. It could be a day when the Pastor asks for volunteers—you know you have the ability to do the job, but you find yourself looking down to avoid eye contact. Or it could be a time you walked into the room and purposely sat in the back. God has created each of us with unique gifts and abilities. There is nobody like you. With this in mind, we must overcome our urge to be a wallflower, and we must passionately allow the Lord to use us to bring light into the world. How can you let your light shine today?

Prayer: Dear God, help me to rise and shine in the midst of all darkness. Amen.

Reverend Shelley D. Best

October 17

DON'T EVEN TALK ABOUT IT

Scripture: 2 Timothy 2:16 (NIV)
Avoid godless chatter, because those who indulge in it will become more and more ungodly.

Gossip! Gossip! Gossip! We are living in times where it seems that talking about other people's personal business and immoral behavior has become a national obsession. The evening news, instead of focusing attention on many important world events, spends valuable airtime discussing the sins of public officials and superstars. With all this public discussion of ungodliness, we of faith could be led to believe that we too should speak of such things. However, the Word of God teaches us to do our best to avoid such chatter because when we talk about the immorality and sinfulness of others, we desensitize ourselves to such ill behaviors and become vulnerable to them ourselves. My grandmother, a faithful woman of God, often said, "If you can't say something nice, say nothing." So, the next time people gather around the water cooler at work to discuss office antics, we should hold our tongues and keep our faith.

Prayer: Dear God, help me to hold my tongue and to avoid conversations that dishonor you. May I speak only that which edifies and glorifies you. Amen.

Reverend Shelley D. Best

October 18

EVERY LITTLE BIT HELPS

Scripture: 1 John 3:17 (NIV)
If anyone has material possessions and sees his brother in need but has no pity on him, how can the love of God be in him?

One afternoon, my goddaughter and I were standing in line at a popular hamburger restaurant. In the next line, we witnessed an elderly woman dressed in frayed clothing diligently counting the change in her hand. On her face was an expression of deep contemplation and calculation, for she did not have enough to meet her needs. The Holy Spirit moved in our hearts—my goddaughter and I knew we would not be able to change the woman's economic status, but we could help feed her today. My goddaughter looked at me with those, "may I please eyes," and I immediately handed her a bill to cover the woman's lunch. She walked across the aisle and with pure love she said, "This is for you." With that, the woman's face lit up with joy, and we knew we had made a difference. What can you do today to show someone less fortunate that you care?

Prayer: Dear God, help me to be my brother and sister's keeper. Amen.

Reverend Shelley D. Best

A FRUITFUL LIFE

Scripture: John 15:5 (NIV)
"I am the vine; you are the branches. If a man remains in me and I in him, he will bear much fruit; apart from me you can do nothing."

One of the most wonderful aspects of the Christian life is the way God plants the Word in us through pastors, teachers, brothers, and sisters in Christ. When we truly receive the Word, it opens our hearts and minds so we can grow into fruitful people. In other words, we become trees, planted by the water, that when rooted, bear fruit. In my moments of personal frustration over the challenges faced with living, I take a personal inventory to reflect on the ways I am fruitful in God's kingdom. When I examine the fruit of my tree, I am always flooded with joy, and I know that no matter what sorrows I endure, there is an awesome blessing in knowing I have been used by God to bear fruit. What fruit have you borne for the Lord today?

Prayer: Dear God, help me to always remember that the purpose of my life is to bear fruit. Amen.

Reverend Shelley D. Best

GOD WILL WORK IT OUT

Scripture: Proverbs 3:5, 6 (KJV)
Trust in the Lord with all thine heart; and lean not unto thine own understanding. In all thy ways acknowledge him, and he shall direct thy paths.

Trust is a word many of us have a hard time living. To trust is to lie helplessly, face down. It means to surrender. To many of us who have been hurt or betrayed by those we love, the notion of trusting anyone, including God, is a hard pill to swallow. Unfortunately, until we learn to trust in the Lord, we will continue to try to do things our way, thus making our lives more complicated than necessary. When we realize that by accepting Jesus Christ as our Lord and Savior, we have given our life to the Lord, the idea of trust comes clear. If we remember that God is the one who is in the driver's seat, and we are merely passengers, we can be sure that the Lord will get us where we need to be, at the appointed time, safely. Can you let go and trust God to direct your life?

Prayer: Dear God, help me to trust you completely with my life. Amen.

Reverend Shelley D. Best

DON'T GIVE UP

Scripture: Galatians 6:9 (NIV)
Let us not become weary in doing good, for at the proper time we will reap a harvest if we do not give up.

Church work is a never-ending process. There are people to visit, prayers to pray, things to fix, lessons to learn, and funds to raise. The more you learn about the Lord, the more you learn how much you do not know. The more you study the Word, the more you know you need to study. You can do your best to love people and mind your manners, but there will always be folks who do not like you, who talk about you, and who crucify you like they did Jesus. There may be times when you feel like giving up, but keep your eyes on the crown and know that your labor is not in vain. God has already ordained the perfect time for your blessing to manifest. This may not be the time for it to come, but as long as you remain faithful and do not give up—God promised you the reward.

Prayer: Dear God, restore me, revive me, and re-energize me as I continue to yield to your Holy Spirit. I thank you for strengthening me in my inner man with might that your plan and purpose for my life will be fulfilled today. Thank you for making me more than a conqueror. As I face this challenge, I walk in victory. Amen.

Reverend Shelley D. Best

GOD WILL TAKE CARE OF YOU

Scripture: Psalm 37:25 (NIV)
I was young and now I am old, yet I have never seen the righteous forsaken or their children begging bread.

The job market is not what it used to be. Large corporations that had the reputation of never laying off people are now downsizing, and reorganizing. Other companies that once had the corner on the marketplace are closing their doors. Individuals with graduate degrees are standing in the unemployment line. But we who love the Lord and are serving Him with our lives must cling to the Word. No matter what a situation may look like, we must remember that God promised to take care of us. With that in mind, we should each thank the Lord from the depths of our hearts for our daily bread—for He promised neither we nor our children would have to beg for it. And remember, *God is not a man, that he should lie . . .* Numbers 23:19.

Prayer: Dear God, I thank you for supplying all my needs, day by day. Amen.

Reverend Shelley D. Best

WHAT IF VERSUS WHAT IS

Scripture: Matthew 6:34 (NIV)
Therefore do not worry about tomorrow, for tomorrow will worry about itself. Each day has enough trouble of its own.

Think of how much energy you have spent in your life worked up over something that might happen. Many of us focus countless hours and conversations saying, "what if this happens or what if that happens?" As we focus on negative possibilities, panic can take over and cause us to jump overboard, even before the boat is sinking. The Word of God tells us not to worry about the "what ifs" of life. For "what if" only exists in the next moment, hour, or day and "what is" is the only thing we can actually impact. Therefore, we should not allow ourselves to worry, for it reduces our life span through ulcers, high blood pressure, and heart disease. Allow faithful thoughts to overtake worry, then wait and see what your God who loves you will bring to pass.

Prayer: Dear God, help me release my worries about tomorrow and build up my faith today. Amen.

Reverend Shelley D. Best

WORKING FOR JESUS

Scripture: Colossians 3:23 (NIV)
Whatever you do, work at it with all your heart, as working for the Lord, not for men,

How many times are you tempted to cut corners in your work? When your boss is away, do you extend your lunchtime? When no one is looking do you overlook your mistakes? If your phone is not being monitored, do you spend company time speaking to friends and family members long distance?

We must remember that when we gave our life to Jesus Christ, He became our Lord and Savior. As Lord, Jesus became our permanent employer, who places us in various temporary positions here on earth, where we are called to be ambassadors and witnesses. Because we owe Jesus everything and love him with our heart, mind, and soul, we are called to put passion into our work, for our ultimate boss is the One who "sits high and looks low."

Prayer: Dear God, help me to remember that you are my Employer, my Evaluator, and the One who issues my raises. Amen.

Reverend Shelley D. Best

October 25

A LIVING SACRIFICE

Scripture: Romans 12:1 (KJV)
I beseech you therefore, brethren, by the mercies of God, that ye present your bodies a living sacrifice, holy, acceptable unto God, which is your reasonable service.

When I think of human sacrifices, I am reminded of the Tarzan movies I watched as a child. In many of the movies, I can remember a lovely lady tied to the stake prepared for the end of her life, as she knew it. When we come to Christ, we are urged to offer our bodies for service in the Kingdom as living sacrifices. The old personality and lifestyle must go so that the new mission and role in the kingdom will come. We are living sacrifices, because without Christ—we would be dead in sin, belonging to the enemy who does not love us. It is wonderful to know that Jesus loves us and will use our sacrificed lives not only for our good, but also for the good of the Kingdom of God. Will you be a living sacrifice for Jesus today?

Prayer: Dear God, help me to surrender my will, so your will can be done in my life. Amen.

Reverend Shelley D. Best

CHANGE YOUR MIND---CHANGE YOUR LIFE

Scripture: Romans 12:2 (NIV)
Do not conform any longer to the pattern of this world, but be transformed by the renewing of your mind. Then you will be able to test and approve what God's will is—his good, pleasing and perfect will.

What do you spend your time thinking about? The Bible says, "As a man thinketh, so he is." If you think about negative things, you will be a negative person. If you think about positive things, you will be a positive person. If you think about joyful things, you will be a joyful person. If you think of depressing things, you will be a depressed person. Paul, in his letter to the Romans, is urging you to stop thinking about life the way people of the world think. You are being called to transform your life—by making your mind new, through the Word. By learning the Word of God, you are reprogramming your thoughts. By changing your thinking, you will ultimately change your actions and habits. And through those changes, your life will change. If you change your mind—you can change your life.

Prayer: Dear God, help me to diligently study your Word to transform my life. Amen.

Reverend Shelley D. Best

October 27

HARVEST OF THE HEART

Scripture: Mark 4:20 (KJV)
And these are they which are sown on good ground; such as hear the word, and receive it, and bring forth fruit, some thirty-fold, some sixty and some an hundred.

October is harvest time. How is your garden growing? Are you prayerfully preparing the soil of your heart garden? That is the way to receive the divine seed of God's Word. Is the Gospel of Christ sown in your heart?

When God's seeds of truth are planted in a prepared, receptive heart, the Word takes root and produces increased faith and good works in our lives.

Be thankful that God's Word does not return to Him void. His Word accomplishes His desires for us.

Prayer: Dear Lord of the Harvest, teach me to receive the truth of your Word in the garden of my heart each day. In Jesus' name. Amen.

Barbara L. Quarles

WALK TOGETHER CHILDREN

Scripture: Isaiah 40:31 (KJV)
But they that wait upon the Lord shall renew their strength; they shall mount up with wings as eagles; they shall run, and not be weary; and they shall walk, and not faint.

The message of the old Negro spiritual "Walk Together Children" is one of hope, unity, and tenacity. As African Americans, we have forgotten how to walk together.

Walking together speaks of our need for togetherness and oneness. As a people, our voices have been raised in harmony, while bound together in the ships during the Middle Passage, while working the cotton fields, and while walking together through the streets of this country during the Civil Rights Movement. We have received courage to continue from one another. There is power in numbers, but the greatest power is in numbers unified in purpose and blessed by God.

We still have a long and difficult walk—but we are in this journey together. We need each other. We belong to each other. We share a common destiny and bond, and we cannot go it alone. Let us continue to walk together, for God has promised a "Great Camp Meeting in the Promised Land."

Prayer: Help me, Lord, to keep on walking and do not let me be afraid to take a righteous stand for justice and equality. Amen.

Reverend Carolyn H. Dixon

October 29

FOR THE CHILDREN

Scripture: Matthew 19:14 (KJV)
But Jesus said, Suffer little children, and forbid them not, to come unto me: for of such is the kingdom of heaven.

The password for October is "trick or treat." We give our children treats of material things, thus we play a horrible trick on them. Emphasizing materialism instead of spirituality, we are guilty of tricking our children into believing that things are more important. We deny them God's blessings. Our misplaced priorities have resulted in our children becoming spiritually impoverished.

Too many young people feel hopeless, empty, and unfocused. Their eyes light up only when they have been stimulated by glitter, violence, and sexual innuendo. They seek immediate gratification rather than the lasting rewards of Christian character. Jesus rebuked His disciples when they attempted to prevent the children from coming to Him. We too are being rebuked for the same reason. We must change our focus. Only by bringing our children back to God will the true light return to their eyes. Only then will they light up in their knowledge of God and His love for them. Only then will they know their place in His Kingdom and His divine plan and purpose for their lives.

Prayer: Dear God, use me to bring children to you. Amen.

Reverend Carolyn H. Dixon

October 30

THE PROMISE

Scripture: Matthew 28:20 (KJV)
Teaching them to observe all things whatsoever I have commanded you: and, lo, I am with you always, even unto the end of the world. Amen.

Have you ever been in a situation when you did not know what to do, what to say, or were to turn? Have you been bombarded with questions, but had no answers? Have you ever felt like you were against a wall, with no way out? During those situations you needed someone to talk to so you called your friend and discovered she was not available. When the phone rang you thought they had answered, but you were disappointed to discover the voice was not live but Memorex. How did you feel? Did you feel like crying? Did you feel alone or did you get angry with that person for not being there? I am sure we have all been at a crisis point in our lives. But we can be assured that if we are acquainted with Jesus, He will always be available to us. He can always be reached. Jesus promised that He would always be with us. It was not a conditional promise, nor was it a provisional promise, it is a perpetual promise. We can rejoice in His promise because according to His Word, He promises to hear us when we pray, He promises to supply our need, give when we ask, open when we knock, and to prepare a place for us in His Kingdom where we can live with Him forever.

Prayer: Dear Father, thank you for your promises. Amen.

Geraldine J. Walker

October 31

November

And it shall come to pass, if ye shall hearken diligently unto my commandments which I command you this day, to love the Lord your God, and to serve him with all your heart and with all your soul, That I will give you the rain of your land in his due season, the first rain and the latter rain, that thou mayest gather in thy corn, and thy wine, and thine oil. And I will send grass in thy fields for thy cattle, that thou mayest eat and be full.

Deuteronomy 11:13-15

Eastern North Carolina Episcopal District
Table Of Contents

THE SOURCE OF MY SUPPLY

Scripture: Psalm 37:3 (KJV)
Trust in the Lord, and do good; so shalt thou dwell in the land, and verily thou shalt be fed.

I came in from work one evening, and my kitchen was full of young people. My oldest child said, "Mama, the guys didn't get paid, so they have not eaten since yesterday. They are broke and hungry. I told them my mama would feed them." She was confident that that I would feed her friends.

I was not so confident. I barely had enough to feed my six children. Now with 15 more of my daughter's friends this was impossible. But my only response to my daughter was, "Okay, fix dinner." I went to my bedroom and prayed, "Lord, please let there be enough food for all of them, they're away from home, hungry, and they are somebody's children. I'll eat a peanut butter and jelly sandwich, just feed the children."

A while later I returned to the kitchen. Everyone had eaten, declared they had enough to eat, thanked me, and said good-bye. I went to the stove to see how this could be and to my surprise there was enough dinner left for me. I thanked God for His goodness and promised to never complain about my lack of food, but to always feed the hungry. One of the young men still tells everyone about the family who fed him when he was hungry. He is still amazed.

Prayer: God, thank you for your amazing grace that is sufficient to provide food for the body and the soul. Amen.

Lottie D. E. Clinton

November 1

HELP IN THE TIME OF TROUBLE

Scripture: Psalm 46:1 (KJV)
God is our refuge and strength, a very present help in trouble.

This Bible Verse has proven to be a true testimony in my life. As long as we know that we can trust God when the perplexities of life seem to overcome us, we can prevail. But when we become doubtful and fearful, we no longer rely on His strength and tend to rely on our own.

My husband was quite ill in the hospital. I was somewhat fearful and anxious as the medical complications had taken their toll on him. I solemnly watched him as I began to reflect upon his life as a minister of the Gospel. He pastored for 32 years. He lived an exemplary life and truly loved God's people. I prayed for God to spare my husband's life. I needed him. We had no children. What do I do if he leaves me? I will be alone.

Then I began to ponder my selfish thoughts. I must believe that God would give me strength in my trouble. A sudden calm came over me and I could feel God's presence giving me that inner strength to accept whatever happened. My husband passed away, but I have realized how important it is to depend upon God. He is always there to be our strength and stay.

Prayer: Dear God, thank you for helping me to accept those perplexities of life and giving me your promise to be with me always. Amen.

Posey Johnson

November 2

PRAYER WORKS

Scripture: Proverbs 15:29 (KJV)
The Lord is far from the wicked: but he heareth the prayer of the righteous.

When you know what God has done for you through prayer you can tell the world that prayer works. Prayer is communication with God. The purpose is not to enlighten God on our situation. God knows what is going on. The purpose is to give God the authority to move on our behalf.

Prayer edifies our spirits. If we talk to God and give Him the opportunity to speak to our hearts, God will give you solutions and answers that your natural mind could never conceive.

In 2 Samuel Chapter 22, David in his distress called out to the Lord. It says God came down on a bolt of thunder and defeated David's enemies.

In Daniel Chapter 10:12-14, it says Daniel fasted for days waiting for an answer to his prayer. When Michael, the angel, arrived he told Daniel that God heard him when he when he first called out. God hears our prayer, and He responds.

Prayer: Lord, thank you for giving me a way to communicate with you directly through prayer. Lord, I thank you that you answer my prayer. Amen.

Carolyn Varner

November 3

PRAY WITHOUT CEASING

Scripture: 1 Thessalonians 5:17 (KJV)
Pray without ceasing.

Everyday of our lives, through the good times and bad, we engage in various conversations with family, friends, and foes, but our greatest conversation should be with Almighty God, our Father; for He is the only one that can supply our every need.

We should commune with Him through prayer, for our highest privilege is to talk to God. Jesus prayed in the Garden of Gethsemane, Mark 14:32. If Jesus had to pray, we also should pray.

Consider the disciples, they walked with Jesus, saw Him do many miracles, and heard great wisdom come from Him. But when they had the opportunity what did they ask? Teach us how to pray. They saw something in Jesus. I believe they saw that the success of His ministry was His prayer life, His constant communication with God, the Father.

Prayer: Father, teach me to pray. Amen.

Vera B. Andrews

STOP WORRYING—START PRAYING

Scripture: Philippians 4:6 (NRS)
Do not worry about anything, but in everything by prayer and supplication with thanksgiving let your requests be made known to God.

Our lives are filled with many issues and concerns. There seems to be so many weighty issues to consider in our lives. Consequently, we are in a constant state of anxiety, but God's Word clearly states that we are not to worry about anything. How did we get so off track? When did we start worrying about everything and stop praying about anything? Maybe a better question is how do we get back on track?

Jehosphat, the king of Judah, had a host of enemies to come against his kingdom. Jehosphat sought the Lord. The Lord's replied, . . . *Do not fear or be dismayed at this great multitude; for the battle is not yours but God's,* 2 Chronicles 20:15.

That was all the people of Judah needed to hear, they immediately began to praise the Lord. The next day Jehosphat appointed singers to go out before the army to praise the Lord. Judah's enemies were defeated.

God wants each of us to cast our cares on Him and to stop worrying. When we do this, God promises that, . . . *the peace of God, which surpasses all understanding, will guard your hearts and your minds in Christ Jesus,* Philippians 4:7. So stop worrying and start praying.

Prayer: Father, today I cast all my cares on you. I will rejoice in you and allow your peace to replace my worry. Amen.

Jonathan Douglas, Sr.

November 5

KINGDOM BENEFITS

Scripture: Isaiah 55:1 (KJV)
Ho, every one that thirsteth, come ye to the waters, and he that hath no money; come ye, buy, and eat; yea, come, buy wine and milk without money and without price.

Can you imagine a place where as believers, we can inhabit where there is no need for a monetary exchange for goods? Certainly in the world, nothing is free. Everything has a cost attached to it. In our times, there is a separation between those who have and those who have not; and the gap is increasingly widening.

God however, has another plan in mind for those who are the called according to His purpose. He has ordained that we shall inhabit the land that flows with milk and honey. Many believe that this is illustrative of our heavenly benefits, once we take off this earth suit. But, God has ordained in His Word that these are our covenant rights and benefits now.

We can receive these benefits as a result of the sacrifice Jesus Christ made on the cross. We, who are thirsty can come to the waters and drink the nourishment of the Holy Word of God. We can make our heartfelt desires known to Him and He will supply all of our needs according to the power that is vested in Him.

Prayer: Father, all that I need is found in you. You are my source and sustainer. You supply every need according to your tender mercies and lovingkindness for my life. Amen.

Janice McMillian

November 6

VISION OF GOD

Scripture: Psalm 92:1 (KJV)
It is a good thing to give thanks unto the Lord, and to sing praises unto thy name, O most High:

Sometimes we wish we knew the future. We think knowing the future will help us make it through the present, but I wonder if that is really true.

Consider the life of Joseph, Genesis Chapters 37-47. I wonder if he would have ever attained the heights he did had he known all the trials and tribulations he would have to encounter. Each situation in Joseph's life was necessary to make him who he was. The situation taught him how to lean and depend on God, knowing the divine providence of God would see him through. Given the choice, I am sure Joseph, like most of us, would have chosen an easier road.

As a minister's wife for thirty-one years, I have felt the apprehension of each new assignment. But God knew each new assignment brought new blessings. Each new assignment raised my level of commitment. I could not see it in the beginning and sometimes not even when it was happening, but God sees around every one of my corners. He has perfectly orchestrated my life to fulfill His purpose. It is merely my job to give thanks to the Lord and sing praises to His Name.

Prayer: Lord, thank you for seeing into my tomorrow and providing for my today. Amen.

Delma S. Jones

November 7

AN ENDURING PRINCIPLE

Scripture: Isaiah 40:6, 8 (KJV)
All flesh is grass, and all the goodliness thereof is as flower of the field: . . . The grass withereth, the flower fadeth: but the word of our God shall stand forever.

There are great men that we worship. Men like Abraham Lincoln, Mahatma Ghandi, John Kennedy, Martin Luther King, Jr., Malcolm X, and Robert Kennedy have been made heroes in our minds. These men live on in our minds and hearts because of the principles which governed their lives.

These men are worthy of our admiration and respect for the sacrifices they made and the work they did. However, we cannot make men or their legacies bigger than the Word of God. We have begun to teach our children the principles of Malcolm X instead of the Word of God. Our children are learning speeches by Martin Luther King, Jr., rather than Scripture.

We must realize that the only enduring legacy is the Word of God. Man is like grass and will be cut down, but the Word of God shall stand forever. We must begin to undergird our children with the Word of God. We must give them a foundation of spiritual principles and deliver them from cute slogans. The Word of God is the enduring principle.

Prayer: Lord, your Word will stand forever. Ground me in your enduring principles now and forever. Amen.

Blossie English

November 8

THE DEPTH OF GOD

Scripture: Isaiah 40:27 (NIV)
Why do you say, O Jacob and complain, O Israel. "My way is hidden from the Lord; my cause is disregarded by my God."

The Lord is the everlasting God, the Creator of the ends of the earth. He will not grow tired or weary, and His understanding no one can fathom. It is so hard to imagine the depth of God that we look elsewhere from time to time when we are in trouble, pain, and distress. We look to the world's systems to be all encompassing in our lives. But God is always in our presence, whether we acknowledge it or not.

God is standing with open arms, ears, heart, and soul. He understands and forgives us when we fall short. Those who hope in the Lord will renew their strength. The spirit man gets tired even to the point of giving in. We must know that the Lord will strengthen us and empower us with wings like an eagle. He wants us to walk in love to the end knowing we have eternal life with the Father.

Prayer: Lord, while I cannot comprehend your depth, help me to embrace it in my life so that my hope would always be in you. Then, Lord, restore a child-like spirit in me. Amen.

Anonymous

November 9

A CLOSE ENCOUNTER

Scripture: Luke 18:18 (KJV)
And a certain ruler asked him, saying, Good Master, what shall I do to inherit eternal life?

At first glance, it seems that the rich young ruler in this parable had the right idea. He came to Jesus sincerely, wanting to know what he needed to do to inherit eternal life. The ruler was a moral man. Not only did he know the law of Moses, but he had kept the law from his youth. But when Jesus asked him to go a step beyond keeping the law and give of his material substance, the young ruler walked sorrowfully away. The rich young ruler allowed things to come between him and eternal life.

He is not unlike us today. We place such a value on things that we pass over the priceless gifts a life in Jesus offers us. The call to Christianity is a call to total commitment and dependence on God.

As we gather with friends and family during this holiday season, draw closer to God. Look for ways to reach out to others and do not walk away from Jesus because you think the stakes are too high. Jesus willingly gave Himself so that we could have eternal life; let us willingly give of ourselves to bring others to Him.

Prayer: Heavenly Father, give me grace to share of my substance with those less fortunate than I and give me the strength to renew my commitment to you, no matter what the cost. Amen.

Sylvia D. Smith

November 10

GIVE GOD FIRST PLACE

Scripture: Matthew 6:33 (KJV)
But seek ye first the kingdom of God, and his righteousness; and all these things shall be added unto you.

Today many people are seeking first the kingdom of pleasure and possession. The love of possessions has captured the heart of millions. Possessed with the love of money, people are selling their souls to obtain material wealth.

Obtaining wealth has taken the place of family life, training our children, even knowing God. We are so caught up that at times, we do not even recognize when our priorities get off track. It is easy to understand why they get off track. It happens when we do not seek the Kingdom first and allow God to add things to us. We put the wrong emphasis on acquiring and maintaining possessions when we do not seek the Kingdom first.

Jesus promised all these things shall be added to us if we give Him first place. It is time to get our priorities back in line and put God first in every aspect of our lives.

Prayer: God, be merciful unto me, bless me, and cause your face to shine upon me as I put your Kingdom first. Amen.

Rebecca Wright

November 11

CAST DOWN FROM EASY LIVING

Scripture: 1 Corinthians 10:12 (NIV)
So, if you think you are standing firm, be careful that you don't fall!

Let us be realistic about the record of our lives as children of God. Though we belong to Christ and seek to put our trust in Him, on occasion we stumble and fall. It seems that it is when we are most sure of ourselves that we slip. We find ourselves frustrated, on our backs pawing away like sheep trying to right ourselves with efforts that are futile.

One thing that causes us to fall is the way we forever look for the soft spots in life. The sheep that choose the comfortable rounded hollow in which to lie down may often be the very sheep that end up cast down. It is in the soft spots of life that it is so easy to roll over and lose the ability to right ourselves.

In the Christian life there is danger in always looking for the easy place, the cozy corner, comfortable position where there is no difficulty, no need for endurance, no demand for self-discipline. The times when we think we have it made may actually be the times when we are most susceptible to danger.

It is from this danger that our Good Shepherd protects us. His Word reminds us of His power over sin, death, and the devil.

Prayer: Almighty God, lift me, challenge me, and lead me. In Jesus' name I pray. Amen.

Catherine H. Whitley

THE GREATER ONE IS IN ME

Scripture: 1 John 4:4 (KJV)
Ye are of God, little children, and have overcome them: because greater is he that is in you, than he that is in the world.

As Christians, we do not realize the power we have. We forget or have not come to the point of understanding that when God created man, God put everything under man's control. We have dominion and control over those things that plague us, over situations that defeat us, over circumstances that stop us.

Consider this, God is everything and once we accept Him, He places His everything in us. We are never left helpless. The Greater One is in us. If we humble ourselves, stay daily in the Word, and allow the Holy Spirit to take control, we do not have to worry about anything.

We have dominion and control, but we must exercise this power, or the devil will convince us we do not have it. Do not let the devil take what God has given you and use it against you. Walk in the authority and power that having the Greater One in you gives you over the world.

Prayer: Dear God, thank you for your precious Holy Spirit which gives me the power to walk in my created position. Amen.

Ida Carmore

JESUS CAN DO IT

Scripture: Philippians 4:13 (KJV)
I can do all things through Christ which strengtheneth me.

We must learn to depend on God unconditionally, even for the simple things. I taught my daughter to pray for the things she needed. For example, one evening we were on our way home in the middle of rush hour traffic and she had to go to the bathroom. I told her to pray and ask Jesus to help her make it home. She prayed, and she made it home.

It may seem silly to pray for such a small thing, but I use the small things as faith building exercises. If I can believe for the smaller things, when the large problems appear in my life, I will be so use to depending on Jesus that it will come natural.

It is so easy to feel we must do something to make things right or fix it. I challenge us to stop trying to help Jesus. He can do it all and He will do it all. We must ask His Spirit to go before us and allow Him to guide us through the storm to peace.

Prayer: Heavenly Father, humble my spirit and teach me to depend on you. Help me to show love and peace and to be thankful. In the name of Jesus I pray. Amen.

Jeryl Z. Anderson

November 14

LOVE

Scripture: John 13:34 (NIV)
"A new command I give you: love one another. As I have loved you, so you must love one another."

When Jesus was asked to identify the greatest teaching of all time, He answered, "to love God and others." Love was the central core of His teachings. It is therefore natural that Jesus would expect genuine love to dominate the lives of those who claim to follow his teachings.

A story is told of a devoted and beloved Bishop who spent his life in Africa. During this man's first year on the mission field, he was a failure. He held in contempt the very people he was sent to help. He was impossible to get along with and was about to be sent home.

The overseas committee decided to give him another chance on conditions that he read 1 Corinthians 13 (the love Chapter) every day for a year. He did. His life was transformed. His work prospered and many were brought to Christ through his love for others.

The responsibility to love rests upon all Christians. It does not matter what our occupation may be. It does not matter what status in life we may hold. It does not matter if others do not care for us. We have but one great responsibility, to love one another.

Prayer: God, thank you for your gift of love. Help me to love those you send my way so that they might see your Son in me. Amen.

Doretha Morgan

November 15

WITNESSING

Scripture: Matthew 28:19, 20 (KJV)
Go ye therefore, and teach all nations, baptizing them in the name of the Father, and of the Son, and of the Holy Ghost: Teaching them to observe all things whatsoever I have commanded you: and, lo, I am with you always, even unto the end of the world. Amen.

Upon accepting Christ as our personal Savior, we are given the command to preach the Gospel to every creature. We must witness to others, sharing with them the love of God; sharing with them that . . . *God so loved the world, that He gave His only begotten Son, that whosoever believed in Him should not perish, but have everlasting life,* John 3:16.

We have been commissioned to help save the world for Christ. We must tell the "Good News."

In order to be true witnesses we must bear in mind that we must be clean vessels. We must live a Christian life of love and obedience though God's Son, Jesus Christ the Savior. We must witness at all times and in all places. God has chosen us to bear witness, and we have been given the divine authorization to be ambassadors for Christ.

Prayer: Dear God, my Heavenly Father, as I go forth and witness, let others see that you truly live within me. Amen.

Artelia M. Perry

A LIGHT SET ON THE HILL

Scripture: Matthew 5:14, 16 (KJV)
Ye are the light of the world. A city that is set on a hill cannot be hid . . . Let your light so shine before men, that they may see your good works, and glorify your father which is in heaven.

As missionaries we are on a mission for Christ. In the 21st century our lights need to shine everywhere we go — in our homes, churches, jobs, and communities. To follow God's leadership we must follow Him wherever He leads us. We must walk in the light of Jesus because He is the Light of the world. Walking in the light of Jesus means we are willing to teach our children what is right and wrong, then discipline them when they are wrong. We must teach them how to respect themselves, their teachers, preachers, parents, and all adults.

When we are in the light, we must not go along with everything, but we should stand up for Jesus and truth. We must live so God can use us here in the earth to help those who are less fortunate than we are. We should never be ashamed or afraid to worship Jesus in spirit and truth, for His grace and mercy brought us safely thus far. So let us shine for Jesus.

Prayer: Lord, teach me how to love others. Help me to let your light shine in me. Help me to have such a shining light that I can reach lost souls and tell them about Jesus. Amen.

Wardell Brown

November 17

STOP, THINK, THEN THANK

Scripture: Psalm 105:1 (KJV)
O give thanks unto the Lord; call upon his name; make known his deeds among the people.

The week before school was to begin, I saw two co-workers. They asked the dreaded question, "Are you ready to go back to work?" "No, I am not," I answered, explaining that we needed at least another week to be out. They readily agreed with me. After exchanging pleasantries, my co-workers went on their way, but I was stopped in my tracks.

What was I thinking about? There are people without jobs. There are people without homes and food. I had begun to take my comfort for granted. I was beginning to forget the price my God had paid so that I could have the abundant life.

Right there in that spot I began to give thanks to God for a safe summer vacation, my job, co-workers, the ten minute drive to work, the children, books, chalk, crayons, my car, bus duty, staff meetings, and everything else I could think of. I learned a simple lesson about complaining: stop, think, then thank God!

Prayer: Father, you have given me so much. I pray that I will not take any of it for granted. Help me to exercise thankfulness today for all the glorious things you have done. Allow me to proclaim your wondrous works to the world. Amen.

Viola L. Freeman

November 18

THANKSGIVING REASONS

Scripture: Colossians 2:7 (TLV)
. . . Let your lives overflow with joy and thanksgiving for all he has done.

As we approach the Thanksgiving season we spend a lot of time thinking about why we are thankful, but are we really thankful? We have become so comfortable in the everyday things that we forget to thank God that we are able to move, breathe, care for ourselves, or have someone to care for us. Eventhough we have the promise of eternal life, our next breath in this earth is not promised to us.

If we honestly assessed our lives, we have a whole lot to be thankful for. If you cannot think of anything else, think about Jesus and what He has done for you to begin your thanksgiving. Isaiah 53:5 says, *. . . he was wounded for our transgressions, he was bruised for our iniquities, the chastisement of our peace was upon him; and with his stripes we are healed.* Our God, who was without sin, took on our sin. He allowed Himself to be bruised so that we would not have to. If that was not enough, He took on our disease and sickness so that we are healed. We do not need to look for another reason to be thankful—Jesus has given us plenty.

Prayer: Dear God, keep me in remembrance of all I have to be thankful for, your love, your peace, and your joy, so that I might come before you with thanksgiving and sing praises unto your name. Amen.

Gloria J. Smith

November 19

COUNT BLESSINGS AND GIVE THANKS

Scripture: 1 Thessalonians 5:18 (KJV)
In every thing give thanks: for this is the will of God in Christ Jesus concerning you.

The story was told of a man who never failed to pray over his food at mealtime. One day he had only a drink of water, however, he asked for his usual blessing. An observer inquired, "Why ask blessings when you have only water." It was apparent the observer gave little value to water or to the source from which it came.

Had the observer thought about the purpose of water instead of looking at the man's lack, he would have understood why the man gave thanks. Water is a thirst quencher, a cleanser, and a stimulator for growth for which we should give thanks.

As Christians, we must be cognizant of the purpose and source of all things in our life and give thanks. We must stop focusing on our lack and realize how blessed we are when the simple things we have satisfy our need, cleanse our minds, and stimulate our spiritual growth.

Prayer: Lord, there is a purpose for everything that is in my life. Make me keenly aware of that purpose so that in all things I would give you thanks with all my heart. Amen.

Lula B. White

THANK YOU GOD

Scripture: Psalm 95:2 (KJV)
Let us come before his presence with thanksgiving, and make a joyful noise unto him with psalms.

The Word says we should come into the presence of God with thanksgiving. I had to consider what that meant. After all, God is everywhere. We are always in His presence. Then I realized we are to be thankful in all things and in all places.

When we are thankful in all things, others will see God's presence in us. What better gift could we give our family, friends, and co-workers than to show them the presence of God.

Prayer: I am so thankful to you, dear God, for your presence in my life. I thank you for the peace of mind I receive in your presence. I pray that I would let your Holy Spirit live in me. I know that you are always with me. I am grateful for all the blessings in my life. Amen.

Annabell M. Fearrington

November 21

BE THANKFUL—PART I

Scripture: Exodus: 15:22, 23 (NIV)
. . . For three days they traveled in the desert without finding water. When they came to Marah, they could not drink its water because it was bitter . . .

The Israelites had witnessed miracle after miracle— being set free from slavery, crossing the Red Sea, and manna raining down from heaven. Yet, they never seemed to learn how to be truly thankful for all God's provisions.

The incident described in the Scripture above occurred three days after the Red Sea experience. Right after the children of Israel had crossed the Red Sea and watched as Pharaoh's army drowned, they praised and thanked God for their deliverance. But three days later, they had forgotten what God had done for them. They could not see that the God who parted the Red Sea was also able to give them water to drink. These people were ungrateful.

It is the same way today. It is easy for us to give praise and thanksgiving to God when everything is going well, but when things get rough, then we begin to grumble and complain. We think, "I pray and go to church why is this happening to me?" Our testimony in the valley should be the same as it is on the mountaintop. If God is on the mountaintop then He is in the valley.

Prayer: God, you are the Lord of my valleys and my mountaintops. Teach me to be thankful whatever my circumstances so that I might come out of my valleys never to return there again. Amen.

Anonymous

November 22

BE THANKFUL—PART II

Scripture: Exodus: 15:24 (NIV)
So the people grumbled against Moses, saying, "What are we to drink?"

God is tired of our grumbling, complaining, and never being satisfied. We are always wanting more, bigger, and better, never being content with what we have or where we are in our lives. God wants us to learn to be thankful. The children of Israel wandered around in the dessert for 40 years because they never learned to be thankful to God. The Word of God says that we should give thanks in all circumstances for this is the will of God concerning us in Christ Jesus, 1 Thessalonians 5:18.

God has done so much for us, and He gives us so much. Yet, when things start to heat up a little, we forget about those times, just like the children of Israel. We forget the times He made a way out of no way. We forget the times He opened doors we could not even see. We forget all that—instead we focus all our energies on how bad our current situation is. Well, the same God who made a way for you and opened doors for you is the same God that will do it again this time. We must learn to be thankful or we will continue to wander around in our desert, just like the Israelites.

Prayer: Dear Lord, when things get a little rough and I do not see an answer, let me not forget all those times you have moved on my behalf—the doors you have opened and the situations you have stilled. Let the remembrance of your past deeds calm my heart. Amen.

Anonymous

November 23

GOD'S PRESENCE

Scripture: Psalm 139: 7, 8 (KJV)
Whither shall I go from thy spirit? Or whither shall I flee from thy presence? If I ascend up into heaven, thou art there: if I make my bed in hell, behold, thou art there.

A daily morning walk in autumn is a great time to talk with God. It is a great time to give Him thanks for the sight of a new day. Give Him thanks for His gift of hearing, seeing, and touching. As the autumn winds blow, cooling, refreshing, calming, and soothing, God's presence is certainly felt. We cannot see the wind, but it is definitely present. We cannot see God, but we see the results of His presence in our lives. Sensing God's presence in our lives allows us to face calmly and without fear, whatever the future holds, always confident that nothing can ever separate us from God's love. He is everywhere.

Prayer: Dear Lord, I thank you for the things I cannot see, but know they are there. I thank you for your presence in my life, for keeping me safe and out of danger, for keeping me comforted in times of trouble, and keeping me through my good times and bad. Thank you for always being with me. Amen.

Jane Brickhouse

IF YOUR RIGHT EYE OFFEND THEE

Scripture: 1 Samuel 16:7 (KJV)

. . . look not on his countenance, or on the height of his stature; because I have refused him: for the Lord seeth not as man seeth; for man looketh on the outward appearance, but the Lord looketh on the heart.

If you had to choose someone to do an important job for God, what would be your criteria? What does a person with a godly purpose look like?

Samuel was a godly man. He knew the Lord and thought that he knew the kind of person that God would choose for His purpose. Samuel was wrong, as we most often are, when we use our natural eyes to look at people, trying to decide whether or not they are worthy of God's time. The fact is that the Lord never uses the criteria that men use. We say things like, "He is so nice and gets along well with everyone." Or, "she is a born leader, I knew a person of her breeding would do well." We confuse spirituality with personality, natural ability, and wealth with spiritual purpose and value. God confounds us when He chooses people who, according to the world's standard, are unimpressive. He does not care how your resume reads or how people thought you would end up. He wants someone who is willing to submit everything they have, or do not have, to Him and allow the Holy Spirit to do the grooming for the position.

Prayer: Father, thank you that you are holy and your ways are right. Teach me to renew my mind that I would not be swayed by a person's outward appearance or worth. Amen.

Alisa Ginyard

November 25

AN INSPIRATION FOR WORSHIP

Scripture: Ephesians 5:25 (KJV)
Husbands, love your wives, even as Christ also loved the Church, and gave himself for it;

Do you know someone with a good marriage? I am talking about a couple who reminds you of Christ and His church. That is the measure that the Word of God gives us. A good marriage inspires worship.

If you have a Godly mate, there are times when you will know more about who God is as a result of that persons life. You will know the tenderness of God, the sacrificial nature of God, and His unconditional love. You will begin to see how our Father gently changes us through years of patience, without being harsh. As you become one flesh, it will become obvious that this is how we conform to the image of Christ, through time spent with Him. A godly marriage is the sweetest institution that God gave us. Why would Satan be attacking so many if this were not so?

If you are single, enjoy watching marriages, but know that marriage, if not entered into wisely, shows the devastation of a broken relationship with the Father. If you are married, strive to be an example that will cause others to know the Lord. Understand that as you long-suffer through trials, so does Christ suffer long with us.

Prayer: Father, I praise you for an opportunity to enter into an earthly union that at its fullest potential, points me to you. Thank you for marriage. Amen.

Alisa Ginyard

November 26

HOW TO LOVE

Scripture: Romans 5:6 (KJV)
For when we were yet without strength, in due time Christ died for the ungodly.

In most of our lives there is someone that we love who is unlovely. It could be that child who makes the bad choices which keep you on your knees and full of pain. It could be a daddy who will not give up the bottle and embarrasses you with his name in the paper. Maybe it is a husband who cannot seem to hold down a job and would not show his face in church for his own funeral. What about the sibling who keeps showing up in your clean, affluent, neighborhood with the ghetto ways that you have taken special pains to suppress in your life?

Of course we could go on naming them, but you must know that you are the unlovely loved one in God's life. How He deals with us is the example of how we are to deal with the unlovely in our lives. What did He do? He sacrificed Himself for us—His pride, His comfort. Let us say He gave all that He could to put us in right standing. Well, that is to be the goal of born again believers, reconciling other unlovelies (like yourself) to God through Jesus. But we can only do it using His methods. You have got to come down, get your hands dirty, and maybe even bleed a little.

Prayer: Lord, thank you that you are able to look beyond who I am or what I have done, and you love me anyway. Amen.

Alisa Ginyard

November 27

GRADUATING FROM CHRISTIANITY 101

Scripture: Hebrews 5:12 (KJV)
For when for the time ye ought to be teachers, ye have need that one teach you again which be the first principles of the oracles of God; and are become such as have need of milk, and not of strong meat.

Most of us are saved, go to church regularly and work diligently in the church. This is what I call Christianity 101. We will never graduate from it, or get closer to God, until we learn to crucify our flesh. In order to grow in the Lord, we must understand that our feelings are insignificant. Paul says that we must die daily.

To overcome our inclination toward evil, we must define the sin we are struggling with. It could be lying, cheating, or stealing. Whatever it is, we must face it and defy it. To grow in Christ—to graduate to the next level—we cannot allow our fleshly desires to be in control. In John 6:63 we see that the Spirit gives life, the flesh counts for nothing.

Continued growth and graduation to the next level requires an understanding that in our flesh dwells no good thing, Romans 7:18. But we know that we can overcome the flesh through Christ. We can not defeat the flesh in our own strength, but God's grace is sufficient. The Holy Spirit that lives in us is a powerful weapon in our war with the flesh. Activate it and graduate to a closer walk with God.

Prayer: Lord, keep me growing closer to you. Amen.

D. Diane Proctor

November 28

LESSONS IN LEADERSHIP

Scripture: Nehmiah 1:4 (KJV)
And it came to pass, when I heard these words, that I sat down and wept, and mourned certain days, and fasted, and prayed before the God of heaven,

In order to win the world for Christ, great leaders are needed. Leadership begins in the heart. The leader must have a heart for the people. An excellent example of this is Nehemiah. His compassion for his people caused him to sacrifice his position, his comfort and his standing in the community. His compassion for his people made him usable by God.

Nehemiah teaches us many lessons in leadership. He shows us that:

- a great leader feels and hurts, Nehemiah 1:4;
- a great leader fasts and prays for the community, Nehemiah 1:4; and,
- a great leader is bold, yet humble, Nehemiah 2:4.

Those who are able to lead must step forward as Nehemiah did to save our people from reproach. And those who know that their motives are not correct must step out of leadership positions so as not to hinder our people.

Prayer: Thank you, Lord, for lessons in leadership that can be learned from your servant Nehemiah. I learn the greatest lessons on leadership from your Son and my Savior, Jesus Christ. Amen.

Reverend Frances M. Draper

November 29

BEING AN EFFECTIVE WITNESS FOR JESUS CHRIST

Scripture: Acts 1:8 (KJV)
But ye shall receive power, after that the Holy Ghost has come upon you: and ye shall be witnesses unto me in both Jerusalem, and in all Judaea and Samaria, and unto the uttermost part of the earth.

Jesus commands me to be a witness for Him in everything that I do and all that I say. Being an effective witness for Jesus Christ includes:

1. Accepting Jesus Christ into my heart as Lord and Saviour, Romans 10:9, and developing a personal relationship with Him using His Word;
2. Receiving training, even as the disciples received training when Jesus sent them out, Matthew 10 and Luke 10; and,
3. Listening for the instructions of the Lord in spreading the Gospel of Jesus Christ, John 10:3-5.

As an Ambassador for Jesus Christ, I must have daily contact with Him to receive strength, correction, and instruction. Since I am doing His work, He determines the priorities and the methodology to accomplish my goals.

Prayer: Heavenly Father, I ask forgiveness for all of my sins of word, thought, and deed. Please create in me a clean heart and renew a right spirit inside of me so that I may be used by you to disciple others. In Jesus' name I pray. Amen.

Janice L. Guinyard

November 30

December

For God so loved the world, that he gave his only begotten Son, that whosoever believeth in him should not perish, but have everlasting life

John 3:16

South Atlantic Episcopal District
Table Of Contents

DWELL ON GOD'S GOODNESS

Scripture: Psalm 103:2, 3 (KJV)
Bless the Lord, O my soul, and forget not all his benefits:
Who forgiveth all thine iniquities; who healeth all thy
diseases;

Have you ever met Christians who seemed to find joy in complaining about their troubled lives, failing marriages, and poor health? They are experts at finding something to complain about. I am not saying that life is a bed of roses, or that real Christians never go through fiery trials. I am saying that we do not have to give place to the devil by dwelling on the negative things the enemy throws our way.

Complaining only gives the devil more ammunition to defeat us. But, if we resist the devil, he will flee! How do we resist Satan's relentless attacks? We resist him by having faith in God's word, believing that it is true, and making our positive confession unto God. Indeed, Jesus tells us that in this world we will have troubles—but we can rejoice because He has overcome the world.

Daily we can acknowledge many blessings to be thankful for—the gift of life, our families and friends, safe places to live, and food on the table. We must claim the Word of God over our circumstances, praise God for His healing power, and thank God for the efficacious blood of Jesus that redeems us from sickness, poverty, and death.

Prayer: Lord, you have given me power to speak life to my failing situations and circumstances. Help me align my confession with your Word. Amen.

Mayfred Nall

December 1

PLANTING TIME

Scripture: Mark 4:14 (KJV)
The sower soweth the word.

Just as a farmer plants his crop expecting a harvest, so it is with our spiritual mission of sowing the Word of God in the lives of unbelievers. If we want to reap a great harvest of souls in the world, we must plant seeds of the Gospel of Jesus Christ. The more we plant, the more souls we can expect to harvest.

God always provides us with opportunities to sow His Word in the hearts of people. Often, a good place to begin sowing the Word of God is right in our own families. Even in our work places or while attending some of our civic and social functions, we meet people who are hungry for deliverance, hungry for the Word of God—their hearts are fertile ground for sowing the Gospel.

The world is full of lost souls who need to hear about the love of Jesus. You and I are the spiritual gardeners of the mission fields who can plant seeds of God's Word in people who desperately need to know Jesus. We can be assured that as we plant God's Word in hearts of others, it will produce a bumper crop.

Prayer: Dear Lord, help me to sow your Word—the Gospel of Jesus Christ—in the lives of others. I thank you for a great harvest of committed believers who will grow to be your disciples. Amen.

Mary Catherine Christian

December 2

THANK YOU LORD

Scripture: Psalm 92:1 (KJV)
It is a good thing to give thanks unto the Lord, and to sing praises unto thy name, O most High:

I was a little tired, trying to do some last minute shopping at a local variety store. Monica, my nine year-old, was very helpful and followed my directions well. On the other hand, TJ, my precocious six year-old, was excited and full of energy—jumping up and down and talking incessantly. I leaned close to him and in a firm voice I whispered, "TJ, be patient." To my surprise, he pressed his little face closer to mine, looked me straight in the eye and in a determined little whisper said, "Mommy, I only want an Icee," pointing to the Icee counter.

It was such a small request, I gladly acquiesced. As soon as the clerk handed the goodies over, TJ loudly exclaimed, "Thank you Lord! Thank you! Thank you!" A rush of gratitude sprang up in my heart as I witnessed my little boy giving praises and thanks to the Lord. I thought about how often our heavenly Father grants our requests and we adults forget to say "thank you."

As I continued my shopping, TJ's exuberant appreciation flooded my mind. My heart began to sing praises to the Lord, thanking Him for my children and my husband, and above all, thanking Him for His matchless gift to us, the Lord Jesus Christ.

Prayer: Dear Lord, help me keep the Christmas spirit every day as I show gratitude for your presence in my life and for all the blessings you bestow upon me. Amen.

Shirley Boyd

December 3

THE BLESSING OF GIVING

Scripture: Acts 20:35 *(KJV)*
It is more blessed to give than to receive.

During this Christmas season the world is actuated by the sacred birth of the Holy Child in the manger—the deeper meaning of why we celebrate Christmas. Throughout the world, choirs sing of the little child of Bethlehem, peace on earth and good will toward men. Missionaries around the world are praying that the words of these inspiring songs will echo in the hearts of people and bring joy to all.

As we celebrate the birth of Christ Jesus, let us remember this Christmas season as a special time of giving. There are millions of people around the world who are in need of love today, who are suffering untold injustice, sorrow, discouragement, hunger, pain, and hopelessness. They need a touch from Jesus. They need to know of His unconditional love for one and all.

Let us seize every opportunity to minister to the needs of our sisters and brothers, both at home and overseas. As missionaries making sacrifices to give to those in need, may our service to humanity this Christmas season bring us contentment and peace as never before. Let us remember as we bring comfort to those in distress, that it is indeed more blessed to give than to receive, not only at Christmas time, but each day of the year.

Prayer: Dear God, as I celebrate the birth of your Son Jesus, endow me with unconditional love for my fellow man. Direct me as I spread joy to your children during the Christmas season and throughout the year. Amen.

Ethel S. Kilgore

December 4

HUMBLE THYSELF

Scripture: Luke 18:14 (AMP)
. . . He who humbles himself will be exalted.

     The prayer of the Pharisee was unacceptable to God because he prayed out of a spirit of pride and haughtiness. Jesus gives a lesson in parable concerning humility, pointing out the misguided actions of the proud Pharisee. This man sought self-aggrandizement based on his erroneous perception of his own personal goodness and worthiness. On the other hand, the repentant tax collector humbled himself and prayed with humility and penitence, which pleased God.
     What do we really have to be spiritually proud of, we have not merited God's grace or His blessings? As Christians, we must remember that our righteousness is as filthy rags to God. Our appeal to God must invoke His mercy and unmerited favor. God has promised that if we humble ourselves in His sight, then He will exalt us in due season.

Prayer: Dear Lord, give me a humble spirit, as I come before you to always give thanks in all things. Amen.

Bertha Howard-Bray

December 5

GREATER LOVE HAS NO MAN

Scripture: John 15:13 (KJV)
Greater love hath no man than this, that a man lay down his life for his friends.

Our youngest son desperately needed a kidney transplant. He had been on painful dialysis for about two years. One night, we received a call from our eldest son. He informed us that after talking things over with his wife, they decided that he was the best donor for his brother. They even went ahead and made all the hospital arrangements.

On the day of the surgery, our sons were in good spirits and we all felt God's power as we prayed together in the hospital. I recalled John 15:13. Truly my eldest son was laying his life down—placing himself in a life threatening situation to help his brother gain a new lease on life.

After about two hours, the surgeon came out and said, "The surgery was a great success! The kidney began functioning right there on the operating table." The wonderful news caused my husband and I to mightily thank God for our two wonderful sons and daughter-in-law.

Five years later, our youngest son is the picture of health. And my eldest son and his wife have been blessed with two beautiful, healthy children. To God be the glory!

Prayer: Thank you, God, for your Son Jesus. His example of unselfish love teaches me that there is no greater gift than a man who will lay down his life for another. Amen.

Dorothy S. Johnson

December 6

PUT JESUS IN YOUR HEART

Scripture: Psalm 119:11 (KJV)
Thy word have I hid in mine heart, that I might not sin against thee.

The story is told about a mother and her five year-old daughter, who were shopping on Christmas Eve. The mother waited until the last hours of shopping time because she had very little money to spend.

While strolling down the aisles, the daughter was overtaken with adoration for the baby doll she saw in a nativity set. She removed the baby doll from the manger and began kissing it. She hoped so very much that her mother would buy it for her. To her disappointment, her mother requested that she put the doll back in the manger because they did not have the money to purchase the doll. The child became very upset and began to cry sorrowful tears.

Another shopper who witnessed what had happened, felt compassion for the child and the mother. So the shopper purchased the nativity set and gave the baby doll to the little girl. Each Christmas since that time, the lady has displayed the nativity scene in her home without the baby Jesus doll. When she is asked "where is the baby Jesus?" her reply is always, "He's in my heart!"

Prayer: Dear God, help me to always keep Jesus in my heart. May I remember to give heartfelt gifts to others and to proclaim that Jesus is in my heart throughout the year. Amen.

Mary Hicklin Jones

December 7

A CHILD IS BORN

Scripture: Isaiah 7:14 (KJV)
Therefore the Lord himself shall give you a sign; Behold, a virgin shall conceive, and bear a son, and shall call his name Immanuel.

Through the unmerited grace of God, He sent to mankind the Gift of Life. After sin entered the world through one man's unrighteousness, God Himself covered sin with the first animal sacrifice. Little did man know that this was a sign of the coming Savior who would come into the world, born of a virgin, and His name would be called "Emmanuel," meaning "God with us."

We must first understand the purpose of the newborn King's birth before we can appreciate it. What greater love can we find that one should lay down his life for all? This is the way that God chose to reconcile us back to Himself. The full glory was not found in Jesus' birth, but rather in the purpose of His birth, which was to die for the remission of our sins. Jesus Christ, the only begotten Son of the Father, born as the precious Lamb of God, was slain before the foundation of the world and died to become our Savior and our Lord. The choice to accept His gift salvation is available to us.

Prayer: Lord, thank you for sending your Son Jesus who was born into the world to save me from sin. I pray that He is visible in my life so that others will know the Good News of His birth. Amen.

Sylvia C. Glenn

December 8

BECOME A LIVING SACRIFICE

Scripture: Romans 12:1 (KJV)
I beseech you therefore, brethren, by the mercies of God, that ye present your bodies a living sacrifice, holy, acceptable unto God, which is your reasonable service.

Have you ever asked the question, "What is God's will for my life?" In order to receive an answer to this question we must first be totally submitted to God, acknowledging Him as Lord of our lives. Before we can begin our assigned mission to go out and win souls for Christ, we must first lay down our own selfish will and accept God's will for our lives.

It was not until I totally committed my life to Christ, repented for my sins, and turned everything in my life over to Christ, that I then began to understand what God's will was for me. As I continued to study and meditate on God's Word and pray, God's will for my life became clearer and clearer each day.

No matter what you have done or who you are, God can use you. You must be willing to commit yourself to Christ Jesus as a living sacrifice. We must do more than verbally proclaim our commitment. We must be doers of the Word and as doers of the Word, we will effectively win souls to the kingdom of God.

Prayer: Lord Jesus, help me to be sincere in all that I do for you, as I make my body a living sacrifice unto you. O Lord, use me at all times to do your will. Amen.

Barbara J. Moore

December 9

ANOINTED TO FULFILL THE MISSION

Scripture: Luke 4:18, 19 (NRS)
The Spirit of the Lord is upon me, because he has anointed me to bring good news to the poor. He has sent me to proclaim release to the captives and recovery of sight to the blind, to let the oppressed go free, to proclaim the year of the Lord's favor.

When God calls us to work in His name, He anoints us for the job. The Holy Spirit empowers us to go into all the world and witness in the name of Jesus Christ. If Jesus, the Chief disciple-maker, had to be anointed with the Holy Spirit to perform His mission on earth, then we too must first be anointed before we can fulfill the mission in our time. Whether we are called to be apostles, prophets, evangelists, pastors, or teachers, without the anointing power of God's Holy Spirit, we are spiritually powerless. Without the anointing of the Holy Spirit we cannot go forth as co-laborers with Christ to save lost souls.

Prayer: Father God, I ask you to fill me with your anointed Holy Spirit, which enables me to witness in Jesus' name and compels the unsaved to repentance. Amen.

Annette Watts

UNEXPECTED OPPORTUNITIES TO MINISTER

Scripture: Ephesians 4:2 (NIV)
Be completely humble and gentle; be patient, bearing with one another in love.

My husband and I had just begun to enjoy our empty nest; our two daughters were busy developing their professional careers. One day, he went to visit his mother and found her lying on the floor where she had fallen—she was all alone and confused. We knew that we would have to take her to live with us, indefinitely. I found myself praying, "Lord, give me the strength to be the daughter to my mother-in-law that I need to be and endow me with unselfish love for this task."

God has given me many opportunities to be the daughter she never had. Since my mother-in-law has been with us, I have had to exercise humility, gentleness, patience, and forbearance, as well as a constant schedule adjustment. But I thank God for this opportunity to serve and grow spiritually—if I do not demonstrate the character of Jesus in my own home, how can I be a missionary in the world? I pray that God will continue to grant me wisdom and direction in this new opportunity to serve.

Prayer: Thank you, Lord, for bringing about changes in my life that afford me the opportunity to minister to those who need me. In the comfort of my daily routine, keep me ever mindful that my blessings of health and strength are blessings to be used to help others. Amen.

Mayfred Nall

December 11

ANSWERING THE CALL

Scripture: Isaiah 6:8 (NIV)
Then I heard the voice of the Lord saying, "Whom shall I send? And who will go for us?" And I said, "Here am I. Send me!"

Doubt and fear can play a major role in hindering us from our call to service. Instead of pressing forward to answer the call of God, we often look back, remembering where we were, rather than keeping our eyes on how blessed we are to be used by our loving Father. Our relationship with God will never be complete if we allow past sins and feelings of guilt to control us.

The prophet Isaiah felt ruined and unclean in the presence of the Lord. Yet, in spite of how insignificant and unworthy he felt, God used him in His service. Likewise, God will use us—in spite of our feelings of guilt and shame. We too have been saved for service. God did not expect Isaiah to stay in the temple after his conversion experience. God expected him to fulfill his calling. No less is expected of us. God has saved our souls so that we can go forth serving Him by ministering to others. Like Isaiah the prophet, when the Lord calls, will your answer be, "Here am I, send me?"

Prayer: Father, I thank you for your saving grace and the opportunity to answer your call to serve you by serving others. Amen.

Rosetta Dunham

December 12

SOW THE GOOD SEED

Scripture: Matthew 13:8 (NRS)
Other seeds fell on good soil and brought forth grain some a hundred-fold, some sixty, some thirty.

The missionary is to sow the good seed of the Gospel of Jesus Christ in the world. The world's uncultivated soil in which the missionary plants the seed of hope is the heart of humankind. God has promised that the Gospel or the seed of hope shall not fail. Since Christ lived a sinless life, yielding not to temptations and rose to glory over death, we have the assurance that the promises of Christ are true.

Knowing that God's love will never fail, missionaries can continue to march forward on their missionary journey, sowing the good seed of the Gospel of Christ. Let us never get weary, tired, or faint as we march and spread the Gospel; for no other mission will lead lost souls from death to eternal life. Go forth understanding the mission unto which you are called to win the world for Christ. The missionary journey is a walk that does not end in a few days. It is a walk that continues until the flesh can walk no more. The missionary's task is always to reflect the love of Christ; for therein is the righteousness of God revealed.

Prayer: Dear Lord, bless me to continue to sow the good seed—the Gospel of Jesus Christ. Keep the mission ever fresh before me, so that I will not become weary in well-doing, but will continually remember the great rewards of earthly joy and eternal life that await me. Amen.

Ruth L. Thompson

December 13

GO TELL IT

Scripture: Isaiah 40:9 (KJV)
O Zion, that bringeth good tidings, get thee up into the high mountain; . . .

  This season is an excellent time to focus on sharing the Good News—a time to go and tell it. Like the shepherds who visited the baby Jesus, we have a mission to go and tell what we have seen and heard, what we know, and what we have experienced in fellowship with God through Christ Jesus. In fact, we are compelled to go and tell the tidings of great joy that were brought forth on the first Christmas day. Oh how greatly our lives are spiritually enriched and fulfilled because of that blessed event.

  The expected behavior of Christian missionaries is expressed in the song, "Go Tell it on the Mountain." Whenever we go and tell the good news about Jesus Christ, we take an active role in reaching people and making a difference in a world where so many need to hear the story of Jesus' love. The Lord wants us to serve Him by reaching and teaching others all that he has taught us. May we accept as our duty and joy, the mission to "go tell it" as we spread the Good News of great joy on Christmas day and throughout the year.

Prayer: Dear Heavenly Father, as I go tell it, may those around me see a God who cares for me, as I use my resources to do the work that you would have me to do. Amen.

Vivian W. Brown

WHAT DO YOU WANT FOR CHRISTMAS?

Scripture: Luke 1:46, 47 (KJV)
And Mary said, My soul doth magnify the Lord, And my spirit hath rejoiced in God my Saviour.

Faithfully about this time of the year, each one of my three sons asks, "Mom, what do you want for Christmas?" And each year they try to do more than I ask. It seems so important to them that I know that they love me and that I know they want me to have a joyous Christmas Day. How can I tell them that one of my greatest joys is that they have accepted Christ as their Lord and Saviour? Jesus has purchased their salvation and secured their future, and my joy is indescribable.

When I consider the wonderful gift of salvation, Mary's hymn of thanksgiving and praise expresses exactly what I feel. Whenever I think of the Gospel of Jesus Christ being passed on from my husband and me to our sons, and from them to generations yet unborn, I want to proclaim as the Virgin Mary did in Luke 1:50, *And his mercy is on them that fear Him from generation to generation.*

Prayer: Dear Lord, thank you for allowing my eyes to behold the wonders of your love and my heart to feel the joy of your salvation. Amen.

Ingrid Flack Hunter

December 15

EMMANUEL, GOD WITH US

Scripture: Matthew 1:23 (NRS)
"Look, the virgin shall conceive and bear a son, and they shall name him Emmanuel."

The birth of Jesus, the Christ Child, signaled hope for a world in despair. Today as we face difficult times, we must remember His name is Emmanuel—God with us. God is with us to provide all we need to be successful on this pilgrimage. We must cooperate with God to transform defeats into victories. The transforming of the bitter waters at Marah provides us valuable lessons and proof that our bitter places can be turned into Elims or places of security and restoration. See Exodus 15:23-27.

Often we magnify the tiniest problems in our lives— we make mountains out of molehills. Let us not be saddled with a defeatist attitude, but rather acknowledge our potential and God's love, remembering that we can do all things through Christ who gives us strength, Philippians 4:13. When we glorify God in all things, our spiritual reservoir increases and the Holy Spirit reminds us that greater is He that is in us, than he that is in the world, 1 John 4:4.

Prayer: Dear God, in difficult times, let me be reminded that you are Emmanuel—God with us, and you promised that you would never leave me or forsake me. Thank you, Lord, that I can depend on you. Amen.

Laurenna H. Crenshaw

December 16

HAVE YOU CAUGHT ANY FISH?

Scripture: Matthew 4:19 (KJV)
*And he said unto them, Follow me, and I will make you
fishers of men.*

Peter, Andrew, James, and John were fishermen by
occupation. Jesus summoned them to leave their nets, follow
Him, and become fishers of men. So the four disciples left
their business interests and family ties to follow Jesus.

We must as a body of believers, leave our comfort
zones and go out into the world seeking lost souls, as we co-
labor with Christ to fulfill the mission to win the world for
Christ. The Son of man came to seek and to save that which
was lost. See Luke 19:10. We must be about our Father's
business of catching fish for Jesus Christ. Ask yourself,
"How many fish have I caught for Christ?" Do you know
how to fish for those who are lost in sin? Do you have the
right equipment needed to fish for souls? Some soul in need
of salvation may be in your home, and yes, even in your local
church. Zion, it is time to go on daily fishing trips with Jesus
Christ.

Prayer: O God, help me realize that there are so many who
are not saved. Use me, Lord, to be a fishermen of unsaved
men, women, boys and girls. I ask this in the name of Jesus
the Christ. Amen.

Sandra Coleman Walker

December 17

N

Harmonia
thalia
Yolanda

Rickey
Randy
Wendy

GOD ANSWERS PRAYER

Scripture: Matthew 21:22 (KJV)

And all things, whatsoever ye shall ask in prayer, believing, ye shall receive. Lord you no Their needs you no, The things I ask For I do belive you Some da great my wish

In mid-October my widowed, childless, elderly aunt who lived in another state recognized that her health was declining. It was her desire that I would look after her and her affairs. In my heart I wanted to be of service to my aunt in this matter, but my personal health problems, my family and church responsibilities would not allow me to take on another thing.

As I continued to be faithful to my existing responsibilities, I prayed earnestly that God would give me the answer to my dilemma. My aunt continued to struggle with her health to the point that she was hospitalized for tests. God answered my prayer; the Holy Spirit reorganized my schedule so that I was able to carry out my responsibilities while she received the care she needed.

Prayer: Thank you, Father, for being faithful to your promise, that all things whatsoever we ask in prayer, believing we shall receive. Amen.

Lois M. Parker

Lord I have Children That are highly depressed, it is at The point where they ~~have started~~ are accuseing me For Their their Problems. Lord I am asking To Please grant Their needs, open Their eyes. Lord IF have Put Something in The way of life, so The could not Pull Them selves up. Please Lord Forgive me I am asking you To come into The Life, so They want countinue To accuse me of Their wrong doings.

December 18

WISDOM: A WISE INVESTMENT

Scripture: James 1:5 (NRS)
If any of you is lacking in, wisdom, ask God, who gives to all generously and ungrudgingly, and it will be given you.

In an age when it is acceptable by the world's standards to be a crooked and perverse generation, wisdom is needed in order that we, as a Body of believers, might help win souls for Christ. As we bring many to the knowledge of Christ, God has instructed us that we need only ask for wisdom, and God will grant it to us liberally.

By wisdom the Lord founded the earth, Proverbs 3:19, and by wisdom all of God's works were created, Psalm 104:24. God created us to be productive. We are encouraged to seek and then use God's wisdom as we endeavor to be productive citizens of the Kingdom of God.

As Christians, let us then make every effort to use God's wisdom and then seek to help others do the same. Our reward shall be a lengthening of our days, spiritual riches, and honor from the Lord, Proverbs 3:16.

Prayer: Father, today let me use wisdom as I serve you and others. Amen.

Karen Irick

December 19

STAND ON GOD'S WORD

Scripture: Psalm 10:6 (NRS)
They think in their heart, "We shall not be moved; throughout all generations we shall not meet adversity."

Only a foolish person would think, "I shall never be in adversity." Such people falsely think nothing can hurt them and that they will always be happy and free of trouble. But in these times of so much uneasiness in the world, and not knowing where to turn or what to do, Christians must stand firm on God's Word and pray daily for God's strength. Psalm 27:14 instructs us to *Wait on the Lord: be of good courage, and he shall strengthen thine hearts: wait, I say, on the Lord.* All of us must go through storms in life, but we have the assurance in God's Word that Jesus Christ our Savior has overcome the world. When we stand on the Word of God, we will have the victory. Adversity will surely come into our lives, but we only have to Wait on the Lord; for God is our Helper and our Shield, Psalm 33:20. And when we fall into diverse temptation and trouble, Jesus instructs us to be of good cheer for He has overcome the world.

Prayer: Father God, thank you for helping me to stand on your Word and to wait on deliverance in all situations that would defeat me. Amen.

Queen Esther Major

December 20

CO-LABORERS WITH CHRIST

Scripture: 2 Corinthians 5:18 (KJV)
And all things are of God, who hath reconciled us to himself by Jesus Christ, and hath given to us the ministry of reconciliation;

God uses Christians to do His work—we are workers together with God, as we fulfill our mission of reconciling the world back to Christ—winning souls for His service. Christ, has commanded us to be witnesses to the whole world for Him. Just as the disciples of Jesus Christ were sent out on their mission, as followers of Christ, we too must go out and share the Gospel with everyone, so that they may know the plan of salvation that Christ has given for all.

The needs of our world today challenge each Christian to a personal mission of reconciliation. Sometimes it means a sacrificial, life-changing commitment to the will of God. Our mission as followers and co-laborers with Jesus Christ is to reconcile lost souls back to a wholesome relationship with Christ. It is a mission of hope, love, and life for a lost world.

Prayer: Dear Lord, continue to lead and direct my path as I witness in your name. Wherever I go, may I always lift up the name of Jesus. May my witness and proclamation of your truth cause the unsaved to come to know and accept you as their Saviour and Lord. Thank you, Lord, for salvation. Amen.

Nadine Anderson

December 21

THE GREAT PHYSICIAN

Scripture: Isaiah 53:5 (KJV)
But he was wounded for our transgressions, he was bruised for our iniquities: the chastisement of our peace was upon him; and with his stripes we are healed.

So many times we go about our daily activities enjoying life and taking good health for granted. It is when we are suddenly stricken with ill health, from which we think we cannot recover, that we are able to experience the awesome healing power and mercy of God.

In June of 1997, I was stricken with in intracranial hemorrhage with partial loss of vision in my left eye. This illness most often results in the death of the patient or significant physical impairment. By the grace of God, His tender mercy, and His healing hand, I rejoice in full healing–restoration of my sight, no physical impairment, and the sweet joy of experiencing the spiritual power of the Great Physician in His matchless glory.

If our Lord could raise Lazarus from the dead, then for sure the power of healing is in His Mighty Spirit; for by His stripes we are healed.

Prayer: Father, help me to know and believe in your healing mercies. Let me know that when man says there is no hope, your healing powers are matchless. Help me to remember that when the problem is too big for me, it is just right for you. Amen.

Betty M. Ruth

MINISTERING IN A CRISIS SITUATION

Scripture: Psalm 46:1 (KJV)
God is our refuge and strength, a very present help in trouble.

God calls each missionary to mission work and part of that mission work is ministering to others in times of crisis. My call came on the warm, clear, fall morning of September 22, 1994, at 9:30 a.m. I received a phone call at work requesting that I rush to the hospital immediately because my husband had suffered a traumatic head and facial injury from a car accident. Our nephew, a passenger, escaped without a scratch.

Covington Highway, where the accident occurred, would have normally been very busy, but thankfully no other parties were injured on that tragic day. After thanking God for sparing the life of my husband and nephew, I found refuge in God who sustained me during this critical time, enabling me to minister, not only to my husband, but also to other family members and other patients during my 46 hour vigil.

Prayer: Father, thank you for always being my refuge and strength in the midst of crisis situations. Amen.

Martha Campbell

SHOW AND TELL

Scripture: Philippians 1:27 (KJV)
Only let your conversation be as it becometh the gospel of Christ . . .

Do you remember the kindergarten learning exercise called "show and tell?" Each day, as part of the class activity, a few young students were given an opportunity to bring a precious possession to share with their classmates. I can still remember their little, innocent faces beaming with pride and joy as they held their prize possessions. I can still hear the excitement in their tiny voices as they shared and talked about those things most near and dear to their hearts.

Likewise, we Christians must share with the world our prized possessions: the salvation of the Lord Jesus Christ and the indwelling of His precious Holy Spirit. We must tell the world about God's plan of salvation, the power of the Holy Spirit, and demonstrate the love and character of Jesus through our godly conduct. May we always remember that our lifestyle may be the only Bible that many people will ever read. Hence, we must walk worthy unto the Lord, as living epistles of Christ, holy and acceptable in His sight. Let us glorify Christ in our conversation and conduct so that the world will know that Jesus Christ is Lord.

Prayer: Lord Jesus, I ask that you reveal your holiness to me, and demonstrate your character and love through me. By the power of your Holy Spirit, strengthen me with might in the inner man so that I may tell the world about Jesus. I pray that my godly conduct and conversation will bring glory and honor to you and compel sinners to repentance. Amen.

Sandra Coleman Walker

December 24

WHAT WILL YOU GIVE?

Scripture: Acts 3:6 (KJV)
Then Peter said, Silver and gold have I none; but such as I have give I thee: In the name of Jesus Christ of Nazareth rise up and walk.

Daily, at the gate of the temple Beautiful, the lame beggar would cry for silver and gold, not knowing that his inheritance as a child of God was so much greater than a few worn coins. Contrast the opulence of the temple gates with the image of the impoverished man's frail body, his crippled, shriveled feet and ankles. Imagine this beggar's shame, his pitiful state, his hollowed cheeks, and his dark sunken eyes, as he begged for alms.

Peter fastened his eyes of compassion and mercy on the poor man's frame, spoke to him as a brother, touched him as a friend, and pointed him to Jesus. The lame man was offered something much more valuable than money—Peter offered the poor beggar the precious gifts of hope, faith, and love.

God may put someone in your path today who needs the spiritual gifts you have to share in the name of Jesus. An encouraging word, a gentle touch, and the sincere testimony of Jesus' love can change that person's life forever. Go forth sharing God's gift of love, faith, and hope with a lost and dying world, pointing others to a new life in Christ Jesus.

Prayer: Help me, dear Father, to spread your Gospel and to walk worthy of your calling, as I lead others to the saving knowledge of Jesus Christ. Amen.

Lillian Turner Shelborne Capers (deceased June 3, 1998)

December 25

GOD WILL RENEW THY STRENGTH

Scripture: Isaiah 40:31 (NRS)
but those who wait for the Lord shall renew their strength, they shall mount up with wings like eagles, they shall run and not be weary, they shall walk and not faint.

No matter who you are or how much willpower you have, you will encounter situations in life you just cannot manage by yourself. Human strength will never be adequate as we face all of life's challenges and difficulties. Such trying times make us aware of the need to draw from the strength that only comes from God.

Jesus knew that we could not manage our problems in life alone. Thus Jesus invites us to cast our cares upon Him. He says to His followers, *Come unto me, all ye that labour and are heavy laden, and I will give you rest.* Matthew 11:28.

No matter what you may be facing in life, the secret is to wait on the Lord and look to Him for strength to conquer life's challenges. After we have done all that we can do in a Christian manner to manage a difficult situation, we must then wait on God . . . for in our weakness, God's strength is made perfect.

Prayer: Heavenly Father, give me the wisdom and the patience to wait on you to renew my strength and bring me through life's difficult challenges. When I can see no way out, remind me that Jesus Christ is the way. Amen.

Carolyn J. Steward

CHRIST: THE GIVER OF SALVATION

Scripture: Matthew 1:21 (KJV)
And she shall bring forth a son, and thou shalt call his name Jesus: for he shall save his people from their sins.

As a child experiencing the joy of Christmas, I always hoped to receive many gifts, just as the baby Jesus received gifts of gold, frankincense, and myrrh. It was not until I received Jesus Christ as my personal Saviour, did I understand the meaning of Christ in Christmas. In human form, Christ incarnate (the Word became flesh) was born to Mary as baby Jesus, the Saviour of the world. His mission to save souls led to His death on the cross to pay for the sins of humankind.

The joy of Christmas is knowing that this is the day when Jesus started His mission to offer us a plan of salvation. As a missionary I know that Jesus' mission on earth must continue through His disciples. Having accepted Jesus Christ as my Lord and Saviour, I have the duty and responsibility to answer the call of service to co-labor with Christ and other missionaries, as I seek to make more disciples.

Prayer: Dear Jesus Christ, because you were born, I can say, thank you for my unmerited gift of salvation. Amen.

Sadye W. Potter

December 27

JOY IN THE MIDST OF PAIN

Scripture: Revelation 21:4 (KJV)
And God shall wipe away all tears from their eyes; and there shall be no more death, neither sorrow, nor crying, neither shall there shall be any more pain: for the former things are passed away."

This divine promise and reward that God revealed to the Apostle John has helped sustain me since the death of our youngest son. At times, my pain and suffering seemed inconsolable. I blamed everyone, including my deceased husband and myself for our son's death.

Prior to his death, my son had prepared and delivered a speech on Youth Day at our church. The speech referenced Revelation 21:4, *And God shall wipe away all tears from their eyes; and there shall be no more death, neither sorrow, nor crying . . .* As I read the Scripture, I felt surrounded by God's divine comfort and love as never before. I knew my son was safe in God's arms, enjoying eternal life in a world without tears, suffering, and death; God's promise to all who believe in His only begotten Son.

As I mature spiritually, my mourning is ceasing, for I realize that Jesus Christ bore my grief and sorrow. Daily, I am experiencing God's love, peace, and joy, as I reflect on cherished memories of my dear son.

Prayer: O Lord most Holy, in a world of pain and suffering, I adore and glorify you. Thank you for your precious gift of love, Jesus the Christ, and for your divine promise of eternal life in a world of peace and joy. Amen.

Theodora Shippy Smith

December 28

THE LORD'S BATTLE

Scripture: 2 Samuel 22:33 (KJV)
God is my strength and power: and he maketh my way perfect.

God's people have always had conflict with Satan. When David told Goliath the battle is the Lord's, he did not mean the Lord would merely fight on his behalf. He meant that it was the Lord's battle, and if he allowed himself to be used by God, the strength of the giant Goliath would be powerless against an instrument of God. This godly principle is still in effect today. The Lord does not fight for us to win a battle that we own or engage in for our own ego. When the battle is being fought for God, we need only work, pray, and put our trust in God to win the battle in God's own way.

For David, the battle was against a giant named Goliath. Today we battle with the forces of Satan in the form of temptation to sin. We experience problems at home, in school, at church, and in the community. We toil with financial worries and sickness. Our attempts to work for the Lord are often met head-on by the adversary, Satan. The Lord wants us to remember that when we are working for the Lord, it is God's battle, not ours. Since we are no match for Satan, our task then is to arm ourselves with Scripture, fortify ourselves with prayer, and be filled with God's Holy Spirit.

Prayer: Lord, I am grateful that your Son Jesus Christ defeated Satan at Calvary. I thank you that because of Jesus I have victory over the devil and all his tactics. I am unbeatable in Jesus Christ. Amen.

Ruth J. Scott

December 29

LOVE MOTIVATES FORGIVENESS

Scripture: 1 Corinthians 13:5, 6 (NIV)
It is not rude, it is not self-seeking, it is not easily angered, it keeps no record of wrongs. Love does not delight in evil but rejoices with the truth.

God's love is always at work in our lives. God's love is not rude, but courteous. It makes us considerate of others; for God is unselfish. Love does not gloat over the failure or mistakes of others. Have you ever come in contact with someone who constantly talks about negative things, one who is always talking about a hurtful event that occurred many, many years ago—and the person still holds a grudge? Well, this is not of God. Love keeps no score of wrongs. God's love forgets.

I remember very well a situation that occurred in the local church where I was a member. It hurt me deeply. My first reaction was to seek revenge or to hurt the person who hurt me. I prayed constantly for God to remove the hurt because I did not want to hate anyone or do anything to hurt anyone. God is so good and merciful; for God heard my earnest cry and God answered my prayer. God put love in my heart and through God's Word, I learned to forgive. My healing began when I began to forgive and pray for the person who had wronged me.

Prayer: Lord, help me to walk and operate in your love. Thank you Lord, for the peace you have given me. Help me to say only those things that will bless or bring healing to my sisters and brothers in Christ. Amen.

Barbara J. Moore

December 30

WHAT'S WRONG?

Scripture: Psalm 42:1 (RSV)
As a hart longs for flowing streams, so longs my soul for thee, O God.

"What's wrong with me?" a young mother asked her friend. "I pray and read my Bible the first thing every day. But as soon as I start my busy morning routine, I find myself getting grouchy and snappy with the children and irritable with my husband. Where is the peace and joy that I read about in the Bible? I do not feel like a Christian at all. I feel like a hypocrite."

So many of us go through the forms of the Christian faith—prayer, church attendance, Bible reading, and Bible study—yet we miss out on so much that God had in store for us. Why? There are many possible reasons, but often it is because our personal relationship with God, the Father, has not been nurtured. We go through the outward forms of worship but fail to really communicate with God from the heart.

A yearning to enter God's presence, to commune with God must be preceded by prayer and Bible study to learn God's will for our lives. When we begin to take on God's Spirit and all the accompanying characteristics, then His love, patience, peace, joy, long-suffering, gentleness, goodness, faith, meekness, and temperance will transform us into God's image and likeness.

Prayer: Dear Lord, teach me in all the busy work of daily life, to find the time and sincerity of heart to draw closer to you. Amen.

Ruth J. Scott

December 31

Job - The ~~oldest~~ oldest Book in the Bible

Ramierto yard man
247-8311
or 4609283

1 8007302

dor = highest - helper - A special
representative -

Transgression = Sin Violation.

Knowdledge =

wisdom =

Bernice Worle

2 460 - 2568